PLAIN TALKS

68913

ON

FAMILIAR SUBJECTS.

A

SERIES OF POPULAR LECTURES.

BY

J. G. HOLLAND.

NEW YORK:
CHARLES SCRIBNER & CO., 124 GRAND STREET.
1866.

Entered, according to Act of Congress, in the year 1865, by
CHARLES SCRIBNER & CO.,
In the Clerk's Office of the District Court of the United States for the
Southern District of New York.

JOHN F. TROW & CO.,
Printers, Stereotypers, and Electrotypers,
50 Greene Street, New York.

These Lectures

ARE DEDICATED

TO THOSE

FOR WHOM THEY WERE ORIGINALLY WRITTEN:

TO THE MEMBERS OF THE

LYCEUMS AND LECTURE ASSOCIATIONS

OF THE

UNITED STATES.

PREFACE.

Every accepted speaker before the lecture-associations of the country hears the frequent expression of a wish, on the part of his audiences, to secure in type the utterances of his tongue. My own experience in this respect has not been exceptional; and, in publishing this volume of lectures, I fulfil a promise repeatedly made to those who have heard them from the platform. It seems legitimate to conclude that that is not valueless on the printed page which has been received with favor by many audiences, in nearly every Northern State of the Union. I am sure it will revive some pleasant memories; and I hope it may renew some useful impressions.

These lectures have been written at different periods during the last six or seven years. These years have been eventful ones in American history;

and they have given point and coloring to much that the volume contains. It has not been deemed desirable to introduce changes in the text, in order to adapt it to altered times and circumstances, or to append notes explanatory of incidents and events that have retired from the field of current interest into history. Such lectures as bear the stamp of any time bear the stamp of their own time, and sufficiently explain themselves.

J. G. H.

SPRINGFIELD, MASS., *July*, 1865.

CONTENTS.

SELF-HELP.

THE power of self-help—the power that sits behind, or sits above, all other human powers—the motive force of progress—the mother element of history—is, perhaps, the most interesting and the most wonderful to which we can turn our attention. In it abide the germs of all individual growth and development. Of it are born all the facts and all the phenomena of human civilization.

It is this power which distinguishes man among, or from, animals. Curious philosophers have variously characterized man as a laughing animal, a talking animal, a reasoning animal; but the functions upon which these distinctions are based can hardly be deemed radically characteristic; for all animals laugh, and talk, and reason, in their own way. The power of self-help, however, cannot be predicated of any animal but man—the power to conceive and achieve a higher, better, and rationally more desirable character and condition than he possesses. It is not a development of the animal life at all, but stands above it—stands upon it—and lifts the hand by which man links himself in alliance with God and the angels. All art, all science, all agencies that give man power over nature and over his own destiny, all civilizing forces whatsoever, are emanations of this power. All inspirations from above are addressed to it. All ambitions have root in it. All emulations are suggested and supported by it. It is the main-spring which moves the wheels of the world's industry. It is, in short, the characteristic power of man, and that which crowns him with divine possibilities.

This faculty of self-help, then—this power of building exalted ideals of life and character, and of realizing those ideals by self-elevation to them and into them—the power of voluntary development in the individual and of civilization in society, is that which distinguishes man from all the forms of life we know. It would be delightful to devote the hour to a historical and philosophical consideration of this characteristic power of man. It would be pleasant to draw from biography and from history illustrations of its operation, because the grateful task would be simply to sketch the story of the progress of mankind. We should see how impulsive childhood has, by the inborn power of self-help, risen into rational manhood;—how rude barbarism has, by its patient hands, climbed slowly up the centuries into civilization—how it has constructed and used, and destroyed and reorganized, institutions—how Christianity itself came down to meet and aid it, and to join hands with it for the world's regeneration. But our discussion will take a lower and more practical range.

You are aware that, for the past twenty or twenty-five years, there has been a great deal of talk about self-help, self-culture, self-discipline, and self-made men. The young, and particularly those who have had little to do with the schools, have been addressed through ingeniously written biographies, through anecdotes of humble men who have risen in the world, through proverbs, maxims, exhortations, and appeals in prose and verse—every imaginable thing, indeed, adapted to reach and rouse unlettered ambition. In all the teachings on this subject there has been a measure of truth, and always, perhaps, a laudable motive; but it contains so much of falsehood—it has led so many men into fatal mistakes—it is so mischievous in the social, political, and professional life of this country—that the time is fully come when the public thought should be critically directed to it.

We have had, and we now have, a class of writers whose avowed purpose it is to stimulate the humble to rise in the world,—not to rise into manly excellence in their own sphere; but, irrespective of their tastes and talents, to rise out of their sphere. Biographies of men of genius are written with the direct intent to excite the whole class out of which these exceptional men sprang into an imitation of their efforts. Here and there, doubtless, some worthy nature gets encouragement from these narratives; but the general effect is to start young men into courses of life, and lead them to the adoption of callings and professions, to which they have no natural adaptation.

The lesson of the lives of these men is not left to be gathered by the common sense of their readers; but the biographies are written for the sake of the lesson, and, of course, the lesson is pointedly shaped to its purpose. The idea kept prominently uppermost in these biographies, as in all the teachings of their writers, is, that a man may be anything that he chooses to become; that will, determination, purpose, labor, perseverance, will accomplish anything—all true with relation to some men, and all false with relation to the majority of men. The effect of this upon bright men, who have sense enough to see what kind of a life they are adapted to, and who do not need the stimulus which works like these are calculated to supply, is, of course, not bad; but the stupid, the weak, the obtuse, the slow, are those generally who read the books, and who are influenced by them into a life for which they have no natural fitness.

Let us, for a moment, look at some of the maxims which these biographies are intended to illustrate, and which are in frequent use themselves. "Where there's a will there's a way"—one of the largest lies ever palmed off upon credulous humanity. Everybody has a will to be rich; but there is no way for everybody to be rich; there is no way for one man in ten to be rich. I suppose that at least a thousand men have a will to become President of the United States; but there is no way for one in five hundred of them to achieve the object of his ambition. There is a pretty universal will for social or political distinction; but the laudable ways of obtaining it are not many nor easy.

"Labor conquers all things"—another lie, as it is accepted and used. The power of the laborer must be equal to the power required by his task, or his labor will conquer nothing. Set an ass to carry an elephant's burden, and his back will be broken. The man of few brains cannot do the work of the man of many brains. Labor may read many books, without conquering one of them. Labor may read Shakspere; but labor alone did not write Shakspere, and labor alone, without Shakspere's brains, can never equal him.

"Nothing is impossible to him who wills"—a sentence of Mr. Emerson's, I think, though only a repetition of a Chinese maxim, and about as true as we should naturally suppose a Chinese maxim would be.

Now these maxims, and the biographies and anecdotes which are written to illustrate and enforce them, all say to the boy and the young man this: "You can make of yourself anything you may choose to make. To become a great preacher, or a great lawyer, or a great physician, or a great financier, or a great statesman, all that it is necessary for you to do is to will, to labor, and to persevere." Like the accommodating showman, who was inquired of as to which might be the kangaroo and which the hyena in his collection, they say: "Vichever you please, gentlemen; you pays your money and you takes your choice." All they have to do is to pay the requisite amount of labor, and the key of destiny will be placed in their hands.

It is under spurs like these that multitudes of men come up, and enter into walks of life for which they have no natural fitness. Victims of the false ideas promulgated upon this subject may be counted by thousands in this country—disappointed men—unqualified for the posts they have patiently and faithfully labored to reach and fill, and spoiled for the range of life in which they naturally belonged.

But, before I go further in this direction, I have another matter to discuss, which may be introduced by the proposition that every well-made man is a self-made man. It matters not whether he rise from vulgar poverty, or vulgar riches; whether his roots be planted in high or in humble life; whether he have the advantage of books and preceptors, or whether he acquire his education by direct contact with facts and things; whether he be a day-laborer in the garden of his neighbor, or a life-laborer in the vineyard of his Lord; if he be a well-made man, he is always a self-made man.

I mean, by this, that there is no instituted process by which a true manhood may be manufactured; that there is no educational mill which takes in boys and turns out men; that all who become men of power reach their estate by the same self-mastery, the same self-adjustment to circumstances, the same voluntary exercise and discipline of their faculties, and the same working of their life up to, and into, their high ideals of life.

The popular notion is, that only he is a self-made man who, without the aid of schools, or the regular processes of education, arrives at excellence in knowledge, or who, without the advantages of wealth and culture, achieves high position.

The self-made man is thus, in the popular apprehension, a remarkable man—a most honorable and worthy exception to the general rule. A day-laborer, for instance, acquires in the intervals of his toil a score of languages, and he is dubbed a self-made man, though his acquisitions may be useless to the community in which he lives, and an absolute disadvantage to himself and his family. A man by craft, and cunning, and miserly meanness, may come up from some low place, and acquire wealth, and, through wealth, influence; and straightway people will speak of him as a self-made man. A vulgar wretch, by the arts of the demagogue—by chicanery, and duplicity, and bribery—may arrive at place and power; and he will always find toadies and tools enough around him to glorify him as a self-made man. A peculiar honor seems to be attached to such men as these, as if whatever they might do were more remarkable and creditable than if done by others. The music of a corn-stalk fiddle or a pumpkin trumpet may not be overwhelmingly ravishing in itself; but we are expected to admire it, because corn-stalks and pumpkin-vines are not materials usually drawn upon for the manufacture of musical instruments.

Of self-made men like these, the high places of this country are shamefully full to-day; but the majority of them are not self-made men at all. We have self-made governors, self-made members of Congress, self-made preachers, doctors, and lawyers; self-made sheriffs and justices; self-made mayors and aldermen; self-made scoundrels and self-made noodles of various denominations; but self-made men are by no means so plenty. It would not be safe to predicate genuine manhood of every person who rises from poverty to wealth, or who lifts himself from common life to positions of influence and power. It might bring us into relations which would damage both our comfort and our character, even should we be so fortunate as to escape with our pocket-handkerchiefs and watches.

Though the popular idea of self-made men includes all the classes which have been alluded to, it is applied in a better sense, and more particularly, to those who have arrived at learning and legitimate personal power without the aid of schools. These are called self-made men to distinguish them from college-made men, or "university-men." It would not be difficult to select two men, of equal and similar natural gifts, representatives respectively of these two classes, working side by side in life, and illustrating the difference in the temper and quality of their manhood. It would not be difficult to see why the man who educates himself, without the aid of professional preceptors, always surpasses in personal power him who is simply a college-made man.

Now let me be understood with relation to what —for the purposes of this discussion—I call a college-made man. Let me first repeat the proposition that all well-made men are self-made men; and now let me say that the majority of self-made men are men who have had a "liberal education." A strictly college-made man is one who has adopted and obeyed the arbitrary and undiscriminating laws of the schools for his development; who has submitted himself, with his fellows, to all the prescribed processes; who has swallowed, without a question, the food prepared alike for him and them, and who has gone to the work of his life without a particle of training addressed to his special individuality, or without the slightest knowledge of the relations of his individuality to the world of life upon which he has undertaken to exercise his power. Such are the men who pray by rote and preach by rule; whose individual personal power is absolutely nothing; who are simply tolerated as necessary and cheaply-procured parts of ecclesiastical machinery. Such are the men who make mockery of law; who hold principles subject to precedents, and who forget justice in their blind worship of words and forms and phrases. Such are the men who prescribe the name of a drug for the name of a disease, and who lay down the lives of their neighbors, and would possibly be willing to lay down their own, rather than depart from their old, unreasoning routine.

Such as these I call college-made men, in contradistinction from self-made men. Both from college and from the world outside, noble, self-made men arise—men who know their own individual powers; who intelligently select the nutriment which those powers demand; who understand the relations of their individuality to the life of the world; who place themselves in contact with facts and affairs, and who, with an ideal of excellence before them, which their own imaginations have builded, build themselves up to it, and into it. Such are the men who elect, appropriate, and assimilate, from the wide variety of food presented to them, that which will nourish them, whether it come from the intellectual commons of college-life, prepared and presented by the accredited professional cooks, or whether it be hunted down in the wilderness, and eaten by the wayside.

The prominent characteristic of self-made men is individuality—a quality never characteristic of college-made men. When I say this, I beg you to keep in mind the vital distinction between these two classes which I have endeavored to define, and the fact that self-made men come more frequently from the college than from the world outside. In any process of training to which they may be subjected, they never allow their self-hood to be crushed. They take in that which they need; they reject that which they do not need—that which bears no relation to their individuality. They make themselves, and are not made by others—that is, they voluntarily bring their powers up to the work which they see themselves adapted to do; they feed themselves with relation to their work; they grow from the centre, and organize as they grow; and all the efforts of their life go out on the lines of the relations of their individuality to the world and its affairs.

Power, in its quality and degree, is the measure of manhood. Scholarship, save by accident, is never the measure of a man's power. It may be inferior to his power; it may be greater than his power; it may exist unaccompanied by power at all, as it does in all who are simply college-made. All the positive, progressive thinking and work of this world, are done by self-made men. The life of these men may pass through college-made men—considerably diluted—using them for vehicles, and thus become indefinitely diffusive and effective; but all positive human power abides in and proceeds from those self-nourished, self-sustained, self-educated, self-trained souls that place themselves in vital contact with the things of God and man, and organize and use them according to their respective individualities.

College-made men can tell what they have learned by measure. They can be called up and made to deliver thoughts upon any given subject by platoons. They have profound reverence for authority. They are always loyal partisans. They contentedly abide within the precincts of creeds. Pure scholarship is always conservative. It clings to, and loves to become the ornament of, dominant institutions, and is ever timid of change. It swims easily along the current of peaceful life, but shrinks from emergencies, and shirks the work of revolutions. It does not know how to deal with new questions. It has no vital, sympathetic connection with the life of the world; and shuts its ears to the din, and its eyes to the dust, of its conflicts. It is too often a dead-weight upon social and political reforms. Its life is a borrowed and specific life, and has no power of self-adjustment to the shifting circumstances of a world of change, and the constantly new developments of a progressive age and race. It lives in, and upon, the past; and draws neither motive from the present nor inspiration from the future.

College-made men are very fine ornamental-men—very good things to have for celebrations and occasions of show. They excel in contributions to family newspapers. They collate excellent school-books. They preach unexceptionable sermons to very exceptional people, and reverently put off their shoes among those who have the reputation of tender corns. The self-made men of the world—self-made in college or out of college—may be very rough men—men who will shock your prejudices, and offend your notions of propriety, and scare you by their innovations, and horrify you by their lack of reverence for great names and venerable conventions and institutions; but they are the only men whose productions will possess permanent attractions for you. They are the only men who can feed and stimulate and move you, and satisfy the cravings of your nature. They have original power; they possess individuality: and the only fresh things introduced into the world, from year to year, and from generation to generation, are borne by the hand of individuality.

Having exhibited my idea of the self-made, as contradistinguished from the college-made, man, I am ready to make the proposition that every man's natural organization is adapted to the fulfilment of a certain office in the world. In making this proposition, I only say that God gives every man individuality of constitution, and a chance for achieving individuality of character; that He puts special instruments into every man's hands by which to make himself and achieve his mission. I suppose that the proposition will hardly be controverted by any one. It certainly must underlie all sound theories of human development, even if it be not self-evident.

Every man, therefore, as he has individuality of nature, may have individuality of character; and every man who can achieve individuality of character can be, either in a higher or humbler degree, a self-made man. It is a fact, I suppose, that there is comparatively little individuality of character in the world. The rule is against it, because the influences of the world are against it. We are all soldiers of the king of fashion, and dress in uniform. We march in battalions under the banner of public opinion. We choose our courses and our callings, not with reference to our own powers, but with reference to conventional notions touching the desirableness of those courses and callings. In this way, the individuality of our natures is suppressed and ultimately destroyed. They find in the work which they are set to do nothing to which they bear natural relation. Put a penknife to do the work of an axe, and you spoil at once an instrument that only bears relation to quills and finger-nails; and it is hardly more or less than truth to say that the majority of men put themselves, or are put, to work to which they have no natural adaptation.

We find that, in the world's estimate, certain professions, callings, and trades are held highest—held to be most honorable and respectable. So the whole world rushes after them—rushes into them; so half of the world gets out of its place at once, and loses its individuality; and so half of the world gets made by its calling, and does not make itself at all.

Now, the truth is that every man is respectable, and every man grows in power symmetrically, only when he is in his place. No man is respectable when he is out of his place; no man can grow in characteristic power when out of his place. All thrifty and successful self-making must depend not only upon an intelligent selection of nourishment for our powers, but an intelligent selection of the work which they are best adapted to do.

If you have ever attended an exhibition of horses, you will remember that they are presented in a great variety of size, and style of form and action. One is a truck-horse, another is a farm-horse; one is a family-horse, another a saddle-horse; one is a fancy horse, and another a fast horse. The fast horse is the most popular—the most admired and coveted by the crowd. These different classes of horses are each adapted to a different kind of labor, and can only manifest their individual qualities when put to their legitimate work. They can only properly develop, or make themselves, by that work. Now suppose, with a view to the popularity of fast horses as a class, and not with reference to individual qualities at all, these horses, in all their variety, are entered for the premium on speed. Think what a figure they would make on the course! The real—the only—contest, would be among those that have a natural adaptation to speed; while the remainder would go lumbering along behind, and, by the clumsiness of their extraordinary efforts, would render themselves ridiculous. Boys would hoot at them; dogs would bark at them; and they would come in so far behind that their drivers would be obliged to join in the laugh that would sweep along the line of spectators.

Now drive all from the track, and bring them up in classes; and you will see that we have a very different result. The elephantine truck-horse walks slowly by, the representative of sturdy strength; and there is nothing ridiculous about him now. The docile farm-horse trots quietly along in fitting harness, and proves himself to be a legitimate object of our admiration. The family-horse, at an easy pace, bears over the course his freight of women and children, and he, too, is admirable—nay, he may be lovable. The saddle-horse ambles along under his rider, and we pronounce him both beautiful and graceful. You perceive that all these animals were ridiculous and contemptible so long as they undertook to do that to which their individualities were not adapted; and that all became pleasing and admirable, the moment they took their own place, and entered upon their legitimate work.

Now, suppose all these horses had actually been trained with reference to the popular opinion that speed is the only desirable thing, or the most desirable thing, in a horse. Suppose the truck-horse, for example, had been put to his best as a trotter, through a long course of training: would he ever have made a fast horse? Never; and, what is much more to be lamented, he would have been spoiled for a truck-horse forever. His wind would have been broken, his knees started, and his spirit ruined. In other words, his individuality—thoroughly admirable in itself—would have been destroyed. The same may be said of all the other classes of animals I have mentioned. No possible training could make fast horses of them; and they could only receive training for high speed at the cost of their individuality, and the loss of their ability to do that work well for which they were originally designed.

What a lesson for us is there in this illustration! Bear me witness that the track of American public and professional life is crowded with human truck-horses and farm-horses and family-horses and saddle-horses, all entered for the premium on speed, all making themselves ridiculous by the efforts they put forth to win it, and all spoiling themselves for the sphere to which their native individualities are adapted.

Thousands of these unhappy men were started and stimulated in their courses by such general, indiscriminate counsels as I have alluded to. As boys—as young men—they were told to "aim high," and particularly informed that if they pointed their arrows at the sun, the flight would be higher than it would be if the aim were lower,—another of those precious maxims, by-the-way, of which the world has too many; as if it were not better to knock from a

Virginia fence a respectable gray squirrel, than to spend one's shots on blank blue sky! No man who can hit anything, or who was ever made to hit anything, can afford to waste his arrows upon an object which he knows they can never reach. Even if the acquisition of learning were the grand object of a man, definiteness of aim would serve him better than indefiniteness, though it is not so essential; but when his object is to cultivate that power which is the measure of his manhood, his aim must be determined by the shape of his arrow, the size of his bow, and the strength of his arm.

The prizes of professional and political life are those which the great world of unformed mind is taught to regard not only as desirable above all things, but as obtainable by all men; and, being both desirable and obtainable, to be striven for. The effect has been to crowd professional life with mountebanks and inferior men, and political life with demagogues. It will not be disputed, I suppose, that there are more men engaged in the professions of law and medicine than the country has any need of; more than can obtain a respectable livelihood for themselves. The popular notion—the popular fallacy—is, that if a man is going to make anything of himself, he must be in public or professional life of some sort.

I hesitate to speak of the effect of these false ideas upon the Christian ministry, because it is impossible to judge how far they have been complicated with conscience, honest self-consecration, and motives of beneficence. A young man commences a course of training with reference to a professional life. He proposes, we will say, to become a lawyer. Possibly he has a decided adaptation to that profession; but, midway in his college course, he becomes a religious man. Immediately—with no sufficient regard to the adaptedness of his individuality to the work of the ministry—he determines to become a preacher. I suppose that nine out of every ten occupants of the American pulpit were moved to the choice of their profession by their hearts, without any really competent examination of the quality of their heads. One consequence of this is, that we have a Christian ministry in this country which embraces a larger number of honest, good, pure, self-sacrificing men than can be found, as I believe, in any other class of men in the world. In my judgment the American Christian ministry contains the least corrupted, and the least corruptible, of men; but, alas! I am afraid that not one half of them are self-made—that not more than one half of them have appreciable power as ministers of the Gospel of Jesus Christ. They break down under the effect of labors for which they have no natural adaptation; they rove unfruitful and unhappy from pulpit to pulpit; they fail to command the attention and respect of the world around them; and they have the life-long grief of seeing the work to which their hearts are devoted failing to prosper in their hands.

I will not undertake to decide so delicate a question as this matter involves; but I may be allowed to say that it seems to me as if it were a more Christian thing to be a first-rate Christian lawyer, or a first-rate Christian farmer, or a first-rate Christian shoemaker, than a fifth-rate Christian minister. If a young man becomes religious, and puts his life under the law of love, it is not therefore necessary to his highest efficiency in the Master's service that he become a preacher. Nay, the pulpit may be the place of all others in the world where he would be the most likely to do damage to the cause he loves.

With a respect for the Christian ministry of this country which is as great as Puritan training and a thousand delightful personal friendships can make it, I am compelled to believe that a full half of its members are little more than the creatures of their colleges and the mouth-pieces of their theological schools; that they entered their profession, not because they were adapted to it, or saw themselves specially adapted to it, but because they were moved to it by a mistaken sense of duty, or a false idea of professional life. It seems to me that one of the most pitiful objects in this world is a made-up Christian minister—a manufactured preacher—a man whose individuality has failed to find its appropriate nutriment and its appropriate field of demonstration in his office—a man who is useless where he is, and helpless elsewhere.

Of the over-crowded professions of law and medicine, I speak with less hesitation, because I have to deal with less delicate motives of life. Men go into these professions to get a living, and get a position. Talk to a poor boy about becoming what people call "a self-made man," and he invariably thinks of becoming a lawyer or a physician. Go into any preparatory school: you will find that nearly every boy is aiming at one of these professions. Now if you will reflect for a moment, you will come to the conclusion that the number of really good lawyers and good physicians is comparatively small; and when you have reached this conclusion, you will be able to see how many of them have mistaken their vocation.

In the popular idea, the medical profession is the least showy and attractive of the three which we call learned; but think how rare and peculiar the individuality must be that is perfectly, or even measur ably, adapted to it. Think of the delicate insight that is necessary to judge of temperaments; to detect the true relations of symptoms to diseases in different constitutions; to decide when remedies will assist nature, and when they will not; to draw the line between diseases and disorders; and to discriminate between bodily and mental derangements!—Think of the tender sympathy that is necessary to him who stands beside woman in her hour of trial, and bends over the cradles of suffering children, and moves from house to house, to help poor humanity in its extremity! Think of the strong, serene self-poise that he must sustain notwithstanding this sympathy—the firm equanimity and cheerful assurance which shall enable him to carry confidence and hope to every pillow, and pass through the most terrific trials of heart and nerve and skill in great emergencies! Think of the pure heart, the unswerving honor, the Christian integrity, that should be his around whom the faith and the affections of five hundred families cluster!—who enters into their life, shares their secrets, and has their dearest earthly interests in keeping! Think of all this, and of much more that might be named; and then think of the multitudes of men spawned upon the country every year by our medical institutions; many of them Bob Sawyers and Ben Allens—dissolute and unprincipled; many of them rough and obtuse; some of them who have studied medicine simply because they were not adapted to law or theology—reminding one of the dog that was supposed to be good for rabbits because he was good for nothing else; think of all this, I say, and then marvel not that a distinguished professor—distinguished alike at the dissecting and the breakfast table—has said that if all the drugs in the world were emptied into the sea, it would be infinitely better for mankind and infinitely worse for the fishes!

Notwithstanding this, the profession of medicine is one which I hold in profound and tender respect. My physician shall walk hand in hand with my pastor in my esteem, confidence, and affection; he shall be welcome to my table, my hearth-stone, and my heart: but I utter no more than a self-evident truth, when I say that, because a man passes an examination before a corps of professors, he is not necessarily qualified for a physician, and that there are numbers of the profession who sit in their offices, with their diplomas signed and sealed—aye, and framed and glazed before them—impatiently waiting for patients, who vulgarly look upon their profession as a trade, and in whose medical care it would not be safe to risk a sick horse worth the sum of twenty-five dollars.

Those who know more about the law than I do —worthy representatives of the legal profession—will tell you that it requires a rare organization to comprehend its philosophy, to master its principles and the detail of its facts and forms, and to treat each new question as it arises by successful practice. But common observation is sufficiently suggestive upon this matter. If you will classify the lawyers of your acquaintance under these four heads, as I name them —lawyers of eminence (count them), lawyers of respectability (count them), lawyers of mediocrity (the task grows difficult), and lawyers of absolute inferiority (you can't count them), you will be able to judge how many of them have mistaken their profession. A man has no right to be inferior in his profession, or, rather, he has no right to be in a profession in which he is inferior. Every man who can be a first-rate something—as every man can be who is a man at all —has no right to be a fifth-rate something; for a fifth-rate something is no better than a first-rate nothing.

I have sometimes fancied that the reason why so few are adapted to the three varieties of professional life which we are considering, is, that there was no original provision made for these classes of men. When Eve, our dear, over-tempted grandmother, did that which "brought death into the world and all our woe," she did that which brought physicians into the world and all our lawyers and ministers. If our race had not fallen, it would not have needed ministers, certainly; and a race that would do without ministers, would offer a very unpromising field for the professions of law and medicine. I cannot help thinking that when the golden thousand years, which have been promised us, shall come, professional life will be very much less desirable than it is now. Every man will be as good as a minister, and every lawyer will be—a man; and the favorite professional joke about the existence of an "alarming state of health" will become as serious as it is stale.

But, at this day, it is in politics, quite as much as in the professions, that we see the effect of those unwise counsels, given to the young, which have been noticed in this discussion. A poor boy rises to become a governor, as many a poor boy has worthily risen—as many a poor boy, I trust, may worthily rise; or he has become a member of Congress, or achieved some higher or humbler position in political life. To the young mind, these titles and these positions are so represented as to appear to be the prizes for which their possessors have striven—as a fitting and natural object and reward of their labors. The young have not been taught by their self-appointed counsellors that manhood is the highest human estate; that office can confer honor upon no man who is worthy of it, and that it will disgrace every man who is not. They have not been taught that to desire office, and to labor for it, for the sake of its honors and distinctions, is the meanest of all ambitions, and the most degrading of all pursuits. They have not been taught to distinguish between a self-made man and a self-made governor, and brought to understand that a self-made man is greater than a governor, and that a self-made governor is less than a man. Vital distinctions like these have been ignored; and the consequence is, that boys without beards may be counted by thousands in this country who have already begun their dreams of political distinction—who look upon political distinction as a legitimate aim of life, and who are, of course, growing up into demagogues.

Among all the dangers which threaten this country, I know of none so great as that which arises from the greed of small men for office, and the ease with which they obtain it. When the good and the worthy men of a nation like ours—men who do not need office, but men whom office sadly needs—become disgusted with politics, because of the inferior society and undignified contests into which it introduces them, the country may well tremble with apprehension. When the stable gives law to the library, and the boy who does chores for his board puts his feet upon the parlor-table, and madam stays at home to take care of the baby while Betty makes her calls and goes shopping, it is about time to begin to think of breaking up housekeeping. If the effect of small men in office be degrading to office and disastrous to the country, the effect of office upon small men is quite as disastrous. There is never danger that office will spoil a man who is fit for office. No man who has been spoiled by an office—either by holding it or by losing it—was ever fit for it. A true man is just as much a man when his coat is off as when it is on. Take the coat from a scarecrow—which is simply a bundle of old clothes in office—and you spoil it. In all cases where office injures a man, it is too large for him, and he has no business with it.

Let a man hold an office for any length of time, to which the individuality of his nature and character bears no legitimate relations, and he will be spoiled for the place in which he belongs.

The country is full of these men, or wrecks of men —disappointed, soured, ruined—out of office, out of money, out of credit, out of courage, out at elbows, out in the cold, and usually, I regret to say, exceedingly dry. Ah! if every man who holds, or has held, office in the land, were in the place where he belongs, what a supply of farm-laborers would be given to the great producing interest of this country! What a convulsion would run through the shoe-trade! What a relief would be felt by our mercantile marine! Nay, what an impetus would be given to stone-dressing in some of our public institutions!

In view of the sad effects of the indiscriminate rush into professional and political pursuits, we may well deplore those counsels that are stimulating the ambition of the young everywhere, and urging them into a life which, to half of them at least, must necessarily be unsuccessful and unhappy. God has made all men different one from another. Nature broke her die while moulding you and me as truly as she did while moulding Sheridan. The faculties of our souls differ as widely as the features of our faces and the forms of our frames. Thus, all true self-making must be carried on with relation to this characteristic selfhood.

We see some men rising into a splendid manhood without the aid of teachers—carrying grandly up from their individual nature a corresponding individual character, and finding their place and their work by an unsophisticated instinct. We see others, with the aids of schools and teachers, doing the same thing, perhaps even more grandly; but we see men who went off with these latter, upon the same early educational cruise, coming back razeed—their characteristic upper-deck gone, and that which was their peculiar glory all cut away. One is led by his individuality up into a characteristic development and into his place; the other permits his individuality to be blotted out, and takes, instead, the mixed, incongruous, and undigested and indigestible individualities of his preceptors.

Lest I be thought to undervalue what is popularly denominated education, I devote a few words specially to the subject. All systems of school and college education have the necessary imperfection of regarding and treating men in masses. Classes are formed, not upon a natural but upon an arbitrary basis. The young men who are to be preachers and physicians, and lawyers and merchants, and editors and farmers, and manufacturers and mechanics, are all put through the same text-books, the same exercises, the same discipline. There is no plan of education, except the individual, which can obviate this disadvantage—for it obviously is a great disadvantage. Now the man who educates, or makes, himself, by drawing to himself that which his individuality craves and needs, and by putting himself to the work to which his individuality is adapted, has an advantage, at this single point, over him who goes through school and college, and yields himself wholly to their undiscriminating discipline. There are disadvantages, however, on both sides. The habit of study—of mental labor—and the general knowledge acquired in a systematic education, give the regular student great advantage over the irregular.

Every student can make himself just as well in college as he can out, and he ought to be permitted—nay, made—to do it a great deal better. I pity the poor fellows who have to do their work alone; and I pity quite as much those who permit themselves to be spoiled. As I have said before, scholarship is the measure of no man's power, though the opposite opinion seems to prevail among the teachers of schools and the faculties of colleges. Two men may be exactly equal in scholarship, one of whom will have no more power in the world than a baby, while the other will be a giant, shaking thrones, and moulding the lives and destinies of nations. The difference between these two men will be simply this: one will have sacrificed his individuality or self-hood to his scholarship; the other will have appropriated his scholarship as food for his individuality. Nearly all students, however, make themselves after they leave college. Ten years after a man takes his bachelor's degree, he looks back upon what he learned in college, and the training he received there, as a very small part, and usually the least practical part, of his education. The moment he is beyond college-walls, he drops such books as do not feed him, and seizes upon those that do; and, if he be not injured, he will immediately bring himself into his natural relation to the world's thinking, society, and affairs.

It matters little by what mode a man develops his power, or by what path he finds his place in the world, provided he successfully does both. When John C. Heenan was preparing for his fight with Tom Sayers, he subjected himself to the most rigorous discipline required by the professors of the ring, while his antagonist took his own way in the matter, and did as he liked. When they came to their struggle, it was a question of pluck and muscle; and, the pluck being equal, the larger muscle won, simply because it was larger, and not because it was better. So, in the conflicts of life, it is a question of brains and power. It is not a question how much a man knows, but what use he can make of what he knows; not a question of what he has acquired, and how he has been trained, but of what he is, and what he can do.

In truth, it is in work that a man develops and makes himself, more than in any prescribed or individually chosen mode of training. A man can only become a good accountant—can only develop a good accountant's powers and aptitudes—by the duties of the counting-room. If I wished to make a good woodchopper of a man whom I believed to be good for nothing else, I would not send him to a gymnasium as a preliminary process. I would put an axe into his hand, direct him to the woods, and there let him work it out. Every man's powers have relation to some kind of work; and whenever he finds that kind of work which he can do best—that to which his powers are best adapted—he finds that which will give him the best development, and that by which he can best build up, or make, his manhood.

But there is a higher point from which this subject may be viewed; and, in the moral as in the natural world, the higher the point of observation, the more extended and comprehensive the survey. Christianity, for illustration, regards man from a higher point than any system of philosophy; yet few may be philosophers, while all may be Christians; and it is better to be a Christian than to be a philosopher. So all cannot be preachers and doctors and lawyers, and authors and statesmen and orators; yet all can be men: and it is better to be a man (begging pardon of the women) than to be anything else, for anything else may be something less. It is better to be a self-made man—filled up according to God's original pattern—than to be half a man, made after some other man's pattern. Manhood overtops all titles.

> "The *rank* is but the guinea's *stamp*;
> A man 's a man for a' that."

Labor, calling, profession, scholarship, and artificial

and arbitrary distinctions of all sorts, are incidents and accidents of life, and pass away. It is only manhood that remains, and it is only by manhood that man is to be measured. When this proposition shall be comprehended and accepted, it will become easy to see that there is no such thing as menial work in this world. No work that God sets a man to do—no work to which God has specially adapted a man's powers—can properly be called either menial or mean. The man who blacks your boots and blacks them well, and who engages in that variety of labor because he can do it better than he can do anything else, may have, if he choose, just as sound and true a manhood as you have, not only after he gets through the work of his life, but now, with your boots in one hand and your shilling in the other. There is very much dirtier work done in politics, and sometimes in the professions, than that of blacking boots; work, too, which destroys manhood, or renders its acquisition impossible.

If I have attained the object of this lecture, I have presented to you, and impressed upon you, certain important and intimately related truths, which I will briefly recount:

First. That the faculty of self-help is that which distinguishes man from animals; that it is the Godlike element, or holds within itself the Godlike element, of his constitution.

Second. That God gives every man individuality of constitution, and the faculty to achieve individuality of character, through an intelligent selection of food for the nourishment, and labor for the discipline and development, of his powers.

Third. That those counsels which convey to young persons, indiscriminately, the idea that they can make anything of themselves that they choose to make, are pernicious, from the fact that many will choose to make of themselves that for which Nature never designed them, and will thus spoil themselves for the work to which their individualities are adapted.

Fourth. That a man can never be well-made who is not, in reality, self-made; whose native individuality is not the initial and the dominant fact in his development.

Fifth. That it is a mistake to suppose that a man, in order to be self-made, must necessarily seek the peculiar development that will prepare him for professional or political life.

Sixth. That no man has a right to be engaged in a calling or profession in which he occupies an inferior position, while there exists a calling or profession in which he may occupy a superior position; and that no man is respectable when out of his place, however respectable the place he occupies may be.

Seventh. That a man without a title is greater than

a title without a man; and that a self-made man may occupy, in honor and the noblest respectability, the humblest place in the world, if its duties are only those for which God designed his powers.

There are other truths that I might add to this rehearsal, but they would be hardly more than modifications of these, or correlatives of these. I should be sorry, if, by presenting and insisting on them, I had dampened in a single bosom a worthy ambition. I should regret the awakening in any mind of questions that would prove fatal to a legitimate career. But facts are facts. I am not responsible for them; and I am only anxious that no man, through influence of mine, use them to his harm.

I account the loss of a man's life and individuality, through the non-adaptation or the mal-adaptation of his powers to his pursuits, the greatest calamity, next to the loss of personal virtue, that he can suffer in this world. I believe that a full moiety of the trials and disappointments that darken a world which, I am sure, was intended to be measurably bright and happy, are traceable to this prolific source. Men are not in their places. Women are not in their places. John is doing badly the work that William would do well, and William is doing badly the work that John would do well; and both are disappointed, and unhappy, and self-unmade. It is quite possible that John is doing Mary's work and Mary is doing John's work.

> "Of all sad words of tongue or pen,
> The saddest are these: 'it might have been.'"

Now I do not suppose we shall ever get the world all right on this matter. I do not suppose that all men will find the places for which they were designed, or that, in many instances, Maud will marry the Judge: but an improvement can be made; and if an improvement ever shall be made, it will be through the inculcation of sounder views among the young.

I am sick of the stupid cant by which stupid men strive to inflame the ambition of the youth that are placed under their direction. Far too many of our schools are little better than places for the development of mental and moral fever. Both boys and girls are stimulated, by the infernal machinery of prizes, and honorary appointments, and fear of disgrace, and such counsels as those upon which I have already remarked, to the most ambitious aspirations, the most extravagant expectations, and the most extraordinary exertions. I verily believe that there are but few boys in this country who have not had the idea drilled into them, by teachers or by books, that they can be anything in this world that they choose to be, or really try to become.

The question which a youth is called upon to decide for himself, or which his parents and friends are called upon to decide for him, or assist him in deciding, is not what, with reference to the arbitrary standard of personal and social values accredited by the world, he chooses to be, but what God has chosen to make him. Woe to that youth who finds his choice at war with that of his Maker—who sets his powers to a life-task which they were never intended to perform!

If there be one man before me who honestly and contentedly believes that, on the whole, he is doing that work to which his powers are best adapted, I wish to congratulate him. My friend, I care not whether your hand be hard or soft; I care not whether you are from the office or the shop; I care not whether you preach the everlasting gospel from the pulpit, or swing the hammer over the blacksmith's anvil; I care not whether you have seen the inside of a college or the outside—whether your work be that of the head or that of the hand—whether the world account you noble or ignoble: if you have found your place, you are a happy man. Let no ambition ever tempt you away from it, by so much as a questioning thought. I say, if you have found your place—no matter what or where it is—you are a happy man. I give you joy of your good fortune; for if you do the work of that place well, and draw from it all that it can give you of nutriment and discipline and development, you are, or you will become, a man filled up—made after God's pattern—the noblest product of the world,—a self-made man.

FASHION.

THE proverb that it is as well to be out of the world as out of fashion, is an old one and a mean one; and it has so damaged the world that the alternative is come to be not so bad as it was. Indeed, it were better that a man should be out of the world than in some fashions. I do not speak with particular reference to dress, or manners, or social usage. It does not matter what a fool wears upon his back, or a flirt upon her head; nor does it matter how closely or how universally sensible and sober people imitate them, provided they are comfortable in their habit, and tradesmen drive a thrifty business. It is, of course, very sad to think how often good taste is perverted or ignored in the fabric and form of personal drapery, and how frequently common sense and common honesty are offended by the social customs which fashion ordains; but as uniformity to a considerable extent is desirable, let fashion be the law. It is well enough that a silly queen reign over an unimportant realm. So long as fashion is employed in the shops of the tailor and the milliner, she is engaged in entirely innocent and legitimate business. I am aware that her freaks in these departments often make us all ridiculous; but because they make us *all* ridiculous, there are none left to laugh at us—so we don't care. If fashion had only to do with forms and manners and methods which touch the person and the outer life, it would not be important as a subject of public discussion; but it goes deeper than this, and becomes a power of no mean magnitude in the world's life—even disputing supremacy with Christianity in our civilization.

It will be well for us, at starting, to obtain a sufficient idea of what fashion essentially is, and is not, even if we do not stop to define it fully. Fashion is not public opinion, or the result or embodiment of public opinion. It may be that public opinion will condemn the shape of a bonnet, as it may venture to do always, with the certainty of being right nine times in ten; but fashion will place it upon the head of every woman in America, and, were it literally a crown of thorns, she would smile contentedly beneath the imposition. Public opinion may be opposed to the winecup on the dinner-table, on festive occasions; but fashion places and keeps it there. Nay, fashion and public opinion, in all matters of form, are very often at variance; yet fashion is now, and always has been, stronger than public opinion. Fashion is aristocratic —autocratic; public opinion is democratic. Fashion is based upon the assumed or the admitted right of some man, or of some class, to rule; public opinion is the creature of universal suffrage.

I say that fashion is based upon the assumed or the admitted right of some men to rule. There seems to be in the human mind a native reverence for those who are high in position and social privilege—a native willingness to follow this class in all matters which do not touch the soul's life too deeply. Nay, there is a natural deference, in the majority of minds, to bold assumption of superiority, and bold assumption of the right to rule. The sway of that class which is, or assumes to be, superior, is fashion. What its members wear, the world wears. What their habits are—at the table, in the assembly, on the street—the world adopts. The Empress of France has but to change the position of a ribbon to set all the ribbons in Christendom to rustling. A single word from her convulses the whalebone markets of the world, and sends a thrill to the most frigid zone,—alike of world and woman. The mustaches of the world wax as the Emperor's wax, and wane as the Emperor's are waxed. Coat-collars rise and fall, hats expand and contract their brims, waistcoats change from black to white and from white to black, gloves blush and turn pale, in response to the monthly reports from the Tuileries. Fashion is based on the idea of caste; and the sturdiest democrat in politics is not unfrequently its blindest devotee in his individual and social life.

So, over all the broad realm of public opinion and public conscience, regardless of all recognised rules of taste and propriety, trampling all our democratic theory and practice under feet, Fashion holds her undisputed sway—Fashion, the self-ordained queen over subjects who bow to her, not only with no question as to her authority, but with joyful and unmeasured devotion of time and treasure. She holds in her hands the keys of social destiny. She blesses, and men and women smile; she bans, and they weep. The place where she stands becomes thenceforth holy ground. That which she embraces is sacred; that which she shuns is profane.

We have fashionable sins and fashionable follies, fashionable churches and fashionable schools, fashionable politics and fashionable medicine, fashionable authors and fashionable preachers, fashionable watering-places, fashionable hotels, fashionable streets and fashionable sides of streets. There is no department of life into which fashion does not thrust its hand, and there is no society, unless it be some such conservatory of ugliness as a Shaker community, that does not bow to it. Consequently, or concomitantly, we have a fashionable style of manhood and womanhood, a fashionable social life, and a fashionable literature; and these, as opposed to democracy and a genuine Christian civilization, I propose to make the subject of my discussion.

Here let us define terms a little further. I have spoken of fashion as opposed to democracy and Christian civilization; but by these latter I do not intend to indicate unlike or unrelated things. The popular definition of democracy is something more and something better than "a glittering generality." Democracy is, in a most important sense, practical Christianity, and Christianity is, indeed, the life and soul of a pure democracy. The fundamental idea of Christian society is human equality, and the democratic root strikes into the same soil. Christianity and democracy alike crown men with equal rights and privileges, make them individually responsible, and pass through accidents of birth, circumstances, and position, to lay their claims and their awards upon every soul. They are so closely allied, that a Christian government must necessarily have the democratic element predominant; and a democratic government only needs to lose its Christianity as a controlling power to become a despotism. Wherever, and under whatever form, we find a government that is essentially Christian, we shall find a government that is essentially democratic. I beg you to regard me, therefore, as speaking always and alike in behalf of Christian civilization and American democracy. There is not an influence of fashion which does not tell against both, and both are associated in every advantage gained by either.

What is a fashionable style of manhood and womanhood? It is not always the same in all places, but this is true of it everywhere, I think: that it never demands Christianity, or a regard for popular rights, as an essential element. I have never known a man to be denied the possession of a fashionable style of manhood on the ground that he was an infidel, or an atheist, or a despot, or an oppressor of the poor. I may say, indeed, that I have never known a thorough Christian or an honest democrat to be the possessor of a fashionable style of manhood. A lack of earnestness in any great or useful pursuit, a blind worship of rank and of those who hold it, a childish sensitiveness to the charms of personal adornment, a disposition to magnify above things essential all matters of form and ceremony, a hatred of labor and contempt for the laborer, and a selfish jealousy that walks hand in hand with an undisguised personal vanity—these are the leading characteristics of what may be denominated a fashionable style of manhood and womanhood,—the basis of an outside life, ordered in obedience to an outside law. You will perceive that my definition will establish a great difference between the fashionable man and the polite or gentle man. The fashionable man is often popularly mistaken for the polite man, and, I may say, is greatly interested in being mistaken for him. Indeed, he often mistakes himself for him. The difference between a gentleman and a man of fashion is just as distinct as that between a man of fashion and an unpretending boor. The fashionable man may be, and often is, a brute in his instincts and in his secret life; he may be a cringing puppy among his superiors; he may be the meanest toady of power and place; he may be intolerably insolent among those whom he deems his inferiors; but certainly these things are not possible with a gentleman.

It is not to be denied that genuine ladies and gentlemen frequently associate with men and women who have no further claim to consideration than that they are fashionable, or that ladies and gentlemen give more or less countenance and coloring to fashionable life; but there is no man in all the world more conscious than the purely fashionable man that there is a style of manhood above his, and a style of social life in which he has no home save as a favored or a fawning guest. He is only an imitation of something which he envies. The gentleman is solid mahogany; the fashionable man is only veneer.

The fashionable man, either rich and powerful or allied with those who are, makes social preëminence the end of his life. He dreads poverty, but bows low to vulgar and insolent wealth. All his affinities run in sordid channels. He meanly worships the rich and the powerful, the titled and the gently-bred, and regards all contact with other classes as contamination. His moralities are the fashionable moralities, whatever those may happen to be. If a corrupt and licentious court be the ruling influence, corruption and licentiousness become fashionable with him. If the leading minds are mockers at the Christian religion, he treats it with irreverence and contempt. He calls things good and bad by fashionable names. An earnest Christian with him is a bigot; preaching is cant; prayer is a sort of Puritan snuffle; a life of self-sacrifice to duty is fanaticism; godliness, gloom; conscientious strictness in religious duty or observance, the being "deeply, darkly, beautifully blue." On the other hand, a libertine is only a man of the world; a rich and well-dressed sot only lives too fast, or has an infirmity which renders it necessary that he should be seen before dinner to be appreciated. Swindling by himself and friends is regarded as sharp practice, and obtaining clothes without paying for them, "doing the tailor,"—a very sad joke to one of the parties, but traditionally a good one with the other.

Now for a glance at another picture. Here and there in the world—more numerous in the aggregate than those know who do not love their society—there are men and women whose lives are ordered from within; whose motive and regulating force is love of God and love of men; who are loyal to conscience, earnest in all benevolent enterprise, self-sacrificing, most happy in the communication of happiness, without jealousy and without hypocrisy; who esteem it a more honorable thing to forgive an injury than to resent one; who are humble in their estimate of themselves, and who in honor prefer one another. This, very briefly, is what I understand to be the Christian style of manhood and womanhood.

Now the difference between this and the fashionable style is certainly the difference between antagonistic opposites. The man of fashion is exclusive, and has no sympathy with any but his class or clique. The Christian is universal in his sympathies, embracing in his prayer and in his charitable endeavor every nation, class, and individual. One seeks only to make the world useful to himself; the other, to make himself useful to the world. One seeks for, or seizes, privilege; the other is happiest in ministry. One is a despot; the other is a democrat.

If we approach our second point in the discussion—fashionable social life—we shall find that that which is true of one is true of many. Social life is the interflow of the life of individuals; but social life has individuality. It has its creeds, customs, and conventionalities. It has its store and style of power. It has its currently understood, but capriciously fluctuating, laws. It is a distinct, characteristic thing, to be looked at, turned over, and talked about. If I were called upon to give an opinion upon any form of social life, I should first wish to learn the object of its worship, and, second, the object of its pursuit. I know that a social life which worships God, and pursues the good of men, is a Christian social life; and I know just as well that a social life which worships money, and pursues social distinction as its end, is, in spirit and in fact, an aristocracy. It may have no titles, it may have no civil privileges; but, wherever its power can go,—into all matters, social and religious, political and military,—it will go with the characteristic influence of an aristocracy.

Such is the fashionable social life of America. If it boast no hereditary titles, it is not because it does not desire and worship them. If it have no civil privileges and prerogatives, it is not because it does not feel itself entitled to them. It is, in itself, the result of a conspiracy on the part of wealth and power for achieving and holding social distinction—elevation above the masses of men and the associations of labor. It separates itself from the commonwealth of humanity so far as it may, and believes in its right to rule and use men for its own aggrandizement and convenience.

This fashionable social life has, as I have said, its creeds, customs, and conventionalities. Thronged with jealousies within itself, it is jealous of all outside encroachment and interference. It has its own code of morals, which, more or less strict according to circumstances, is never up to the Christian standard. I do not believe that there is any fashionable life in the world that can justly be called Christian. If I go to the great cities, or even to the little cities, and witness the idleness, the intrigues, the frivolities, and the general self-seeking which characterize the fashionable social life that exists there; or, if I look in upon the wanton wastefulness and the worse than childish greed for display at a fashionable summer resort, I can find nothing that will remind me that man has either a nature or a destiny better than a beast,—nothing that indicates to me that man, as man, has common need of ministry and common privilege. The humanity within me is insulted by assumptions of superiority which ignore the regal supremacy of manhood.

The most intimate sympathy to be found in purely

fashionable society is that which comes through its low tone of morality. Wealth and power and place are considered sufficient in all fashionable social life to palliate, or atone for, almost every crime of which a man can be guilty. Morality is a matter of secondary importance; and there is nothing better understood than the conspiracy among fashionable people to sustain each other in practices which are only justifiable by their own low standard of morals. None of us will be obliged to tax the memory beyond measure to call up the image of a notorious libertine, petted by fashionable mothers of fashionable daughters, because he occupies a high place in fashionable society. None of us will be obliged to go out of his own neighborhood to meet with those whose sole claim to a place in fashionable society is based upon the possession of money won by gigantic frauds, or corrupt contracts, or oppression of the poor. I know of but one garment which the fashionable social life of this country borrows of Christianity. It is that ample mantle of charity which covers a multitude of sins—particularly fashionable sins.

Fashionable society has always been the ally and support of every instituted and profitable wrong. Let any wrong become the permanent source of wealth and power to any class of men, and fashionable society will at once become its defender. We have in the history of the passing times a competent illustration of this fact. If there be in all the world an institution which is both unnatural and unchristian, you will agree with me that it is human slavery; yet fashionable social life has always been in friendly alliance with it. The fashionable society of the North has meanly bowed down to and envied that class at the South whose wealth and position have been based upon the possession and the profits of human slaves; and even at this late day you will find the two classes sympathetic. With the exception of a few wretched politicians, there have been in the North no sympathizers with the great rebellion, undertaken on behalf of human slavery, not found in fashionable society. There has not been a time since the commencement of the great rebellion when it needed more than the striking of the fashionable class out of Baltimore to make that city as loyal as the city of Boston. Almost the only element of Northern society that was at first sympathetic with treason was the fashionable. In the city of Washington—the capital of this great nation—fashionable society even now bemoans the loss of the lordly swaggerers from whom for whole generations it had received its life-blood and law. By the means and through the influence of these men this society had made all reform unfashionable, made labor unfashionable, made Northern men unfashionable, made human freedom unfashionable, made Christianity and conscience unfashionable, made democracy itself unfashionable.

There sits in the White House, to-day, a most unfashionable man. His hands are clean from all suspicion of bribes,—but he is unfashionable. No President since Washington has sought so little to compass private ends and promote personal ambitions as he,—but he is unfashionable. He has but a single aim, which has actuated him through all the weary months of his public life—the restoration of national unity,—but he is unfashionable. With an army numbering a million of nobler and braver men than were ever before marshalled upon the field—an army finer than any king or emperor ever saw—and with a navy that within a year of the time of its creation revolutionized the modes of naval warfare throughout the world—head of a realm of thirty millions, and presiding calmly, conscientiously, and wisely over the history of the most eventful period of the national existence,—he remains a most unfashionable man. Honesty, integrity, patriotism, unflinching devotion to the great cause into which he has cast his life, boldness to do what he believes to be right, charitable moderation toward all,—none of these things have made him fashionable. Nay, occupying a position of moral grandeur which we cannot possibly apprehend, as it will be conceived by the future historian, there are fashionable people about him who regard him with ineffable contempt; fashionable people who owe to his moderation and large-hearted charity their immunity from iron gratings and hempen cravats. Let the nation thank God, that whatever else President Lincoln has been, he has not been a fashionable man.

Fashionable society has not only been the defender of every system of profitable wrong, in this and other countries, but it has been the constant opposer and reviler of humane and Christian reform. The fashionable instinct naturally rises against reform—against any scheme which tends to elevate the people, and relieve them from the rule of those who give law to fashionable life. Reforms are always democratic, and are based upon a recognition of the equality of men; and fashionable society can possibly have no sympathy with them. There is hardly a fact in all history more patent than this: that in the undertaking and prosecuting any humane or Christian reform, the fashionable class are never to be relied upon for aid, while their opposition in one form or another is certain. While this is true, it is just as true that the rule of Christian society, its motive and regulating force, is universal benevolence, which finds no plane of action and no rest save in the sentiment of universal brotherhood—the basis of a perfect democracy. So distinct are the spheres and the atmospheres of these two forms of social life, that the Christian gentleman finds nothing in fashionable society for the satisfaction of his social nature, and the fashionable man finds nothing in genuine Christian social life which is not to him a burden and a bore. Sometimes—quite universally, indeed—compromises are effected between fashionable and Christian social life, for the accommodation of worldly people with tender consciences and Christian people with tough consciences; but compromises of this character are always surrenders upon the wrong side. Christian society, by consenting to an alliance with it, consents to neutralization by it. It is the old and everlasting impossibility of serving God and Mammon.

We, as Americans, profess to be a Christian nation. We profess to believe that we live under a democratic government, and that we are democrats ourselves. We should be startled to learn that we had really been governed for years by an aristocracy; but what are the facts? How much, for the past fifty years, has Christian social life in Washington influenced the legislation of Congress? You know that I ask a question to be sadly laughed at. You know that fashionable society at the national capital has always been able to secure the performance of its behests. In close alliance with every profitable wrong, it has been able to lord it over the Christian element, which, weaker or stronger, has always been present. It has branded good, conscientious, Christian men as fanatics, and they have walked the streets of the national capital despised, proscribed, alone. It has contemptuously barred its doors against those whom posterity will number among its saints and its heroes. It has laughed to scorn those who have dared to speak of a higher than human law, and coupled their names with the foulest epithets which malice could invent. Arrogant, selfish, exclusive, meddlesome, the fashionable society of Washington has used the machinery of the government for its own support and aggrandizement. No unchristian and oppressive measure has ever found its slimy way through Congress, that was not either engineered or aided by the fashionable society of Washington. It has kept its gilded wares constantly in the political market. They have been hawked about by scheming women, who have boasted of successes won by flatteries and favors which degraded them and all who received them. It has never been the fashion to be virtuous in public affairs at Washington. It has never been the fashion to be devoted to the interests of the people there. Morality, integrity, religion, democracy, patriotism—these have only been names in Washington; and the men who have really believed in them, and who have undertaken to incorporate that which they represent into their living and doing, have been regarded with pity or derision.

I am smitten by wonder when I think of the power which bold assumption has in the world—when I see how it moulds the hearts and bends the wills of men. I am smitten by wonder when I see how the masses of men bow to the assumptions of fashionable society. I see everywhere a class of men who assume to give the law of social distinction to the communities in which they live. This law, so far as it reaches, is supreme. The great and the little, the rich and the poor, the old and the young, bow to it, and regulate themselves and their relations by it. It ignores Christianity, moral worth, intellectual culture, personal loveliness—everything most prized in the soul's life and loves and friendships—and decides upon the positions of men and women by its own rule. It shuts out from the circle of its sympathies and support a good man because he is poor; it bids a bad man welcome because he is rich. It ignores the charms of a beautiful and gifted woman because she earns her bread; it accepts an old and ugly remnant of an old and ugly family because she manages to live upon her friends. It kicks the young man of modest worth and noble aims and industries, and kisses the idle lout whose worth is on his back and whose graces are in his heels. It receives a religious sect into favor and frowns upon all others. In every variety of life which it enters, it assumes the preëminence, bending to nothing, and deliberately opposing itself to Christianity as the dominant element in our civilization.

But I hasten to the third point which I have proposed to discuss, viz., fashionable literature. There is fashion in literature. Nowhere, indeed, is it more exclusive or despotic; nowhere is it more mischievous. I make the unqualified statement, that fashion has always insisted on the divorce of Christianity from elegant literature. It has patronized with a lavish hand the mythologies of ancient Greece and Rome, with all their classical and cursed abominations; and, in modern days particularly, it has treated with dainty tenderness the Korans and Vedas and Shasters of swarthier and more insignificant heathen. I will, if you please, admit that, sometimes, as a matter of favor, it has accorded to the sacred writings of the Jews a place by the side of the sacred writings of the Hindoos. Nay, I will go further, and confess that the name of God is sometimes used by the most fashionable writers as a sonorous old noun for the rounding of a period, and that "the sweet Christ," or "the Spotless One," as He is patronizingly called, is worked up very handsomely for ornamental purposes in works of sentiment. But JESUS CHRIST, the personal representative of JEHOVAH on the earth—the very centre and soul of that civilization which embraces the moral, social, and political salvation of the human race—its breath, bread, and life-blood—is a name never heartily spoken by the writers whom Fashion recognizes as her own. It is not fashionable to write a Christian book. It is not fashionable to read a Christian book. To these two facts ambition, when yoked with genius, has almost uniformly bowed, and, having performed its fashionable work, gone forward to its fashionable reward. In vain have I searched the pages of fashionable literature, including much of what we call elegant letters, to find what has seemed to me to be the genuine Christian element. In all the exquisite creations which have found life and immortality in fashionable fiction, I have never met one, so far as I can remember, that was put forward as a genuine embodiment of Christian piety. Lovely women we have had in abundance; women of beauty and brilliancy and virtue; women of amiable dispositions and noble instincts; but of women whose whole lives were ordered by Christian principle, by conscience, by the love of God and the love of humanity, alas! how few!—alas! none!

Here and there some sweet-faced, sad-souled devotee has been developed and described, not because she was pious, but because she was picturesque, and never with sympathetic interest on the part of the writer. We have plenty of caricatures of Christian ministers, and Christian societies, and Christian reforms; but never any examples of what the writer accepts as the genuine article. We have had Chadbands and Stigginses, and Dominie Sampsons and Cream Cheeses —reverend fops and reverend fools without number; and these men have been thrust forward in all fashionable fiction as the representatives of Christianity.

Now, mark you, I do not complain that these characters are presented. I do not believe in shielding a humbug because he wears a white cravat, nor do I claim that in every work of fiction a writer is bound to represent both sides of every subject which he introduces. What I complain of, is, that fashionable writers, throughout their whole lives, criticise and caricature Christian men, institutions, reforms, and practices, which, on the basis of their own ideal, they never seek to embody and represent. They are fond of exposing Christian pretension. I find no fault with this, for if there is anything that deserves to be held up to ridicule and scorn, it is Christian pretension. This is not my complaint at all. I complain that, for anything to be found in their works to the contrary, they consider all Christianity pretension, and all Christians pretenders. They never introduce Christian character, Christian principle, Christian love, and Christian purpose, as golden elements in literary creation and composition.

Let me illustrate. Charles Dickens is a fashionable author, and he is not only fashionable, but popular, and popular, too, with the Christian public. Now no man can admire more ardently than I do the genius of Charles Dickens. No man, according to the measure of his nature, can sympathize more thoroughly than I do with the many lovely characters and the sweet humanities which throng the path of his delightful pen; but, so far as I can learn from his writings, that pen, thrilling to its nib with the genius which inspires it, has never written, in good, honest text, the name of Jesus Christ. And when I say this, I mean all that my words can compass and convey. The Christian element is not to be found in his writings. Christianity is not brought forward, either as a cure or a mitigation of the evils which his eyes are so ready to see, and the woes which touch him with so quick a sympathy. You will find in Dickens travesties of missionary enterprise, and ridicule of various schemes of Christian reform; but nowhere, so far as I can remember, any evidence that he either loves Christianity, or believes in it, as his own and the world's consolation and cure.

I have not read Thackeray to find him better, even when I take into account the sulphurous satire which he points with such deadly fire at the very society which makes him fashionable. It is the fashion to read Thackeray, and the fashion to admire him, though he is far less popular than his rival; and we have to thank him for his exposure of the shallowness and shabbiness of the fashionable life which engages his caustic pen; but he has never, so far as I know, administered any medicine but satire. He has never shown, by direct teaching or by any form of art, the radical cure for the life which he so keenly satirizes and so thoroughly despises. Image-breaker he may be, but no reformer. With his pen of gold he probes every social sore with merciless precision; but he leaves it black with his own ink, and unblessed by any balm.

I name these men only because they are representative men,—because most of the fashionable novel-writing of the time consists of Dickens and Thackeray diluted and flavored according to the feeble necessities of the producers and the flatulent mental habit of the consumers. All that is and all that aims to be genuinely fashionable, ignores Christianity as the matrix of a true literature, and discards the social and political systems which are its offspring as its choicest framework and material.

We have an abundance of theology; we have countless volumes of excellent practical sermons—duly labelled, that no one shall mistake them for elegant literature; we have a planet-full of pious stories, written by goodish men and women, whose stupidity has nullified any honor to Christianity which they may have intended,—but only here and there has genuine genius, inspired and impelled by Christianity, worked freely and honestly in literary creation and composition; only here and there has Christian life been carved out of the world's life, and thrown into a form of art which reveals its transcendent virtue and beauty.

It must be known to you that there is a class of writers in every country who assume to be the fashion in literature. You will find them clustered around a literary institution, or a literary magazine, or united in a literary club or cabal. They constitute what irreverent persons have denominated a mutual-admiration society. We know little of the tie which unites them, but we know that no plummet-line is long enough to sound the depths of their self-complacency, and that no common understanding can understand the understanding that exists between them. We know that while they criticise each other in private, they toast each other in public, and quote each other in print, and that when one of them dies, they sow his grave with eulogies that are kept constantly thrifty by copious showers of Maynard & Noyes. We know that neither man nor woman is regarded as having any position, or any right, in the field of letters without their indorsement, and that neither man nor woman can obtain that indorsement without the acknowledgment of their supreme authority. We know that their principal purpose is the nursing and rearing of reputations—the conservation and canonization of names; and that literary art is never regarded by them as only true and legitimate when it is made the minister of a Christian civilization. We know that they regard, or pretend to regard, the most indifferent productions of their sacred circle as the offspring of genius, and that all men who fail to detect in the productions themselves the reason for their good opinion, are regarded by them as devoid of literary judgment. And more than all this: we know that a modest and self-distrustful public voluntarily disfranchises itself by acknowledging merits which it does not see and cannot feel, simply because it is the fashion to admire or to admit them. We know also that these literary fashionables have multitudes of abject worshippers who regard them fearfully from afar, and others who will crawl upon their bellies for a bow, and become their toadies and tools for a single glass of their Madeira.

All this we know, and yet how well we know that we must go outside of this circle to find the Christian power in literature that is to move the world toward the religious and political millennium. We never find in this circle a power effluent in all directions upon the world of life around it, to melt and mould, to elevate and bless, but a beautiful show of gifts and graces that have conspired together to attract the admiration of tributary gazers.

Now I put it to your candor to say whether it is not true, that, in the opinion of this fashionable literary cabal, this self-constituted court of literature, religion hurts a book? Is not hearty, practical, devotional Christianity regarded by this court as a foreign element? a something which is not at home in elegant literature at all? Is it not true that any literary work which is burdened with a Christian mission is regarded as laboring under a disadvantage? Answer these questions as I know you must answer them, if you are well informed, and you yield essentially all that I claim touching the influence of fashionable literature upon Christian civilization.

It is possible that you will tell me that there are some truly Christian writers who are fashionable. There are, indeed, beautiful names that rise to you and to me, before which even the fashionable bow with reverent admiration. I think of one whose genius was angelic; who swept all the chords of human passion with fingers that shook with the stress of their inspiration; who soared and sang as never woman soared and sang before; whose every uttered word leaped from her lips like a bird, radiant in plumage and glorious in music; yet whose heart was the dwelling-place of an all-controlling, all-subordinating Christian purpose. She looked out upon humanity with a love ineffable even to her. She looked up to Heaven with a Christian adoration to which even her marvellous gift of language could give no fitting expression. Her whole being throbbed and sparkled like the sea, stretching its pure, life-giving sympathies around the world, and tossing evermore its white hands toward the stars. Ah! yes; she soared and sang as never woman soared and sang before; soared and sang at last, English sky-lark though she was, into the golden dawn of Italian nationality, till the attraction of the earth was surpassed, and Heaven drew her home. Elizabeth Barrett Browning! How the pretentious stuff that drapes our mutual-admiration societies becomes fustian in the presence of her queenly robes!

I think of a name nearer home than this—the name of one now living—one of whom I may not speak in such terms as her consecrated genius deserves, because she lives. You have read her books, for they have been read in many lands and many languages—read more widely than the works of any other living writer. In these works she has incorporated the religion of Jesus Christ, as it is incorporated in her own life and character. She has devoted her magnificent genius to the cause of Christian reform, and wields a pen whose power one would as little think of questioning as the power of the sun or the lightning. Under the inspiration of Christianity she writes for humanity, entering as a Christian power into life and character wherever books are read and hearts are open; and she sits to-day the queen of a realm, all of which she has either subjugated or created. In your hearts you have already spoken the name of Harriet Beecher Stowe.

There are others, still, whose names come to you and to me. I might pronounce the name of our Gabriel in drab—trumpet-tongued for the right, trumpet-tongued against the wrong; loving the poor man more than the rich, loving both more than himself, loving God more than all—John Greenleaf Whittier. I might speak of him whose catholic sympathies and whose quick sense of Christian truth and love and justice are as evident in his "Biglow Papers" as in his golden "Vision of Sir Launfal"—James Russell Lowell. I might speak of Charles Kingsley, a great Christian genius, or of John Ruskin, the peerless scholar and Christian leader of art, or of Dr. John Brown, whose "Spare Hours" have linked their Christian arms with your spare hours, I trust, and helped them heavenward.

Now do you ask me if these are not fashionable writers? Do you ask me why writers whom fashionable people praise are not fashionable? Simply because they are Christian and catholic in their spirit, their sympathies, their associations, and their objects, and are as little dependent on fashion for their reward as they are influenced by it in their work. They have a genius which commands respect and reverence even among the fashionable, in spite of the Christian inspiration which informs and the Christian purpose which possesses it. They have nothing in common with those whose sole aim is to gather a reputation and make a name. They may be fashionable in a certain negative sense, perhaps,—in the fact that it would be unfashionable to betray such lack of common sense as to deny their genius. Do you suppose that fashionable writers, and the lovers of fashionable literature, love the objects for which Mrs. Browning and Mrs. Stowe have labored? that they sympathize with Mr. Whittier and Mr. Lowell and Mr. Kingsley? Not at all. They look upon all of them as amiable fanatics, and, while they acknowledge their genius, regard their unselfish devotion to the world of men and women, and God's truth in its relations to them, as an element of weakness.

I have said that it is not fashionable to put Christianity into elegant literature. I may and I should say, here and now, that it is not fashionable to put it into a literary address. It is not fashionable for an unprofessional literary man to deliver such an address as I am now delivering before a literary audience. Have we not men clothed in black and choked with white cravats who are paid for this sort of service? Have we not temples built for it? Is there not one day in seven, ordained for religious purposes from the foundation of the world, in which these temples are thrown open that these men may be vocal in their vocations? These Christian addresses are things that we get done by the year! Is not butter furnished by the season? Are not gas and water paid for by the quarter? Every man to his work in the regular way. No handling of Christianity by common hands, especially literary hands, on ordinary occasions, especially literary occasions. "Ah! don't mingle"—you remember the familiar music.

Now, my idea of the Christian religion is, that it is an inspiration and its vital consequences—an inspiration and a life—God's life breathed into a man and breathed through a man—the highest inspiration and the highest life of every soul which it inhabits; and, furthermore, that the soul which it inhabits can have no high issue which is not essentially religious. There are those who make it their business to promulgate dogmatic Christianity: let them fulfil their calling in the proper time and place. There are adepts in scriptural exposition: let them exercise their gifts on all proper occasions. There are earnest souls whose personal exhortations have power to move men to a religious life: God speed them everywhere. It is of none of these things or of these men that I speak. My point is, that a man in whom religion is an inspiration, who has surrendered his being to its power, who drinks it, breathes it, bathes in it, cannot speak otherwise than religiously. The magician can draw an uncounted variety of wines from a single flask, but the alcoholic base runs through them all. So the religious soul may give forth utterances of various forms and flavors, but one spirit imparts to each its vitality and power.

We never know a man's measure till we take it for his coffin. You will find among fashionable writers such wearing of high-heeled boots, such mounting upon stilts, such sporting of tall hats and riding of high horses, that you will be obliged to get them down and get the tape upon them before you can tell how much space they will occupy. Their names will shine upon the coffin-lid, and they will bury well, and stay buried; but no grave can hold a fruitful Christian genius. We say that Mrs. Browning is dead, we say that Mrs. Browning is buried; but we know that she lives, and that she walks the earth, and wings the air, and sits with us here to-night. The earth is not broad enough, the earth is not deep enough, to bury Mrs. Browning in.

I have thus attempted to expose to you the nature

and the tendency of fashion, as it exists in personal character, in social life, and in literature. I have endeavored to show you that it is essentially aristocratic, and must therefore be opposed to a genuine Christian civilization and a true democracy. It practically denies the rightful supremacy of Christianity in every field, ignores its grand, levelling truths, and maintains, through corrupt convention, an independent standard of morals. It is exclusive, devoted to clique and caste, and thoroughly sympathetic with all systems and schemes of life and all forms of society and government which take power and profit from the many and give them to the few.

In this great hour of our national history, I have chosen this subject that a useful lesson may be won from it. I have tried to speak not as a politician or a partisan, but as a philosopher, who believes in the beneficence of democratic institutions and the conservative power of Christianity. This democratic government of ours was founded by Christian men, on Christian principles. It can only be perpetuated by Christian men, on Christian principles. Whenever it passes into the hands of an aristocratic class, which denies the rights of the meanest man, and sustains itself by the oppression and disfranchisement of the laboring masses, that moment it must cease to exist, and a despotism will take its place. A class that denies a black man the privilege of a man, will deny a powerless white man the same—always and everywhere.

The struggle in this country is now and has been for years between a democracy with a Christian conscience, and an aristocracy fanatically devoted to human slavery. The rebellion originated in a dominating class, with which no Christian democrat in this country can possibly have any sympathy; and the power of that class must be destroyed, utterly, or a Christian democracy cannot possibly be the dominant power on this continent.

The sympathy and the support which the rebellion has received from the upper classes of Great Britain and continental Europe, have been natural and inevitable. The aristocratic classes of Europe recognize the nature of the struggle, and take the side of the aristocratic class of this country. I do not wonder at it; I do not blame them for it; and I do not care a straw about it. We are fighting the great battle of the people—the great battle of democratic and Christian equality against the combined aristocracies of the world, and all that fashionable class, at home and abroad, which sympathizes with them. And when the day of our victory shall come, as it will come, let us remember that if we would secure the national safety forever, we must thenceforward and forever make

Christianity popular. I do not say that we must make Christianity fashionable, for it cannot be, in the nature of things. We must make it popular, and compel every political caucus, convention, candidate, and clique, to bend to it and obey it. When that time shall come, we shall have arrived at the political millennium,—and the time must come.

WORK AND PLAY.

THE human race presents no aspect more interesting than that which it wears in its apron and shirt-sleeves. There breathes no nobler music under heaven than the roar of a great city, in which the din of wheels, and the clangor of hammers, and the cries of the hawker and the auctioneer, and the hurried tread of uncounted thousands upon the pavement, are blunted and crushed and blended into a sublime monotone, that rises and swells, and surges and subsides, from day to day, through all the prosperous centuries. There is nothing more wonderful than that labyrinthine net-work of human interests, spread finely over a continent and more broadly enveloping a world, out from whose indistinguishable intersections run the daily efforts of the earth's thronging millions.

There is an office for every man, and a man for every office. One builds a ship, another turns a spool; one paints a madonna, another decorates a toy; one attends a king, another grooms a horse; one sends a ship to the Indies, another gleans the offal of the streets; one writes a book, another places it in type; one conducts a railroad-train over a hundred miles, another trundles a wheel-barrow up and down a plank. Millions live among the whirl of spindles and the clash of looms; and other millions ply the needles that fashion their fabrics. On cotton-fields and corn-fields, on farms and plantations, in workshops and mills, on the water and on the land—everywhere, everywhere—men and women are at work. The brain and nerve and muscle of the world expend their energy, day after day, in tidal sweeps through every artery of industry; and thus the world's great heart throbs and throbs; and thus it will throb until its strings shall shiver in dissolution.

This is a working world—a serious, earnest, hard-working world; yet it is not all, or not always, so. Rising out of this daily vision of work, and harmoniously blending with it, like variations sporting with, and above, a musical theme, there are other scenes that attract attention. A steamer pushes out into the bay, with music swelling and streamers flying over a happy company of men, women, and children, upon an excursion of pleasure. Under the shadow of a grove the groups of a picnic romp and run, and laugh and chat, through the long summer afternoon. In public halls and private parlors feet move to the sound of the viol through the merry evenings, till they cross the bars of midnight. Children frolic upon the lawn, and boys play at football or cricket upon the common. All over the country, where the snow falls, old and young are sleighing and skating and sliding under the moon; and wherever the surf rolls in upon a pleasant beach, or crystal waters mirror lordly mountains, or the earth bubbles with its mineral treasures, a nation of languid travellers gather during the heat of summer, for relaxation and enjoyment.

So this world is a world of work, not only, but a world of play. Surely something of present interest and permanent, practical value may be said of things which absorb more than half of the time, and all the energy, of the civilized world; and I propose to devote the hour to the discussion of Work and Play, and the illustration of their meaning and their mission.

I have not selected this subject because there is much that is brilliant or amusing to be said upon it, but because there is no man, not too indolent to attend a lecture, who does not possess a practical, every-day interest in it. I have selected it, too, because I believe that the popular notions with relation to it are in many respects erroneous, and in some respects unhealthy and even dangerous. My aim will be:

First, To reveal the relations of work and play to the development of the worker;

Second, The relations of work and play to each other, in securing this development;

Third, Their relations to the health and happiness of the race; and,

Fourth, To suggest something of their ultimate results.

The first thing to be done is to define our terms. What is work, and what is play?

Work is the exercise of the mind, or the body, or both, under the command and control of the will, for the attainment of an object of fancied or real utility.

Play is the exercise of the mind, or of the mind and body, at the instance of impulses originating in the conditions and dispositions of the system, and expending themselves without an object, beyond momentary satisfaction. Work contemplates achievement and acquisition, and has its end outside of, and beyond, itself, so far as relates to the worker's intent. Play, self-moved, seeks for nothing further than present gratification, and has its end in itself. Will is the master of work. It fixes its goal, and then harnesses and drives all the human faculties toward it, or to it. Play removes their harnesses, hangs up the whip, and releases them to the impulses which move them to show the iron upon their heels, to roll in the sand, or to frisk upon the sward. Work, under will, is determined, persistent, and steady; play, under impulse, is volatile, and delights in change.

Now let us go directly to nature for our first lesson in the meaning and mission of work and play. The boy is born into the world a delicate organism—a soft bundle of brains and nerves, and bones and muscles, and vessels and limbs, without will, and without the power of self-support and self-direction. The first months of his life are passed in a kind of unconscious consciousness, and nothing higher is expected of him than that he pull the whiskers of his father, and smile appreciatingly when his mother talks nonsense to him. Soon he begins to grasp, or to reach after, the things he sees—a pearl-button, a coffee-pot, a chandelier, or a church-steeple; and we feel that great progress has been made when he can shake his rattle-box three times and repeat, even if the performance be slightly spasmodic and irregular. The months pass away, and he stands upon his feet; and after a brief and delightful tutelage, he waddles about wherever his impulses lead him. He takes trips of ten feet upon his father's cane, which not unfrequently proves refractory and throws him. He frolics with the kittens, or hugs them to death. He builds block-houses, and knocks them down. He excavates convenient sand-banks. He delights, above all things, in the open air, and runs because he loves to run; but whether within doors or without, he is always in mischief. From morning to night his little muscles are in motion; and when compelled, at last, to go to bed, he relinquishes his play with tears. Year by year, as he grows up through boyhood, the range of his play is widened. He drives other boys four-in-hand, or plays at ball, or slides down hill, or runs races, or wrestles, or goes hunting and fishing.

Now, what makes this boy play? And what does this play do for him?

He plays because he cannot help it—because in the central, motive forces of his nature God has written the command to play. He has no end beyond the gratification of his momentary and shifting impulses. He plays because the life within him exults in action, and delights in expenditure. Tired in one direction of amusing or pleasant effort, he turns toward another; and thus, one by one, or group by group, he calls into activity all the faculties of his mind and all the functions of his body. He has no object, I repeat, in this constant action and constant change; but God has. This play is for the symmetrical development of the boy, of all the powers of which he is the possessor; and no boy without play was ever well-developed, or ever can be. A boy who does not play, and does not love to play, is not a healthy boy, mentally, morally, or physically, no matter how many precious hymns he can repeat, nor how well he can say his catechism. Play is the Creator's ordained means for the development of the child. I am aware that it drives weak-headed mothers crazy, and aggravates the aggregate of the shoe-bill, and makes terrific work with trousers; but it makes men, and, as a general rule, the boy that plays the best, makes the best man.

There is a sad amount of fighting against Heaven in the attempts made by irritable and impatient parents to repress the playful manifestations of their children. Carefully and reverently I declare that God impels, nay, compels, the child to play, and that those who strive to crush the spirit of play in children for the security of their own ease and comfort, or from mistaken notions of the nature and the mission of play, oppose Him as really as when they set themselves against any movement or policy in His moral universe.

Play is a sacred thing, a divine ordinance, for developing in the child a harmonious and healthy organism, and preparing that organism for the commencement of the work of life. I insist upon this, at this point, for I shall call it up again in the course of this discussion; I insist that play is not only an innocent thing in itself, but that it is an essential portion of the divinely appointed means for the development of the race into its highest earthly estate.

In order that our lesson may not be complicated, we will leave the period of study out of consideration, and put our boy to work. Perhaps he has already performed a few tasks about the house, willingly or unwillingly, but they have been so light that he has not seriously felt them. That the work may be simple, we will apprentice him to a trade. This little bundle of organs, grown into compactness and power through the exercise which play has procured, is placed under a task-master. The first day, perhaps the first week, is passed delightfully, because it has the charm of novelty; but, at last, his mind, strained in one direction, and his muscles, exercised in a single style of action, become weary. At this point begins the discipline of work—the bringing of all his faculties under the control of his will. He flinches from his task, perhaps, but his will spurs him on. He looks from his window, and sees other boys engaged in play, and longs to be among them; but his will vetoes his impulses, and keeps him to his work.

Thus these organs that have been developed by play, and this life that will manifest itself in action, bend themselves, under the command of will, to the accomplishment of useful results. Directed by intelligence, and starting from rationally apprehended motives, they take their way along the channels of the world's industry.

Here dawns upon us the mission of work. God, by implanting in the boy the impulse to play, has taken care of his development up to this point. As a boy, he is complete; but manhood demands something further, and he must be trained to self-impulsion, self-direction, and self-control. The organs which play has prepared, work puts to use. Over these young faculties the will is placed in office, and is, itself, developed by the exercise of its functions. The mission of work is never fully accomplished until the will has attained supreme control of all the mental and bodily faculties, and those faculties have become obedient and efficient instruments of the will. Patience, persistence, and power to do, are only acquired by work.

But we are leaving our boy. If we watch him at the close of his daily task, we shall find him very weary, but very ready to play. He has been working in a single direction. A single group of faculties and a single set of muscles have been employed during the day, and before he sleeps, Nature impels him to bring those that have been unemployed into harmony with them. The strain must be released, and the worked and the unworked boy must be reconciled to each other by play, before both can sleep well. So, through the evening the boy is as active as the liveliest, and as boisterous as the noisiest; and at bed-time, if he be not rested, he is ready to rest, and to rest well. He sleeps better at night, and he works better the next day, for this play; and thus, play comes in as the minister and helper of work. The used and the unused faculties are harmonized with each other, and developed together. If the impulse to play between the periods of labor be suppressed, and nothing of the boy be developed save the faculties engaged in his special work, he will become not only the slave of work, but he will be transformed into its creature. Woe to him if he fail to yield to the impulses to play which start up among his unused faculties, until those faculties dwindle beyond the power to give birth to an impulse!

This simple illustration has introduced us to the primary and principal offices of work and play. In this illustration they reveal themselves as coördinately essential in that economy which contemplates the highest human development. The development which God seeks for is the growth and perfection of the power to do. Play does what it can for this object, and work, in widely-varied forms of ministry, does the rest.

Our illustration has not only revealed the primary relations of work and play to human development, but it has suggested something of their relations to each other, and thus brought us to the second point under discussion. I begin with the proposition that work was made for man, and not man for work. Work is man's servant, both in its results to the worker and the world. Man is not work's servant, save as an almost universal perversion has made him such. We need not go beyond the circle of our immediate acquaintances for instances of this perversion. Every variety of work has stamped itself and left its stamp upon society. Almost everywhere men have become the particular things which their particular work has made them. In the place of a broad, strong, symmetrical manhood, we have a weak, crippled, and distorted manhood. We know a thoroughly-worked old lawyer as readily as we do an old fox. We can recognize a Wall-street financier at thirty paces, and can tell a clergyman as far as we can see him. There are very much greater differences between a Yankee farmer and a Yankee sailor than in the length of their trousers. There are round shoulders, and pulpy muscles, and halting limbs, and all varieties of bodily and mental eccentricities, resulting from the slavish pursuit of the different callings. The negroes on the cotton plantations of the South, who carry water to the field upon their heads, become bald upon the spot where "the hair ought to grow" by the weight and friction of the jugs, but they are no more distinctly stamped by their work, and are, in fact, not half so bald, as multitudes of whites who bear heavier burdens of a different kind.

Thus have men become the creatures of their work, and thus has work become to them, in many respects, a curse. When work enslaves a group of faculties, and employs and develops that group to the neglect or the death of all others, then does it surpass and abuse its office. This it is that makes one-sided men, partial men, fractional men. This it is that puts the menial stamp upon men, that brands them with the name of their tyrant-master. This it is which spoils manhood, and debases its subjects to the level of their calling. This it is which too often transforms men into lawyers and financiers and ministers and merchants and farmers and hod-carriers—beings who can do one thing, and nothing else—who are competent in one direction, and babies or fools in every other direction. I say again, that man was not made for work, but work for him, and that its office is abused in the degree by which it hinders the symmetrical development of all his faculties. One of the direct roads to brutality lies through unalleviated and undiversified bodily labor. Let a man be worked and fed as a brute is worked and fed, and he will become brutal. A man using only the faculties demanded by his calling will develop only those faculties. So it is evident that something besides work is necessary for healthful development, after the peculiar period of play is passed.

If, now, we turn to play as the exclusive agent

in the development of the adult, we shall find it still more inadequate than work, because in play there is no purpose and no training of power under will. Up to a certain period of life play is everything that is necessary. Wherever it is suppressed, and the young mind, or the young body, or both, are put into the harness of work, disease or disaster is the result. I know not which to pity most—the infants crowded into a premature development of brain and mind, or the pale faced dwarfs among the factory-boys. Whenever I see a pale, old face on a young body, I know that somebody's wilful ignorance, or somebody's cupidity, needs forgiveness.

Up to a certain point of development, I say, play only is necessary. Beyond that point work must come in with its discipline, or play will degenerate into dissipation. There are few more pitiable objects than men and women who have never had anything to do but to amuse themselves. They are pitiable because useless, powerless, and unhappy. The whole horde of dandies and devotees of fashion—men and women who have no higher employment than ministry to vanity and appetite and passion—are blanks, or blotches, on one of the most beautiful and beneficent schemes of the Creator, and objects of disgust to every healthy soul. As much as many working men desire ease, I have never seen one who did not in his inmost soul despise an idle man, or one who could do nothing.

Play, I repeat, leaves entirely out of consideration one of the principal offices of work, viz., the training of the will. It is all-important that the intense vitality that comes in with manhood and womanhood be under control, and be directed into legitimate channels of expenditure. As childhood is left behind, new passions take possession of the individual; and if he be left to the sway of impulse, he will be almost certain to gravitate toward sensuality. There is abundant life to be expended somewhere—if not in work, then in something else. Impulse will be sure of the mastery if the will be weak and vacillating. Appetite is clamorous, and passion is imperious, and an undeveloped and untrained will, will bend readily under the stress of these motives. It is notorious that, almost without exception, those young men who are never put to work, especially if they have strong vitality in them, sink into vice. The reason is, that exclusive play, after the period of childhood, naturally degenerates into dissipation. The will bends before the strongest impulse, or lends it its aid; and the strongest impulse is born of the strongest passion that happens to be in exercise.

Not unfrequently we have striking instances of this dissipation and degradation, and the corrective influence of work when resorted to for the first time in adult life. We all of us know young men who have led a life of gayety and vice upon the paternal wealth, and we have seen them become the terror and disgrace of a neighborhood, the bane and burden of a home, —given up, as hopelessly debauched, by their best friends. Yet, when some great disaster has whelmed the wealth upon which they have lived, and a great motive of action has presented itself to them, we have seen them sobered in a day, and, under the discipline of labor, become men of character and of power. Among men, these cases may be rare; but among women, cases not dissimilar are abundant. With them, play is more a dissipating and less a debasing habit, and reformation is consequently easier. How many gay girls have we seen—butterflies, giddy, thoughtless, undisciplined creatures—becoming sober, noble, and devoted wives and mothers, when marriage and maternity have put the discipline of work upon them. How, under the motive of a great love, has their work often taken on the character of a great heroism!

So, neither work nor play is sufficient of itself; and now, before I come to the practical discussion of the relations of play to labor in adult life, I recall the question of the essential nature of play. I propose that it has as legitimate functions in the life of the man and the woman as in that of the child, and that, in the discharge of those functions, it is in no sense sinful, thriftless, or undignified. The religious asceticism that has placed its ban upon play in its various manifestations, the hard economy that denounces it as wasteful of time and money, and the stolid dignity that regards it with contempt, are essentially moral nuisances. Play may not have so high a place in the divine economy, but it has as legitimate a place, as prayer. Its direct importance, when we contemplate useful results, is not so great as that of work; but it is essential to the healthful development of the worker, and essential in keeping the machinery of work in order. It is the great harmonizer of the human faculties, overstrained and made inharmonious by labor. It is the agency that keeps alive, and in healthy activity, the faculties and sympathies which work fails to use, or helps to repress. It is the conservator of moral, mental, and physical health.

I have never seen a man who, through a long life of labor, has been playful, giving himself up in the hours of his leisure to the lead of his innocent impulses, who was either bigoted, invalid, or insane. In short, play is as innocent and as legitimate in the man as in the boy, provided, of course, that it start from innocent impulses, and answer its legitimate ends.

I bring out this point with special prominence, because many of the innocent modes of play, like play itself, have been placed under ban by well-meaning people who are possessed by the notion that all time spent in play is mis-spent, and that all money devoted to play is mis-appropriated; who believe that the idle words and the thriftless deeds of play are those for which they are to be brought into judgment. Play is to be resorted to intelligently and conscientiously, without doubt, and should never descend into dissipation. It should always be of that kind and amount which will induce the most perfect sleep; which will the most thoroughly harmonize the functions of the mind and body, wearied and distracted by work; which will best nourish the faculties that work has neglected; and which will best prepare both body and mind for the pursuit of work. This is the mission of play to the worker; and a great blessing would it be to the world could it be intelligently apprehended as such. A great blessing would it be, could the almost universal bondage of the world to the idea that play compromises Christian consistency, and worldly thrift, and manly dignity, be forever broken. A great blessing would it be, could a mistakenly conscientious world look heavenward, and feel the full blessedness of the truth that God smiles upon His creatures at play as benignantly as when they are at work, and that He frowns as indignantly upon that work which enslaves and distorts and spoils them, as upon that excess of play which dissipates or prostitutes them.

We have resorted to Nature for an illustration of the effect of play upon the boy: let us go to the same teacher to learn the united effect of work and play upon the man. The simpler the illustration, the better. We will take the negroes of a cotton plantation. They will sing all day while engaged in their work, and dance all night after it, if they can get a chance. For every hard task they have a song which helps them through. It is in this way that they preserve themselves from disease and insanity. If you would find invalids and lunatics, go among the Yankees, and particularly the Yankee farmers. By this play, these negroes become safe property to own. They follow their instincts and impulses, unchecked by any conscientious or economical considerations; and I wish that all the poor slaves, chained to the oar of labor, would follow them as innocently.

But I can bring my lesson from a nearer point than this. I appeal to you to testify if there do not come to you, at the close of each day's hearty and healthy labor, the desire to play. You go home from your work to your dinner or your tea, and when you rise from your table, (if you are not smokers,) what is your first impulse? Springs there not in you that which tells you there is something which should intervene between that point and sleep? You love that wife, or those children, or sisters, better than all, of course; but is it your supreme desire to sit quietly down with them and spend the evening? Is it the most delight-

U of M

ful thing you can imagine to doze over your evening paper for an hour, and retire to bed as early as you decently can? Never, unless work has killed the best part of you. Do you not feel that you need something besides rest and before it? Is it not habitual for it to occur to you that you have "an appointment," that you must go to the post-office, or go somewhere? Do you not long to get into the open air, and to wander where you list? I know that I touch the experience of every healthy working man present. Now, believe me, this is God's voice in your nature bidding you play, and you have no right to disregard it. It is under this untaught impulse that the slave resorts to singing and dancing. It is this impulse, perverted, which drives the poor toper to his pot-house and his pot-house companions. It is this impulse, under a German education and German habits, that takes the German to his garden and his lager bier; but you, with higher tastes and better impulses, resort to nothing at all but a barren walk in a giddy street, and feel yourselves obliged to make a business apology for that! "They order these things better in France."

I therefore make the assertion, that every intelligent worker—every man and woman whose faculties, under will, are trained and held to the performance of a daily task—should always have regular periods of play.

The practical question now arises as to what this play shall be. It should never be that which is essentially work—that which is felt to be a tax of power, under will. If you have read Dickens, you will remember the picture of Dr. Blimber's young gentlemen as they appeared when "enjoying themselves," walking out in dignified and dressy couples, with the Doctor at their head, and the boys of the street turning summersets in the foreground. There is a great deal of this bastard play, in which the young have been forced into walks which worried them, and tasks which disgusted them, as a relief to study or work. Exercise which has been the severest mental and bodily discomfort has been mistaken for play. I have seen young men working away for dear life at saw-horses, or scudding over barren miles as if a ghost were after them, or swinging dumb-bells, when I knew they were engaged in harder tasks than those from which they sought relief. This "muscle-movement," as it is called, in our colleges, will amount to but little if the element of play do not enter largely into it. A young man, or a young woman, who takes exercise of set purpose for the preservation of health, may in some instances succeed; but the chances are against success, in all cases where the exercise alternates with periods of severe labor, of any kind. The severest exercise may, indeed, be play, but that which is felt to be a task is not play, and can never be made to take the place of it.

The mode of every man's play must be determined by the indications of his tastes, conditions, and dispositions. There are some who enjoy athletic games, and are never so much at home as when on the cricket-ground, or the bowling-alley, or the row-boat. Play of this character has the double power to give mental relief, and preserve and develop physical health and strength. Every intelligent lover of his country and his kind will hail the fresh attention attracted to this kind of play with gladness and gratitude. It is time that this over-worked nation—this nation of narrow shoulders, and flat chests, and weak arms and spindle-shanks—possessed more of the characteristics of physical manhood. Who wonders that strong-handed and strong-minded women assert their rights in the presence of such a race of men as this? Were I such a woman, with such a husband as such a woman invariably has, if she has any, I would assert mine. Why is it that the good men of a city permit the bad men to rule it? Why is it that the respectable men of a ward allow rowdies to keep them from the ballot-box? Because, and only because, they lack pluck and prowess, and are physically afraid of them. The cause of public decency, nay, the cause of Christianity, demands more muscle, and I am glad to see that it is likely to get it.

In such times as these, and in such as seem likely to come, the church militant would find abundant employment for a saintly corps of robust and muscular men.

There are others who most enjoy society, and who find recreation and reward in a genial circle of friends. Much is to be done for the play of the nation by a more generous development of its social life. Work has well-nigh killed out this kind of play. How few are the impulses among the every-day, hard workers of the world to mingle in society! We wander from our work into lonely moodiness, for, though we may have something to receive, we are conscious that we have nothing to give, in social intercourse. How many are there in my audience who shrink from receiving company, and who dread to go into it, because too constant and too much work has spoiled them for social life? Work has exhausted them; work has possessed them, and they cannot get their thoughts out of it. Work has absorbed, drunk up all their vital juices; and if they go to a social gathering, they are either driven or dragged there.

It is in a genial social life that the worker comes into contact with minds developed in various directions. A congregation of sympathies touch him at every point, and stimulate his whole nature into delightful activity. It is in society that knowledge is equalized, and experience harmonized, and all those faculties that work has kept from free development, and those sympathies that work has cursed, are called into demonstration. It is in social life that the adult is always to find his best play, and, until work has destroyed the disposition to play, it is there that he will always seek it. In the mind of the healthy man and woman, as in the mind of the healthy boy and girl, play and society will be inseparable thoughts and things. The moment that work has so far abused a man that he loses the impulse to play, that moment his love of society is lost. So I advise all those who find themselves averse to going into society, to go until they like it, as they will be sure to do, so soon as the mischief which work has wrought shall have been remedied.

Lonely walking, unless among new scenery, cannot be play, except in peculiar conditions of the mind. Routine walking, in order to be play, should always be social walking. It takes two pairs of ears, at least, to enjoy the music of a waterfall, and two pairs of eyes to weigh the gold of a sunset with just appreciation.

To a great multitude, riding is, perhaps, the most delightful of out-door play. The man and woman who carry heavy burdens love to be carried. This love of being carried begins in the mother's arms, and is never outgrown. There is something in the passive exercise of riding, and even in the society of a horse, if one can get no better, that is eminently refreshing. I never despair of a man who really loves the society of an intelligent horse. A man who lives as a man should live, never outgrows his love of playthings, and he should always have them. The little girl plays with her doll, the mother with her baby; the boy plays with his rocking-horse, the man with the living animal; and baby and horse are just as really playthings as doll and hobby.

Happy are ye who own horses, and love them and know how to use them; and happy will you all be when you get rich enough to own and keep one. In the mean time, let your imagination tell you of the horse which is to come. His color shall be bay—dark and glossy, like the throat of a wild pigeon; and his mane and tail shall be black and flowing. His pace, when you wish to be soothed, shall be as gentle as the motion of a yacht under easy sail; and, when you wish to be exhilarated, he shall fly like the wind. He shall draw you and yours over the smoothly-gravelled roads, and learn to know and love his burden. He shall whinny for you in his stall, and inform you in his choicest forms of "horse-talk" that all your admiration of him is appreciated. You will speak pet phrases in his ear, your children shall caress him, and he shall catch their spirit and become playful like them and like you. You will tell him that he is very beautiful; that there is grandeur in the arch of his neck; that there is grace in all his action; and that it is not a sin for a horse to be proud. When, by intimate association with you, he shall become half human, you will make known to him the beautiful truth, that when you were young God gave you ready and active limbs to play with, but now, when work has tired them, He has given you a horse.

Every man, I say again, must determine what his play shall be. I say, *must* determine, because he only can judge what is play to him—what his taste selects, and what his nature calls for—and because there is a duty involved in the matter. To every man who has the power to spend a portion of his time in play, I say that you have no right to spoil yourself by refusing to play. You have no right to prostitute all the noble faculties of your soul, and the powers of your frame, to the offices of work—to become the things, the machines, of a calling. What you are to be careful about is, that your play be that which best relieves your labor, and best prepares you for it; that it do not degenerate into dissipation, nor tend in vicious directions; that, for the time, it drive work from your mind, and be recognized as one of its most grateful rewards.

There can be no radical reform in this matter until the popular mind shall more fully comprehend the intrinsic nature of work and its relations to life. The popular mind is enslaved, and needs emancipation. It is enslaved to the idea that life is work and that work is life; whereas work is but an instrument of life, to be held at arm's-length, and used in such a way that there shall be no damaging reaction. During the hours of labor, the mind should bend to its faithful performance; but as soon as they are passed, it should rise out of work into a free and noble life. The Italian beggar, after obtaining enough for a dinner, contents himself, and gives himself up for the remainder of the day to music and maccaroni. This, you say, is very stupid, and I think it is; but he is more sensible than the Broadway merchant or the Wall-street broker whose whole soul is absorbed by work—who is in it all day, and who dreams of it all night. We need emancipation, if for nothing else than for the sake of a decent family-life. The slave of work becomes an inharmonious element in his own home-circle. It is pitiful to see the thousands scattered all over this country, who, through insane devotion to business, have ceased to be husbands and fathers; who have no part in the family-life but to furnish funds for its maintenance; and who are only treated respectfully by wives and children because they are crabbed and sour, or because they carry the key of the family treasury.

We need emancipation, and the tendency to it is happily evident. It is evident in the more general circulation and entertainment of sound and rational ideas; evident in the growing love of literature and art; evident in the increasing attention directed to physical culture and games and sports. These facts relate peculiarly, perhaps, to the literary and mercantile classes; but there is abundant evidence of approaching emancipation to the tiller of the soil, the artisan, and the operative. The effect of labor-saving machinery must ultimately be to reduce the hours of labor, as it has already mitigated its severity. The work of a day will be crowded into a smaller space; and so soon as our people can learn that gold is not the highest good, and that man is something better than a beast of burden, we shall throw off the shackles which now make our callings our masters, and which reduce our life to one long, unmitigated bondage to work.

I now pass to the relations of work and play to the health and happiness of the race. Use is the condition of health in all the human faculties and functions. We have seen that it is the condition of development; and health is naturally implied in the same condition. When a plant grows strongly and thriftily, it is in its healthiest state: so, when the faculties of the mind and the powers of the body thrive the best, are they naturally the healthiest. Happiness depends also upon the same condition; for a complete human organism, in process of full, healthy development, must be happy, or, in other words, consciously harmonious. Work and play, then, do not stop at development as their direct result to the individual, but they make him healthy, and they make him happy so far as happiness depends upon the harmonious movements of his complicated nature. Utter idleness is but another name for utter misery. As a symmetrical development depends upon the use, in work and play, of all the human faculties, so also do health and happiness. I do not believe the world can furnish a man who has for any length of time been entirely absorbed in the duties of a calling, and is, at the same time, healthy and happy. It is impossible in the nature of things that he should be so.

Here we arrive at a point of importance. Neither development, nor health, nor happiness can be secured, in their full degree, unless the mind be animated by a purpose to secure an object in which it is interested. There must be a glad consent of the mind to the efforts of its life, or use will be nothing better than slavery. Childhood may do without a grand purpose, but manhood cannot. For the accomplishment of this purpose, work is the instrument; to its accomplishment, play is only indirectly, though essentially, tributary. There must be a tendency of the life, starting from an intelligently apprehended purpose, to certain ends or certain results, before everything in a man—

before all things in a man—can move harmoniously. Now the mind of no healthy and sound man can gladly consent to a life of slavery to a calling. It revolts from such a life; and play comes in here, not only as an agent in development, but as a mental relief and a mental reward. If a few hours of work purchase and secure a few hours of play, then is the work sweetened as an exercise, and rewarded as a finished performance.

In this philosophy we shall find at least one of the causes of the discontent and the not unfrequent disaster that attend retirement from business. No man in the possession of his faculties can actually retire from business and be happy. The moment a life loses its purpose, and seeks for its sole enjoyment in play, and the neglect of the use of its powers, that moment it loses its happiness. It matters nothing how rich a man may be: the moment those purposes of life are gone to which the work of his life has been devoted, he will become miserable, provided he have any power left for the fulfilment of a purpose. Your memory will recall many a man who has retired from business only to die, or to become a melancholy invalid. So long as a man retains his faculties, and his control of them, he must remain in harness if he would be happy. He must possess and pursue a purpose, or bid farewell to the zest of life. Here is where the greedy multitude of money-makers make wreck of themselves. They deny to themselves play while the work of their life is in progress, in order to have a few years of play, or uninterrupted ease, at the end of it. When their money is madė, they find themselves spoiled for play, and having accomplished their purposes, life is utterly spoiled for them. The truth is that play, for the man and woman, was never intended to be a steady dish, but the condiment of a steady dish. Play is to be taken every day, or never. The moment that the purposes of life are accomplished, play has lost not only its power but its significance; and a man who has really retired from all business is practically dead.

Independence and self-respect are essential to happiness, and these are never to be attained together without work. It is impossible that a man shall be a drone, and go through life without a purpose which contemplates worthy results, and, at the same time, maintain his self-respect. No idle man, however rich he may be, can feel the genuine independence of him who earns honestly and manfully his daily bread. The idle man stands outside of God's plan, outside of the ordained scheme of things; and the truest self-respect, the noblest independence, and the most genuine dignity, are not to be found there. The man who does his part in life, who pursues a worthy end, and who takes care of himself, is the happy man. There is a great deal of cant afloat about the dignity of labor, uttered mostly, perhaps, by those who know little about it experimentally; but labor has a dignity which attaches to little else that is human.

To labor rightly and earnestly is to walk in the golden track that leads to God. It is to adopt the regimen of manhood and womanhood. It is to come into sympathy with the great struggle of humanity toward perfection. It is to adopt the fellowship of all the great and good the world has ever known.

I suppose that all God's purposes in work and play are fulfilled in the completion of the discipline of the worker,—and the results of work are doubtless laid under tribute for this end; but man's direct purposes culminate in the achievement of ends relating to society, institutions, material necessities, art, literature, and the varied objects of human pursuit.

It is in achievement that work throws off all its repulsive features, and assumes the form and functions of an angel. Before her, like a dissolving scene, the forest fades, with its wild beasts and its wild men, and under her hand smiling villages rise among the hills and on the plains, and yellow harvests spread the fields with gold. The city, with its docks and warehouses, and churches and palaces, springs at her bidding into being. The trackless ocean mirrors her tireless pinions as she ransacks the climes for the food of commerce, or flames with the torches of her steam-sped messengers. She binds states and marts and capitals together with bars of iron, that thunder with the ceaseless rush of life and trade. She pictures all scenes of beauty on canvas, and carves all forms of excellence in marble. Into huge libraries she pours the wealth of countless precious lives. She erects beautiful and convenient homes for men and women to dwell in, and weaves the fibres which nature prepares into fabrics for their covering and comfort. She rears great civilizations that run like mountain-ranges through the level centuries, their summits sleeping among the clouds, or still flaming with the fire that fills them, or looming grandly in the purple haze of history. Nature furnishes material, and work fashions it. By the hand of art, work selects, and moulds, and modifies, and re-combines that which it finds, and gives utterance and being to those compositions of matter and of thought which build for man a new world, with special adaptation to his desires, tastes, and necessities. Man's record upon this wild world is the record of work, and of work alone.

Work explores the secrets of the universe, and brings back those contributions which make up the sum of human knowledge. It counts the ribs of the mountains, and feels the pulses of the sea, and traces the foot-paths of the stars, and calls the animals of the forest and the birds of the air and the flowers of the field by name. It summons horses of fire and chariots of fire from heaven, and makes them the bearers of its thought. It plunders the tombs of dead nationalities, and weaves living histories from the shreds it finds. It seeks out and sets in order the secrets of the soil, and divides to every plant its food. It builds and binds into unity great philosophies, along which run the life and thought of ages. It embalms the life of nations in literatures, in whose crypts are scattered seeds of thought that only need the light to spread into harvests of bread for living generations.

How wonderful a being is man, when viewed in the light of his achievements! It is in the record of these that we find the evidence of his power and the credentials of his glory. Into the results of work each generation pours its life; and as these results grow in excellence, with broader forms and richer tints and nobler meanings, they become the indexes of the world's progress. We estimate the life of a generation by what it does; and the results of its work stand out in advance of its successor, to show it what it can do, and to show it what it must do, to reach a finer consummation. Thus the results of work become the most powerful stimulus of the worker. They inspire emulation; they instruct in mode and style; they feed perennially the springs of ambition.

Great, however, as these achievements are, they

derive their peculiar significance from the fact that they are necessarily and forever less than their author. Work being the ordained means of development to the worker, must always, by an immutable law, leave him higher than his achievement. Never was a worthy work accomplished, above which the worker did not stand with the feeling that by his work he had been fitted for something higher. Every generation that has stepped from its sphere of labor into the shadowy beyond, has walked forth with the results of its work beneath its feet. He who hath builded the house hath more honor than the house. Thus work, in its results, lifts each generation in the world's progress from step to step, shortening the ladder upon which the angels ascend and descend, and climbing by ever brighter and broader gradations toward the ultimate perfection. A new and more glorious gift of power compensates for each worthy expenditure, so that it is by work that man carves his way to that measure of power which will fit him for his destiny, and leave him nearest God.

Among the results of work, we shall find for play, too, a compensating ministry. Work wins the appetite for play, and provides the multiplied means for it. It buys and mans a yacht for play. It purchases a horse for play, and drives him before its door, and gives it the ribbons. It opens houses to the incoming of friends, and carpets floors for them, and fills their ears with music and their mouths with delicacies. Play plays for work, and work works for play. Play assists work by ministering to its delight, and keeping its machinery in order, and work supplies play with implements for its grateful service.

There remains to be presented another thought relating to the ultimate results of Work and Play. Development and discipline have been seen to be their immediate object. What is the object of the development and the discipline? For what purpose must you and I play in boyhood, and then work through a life-time, bringing all our powers under the control of will, bending our whole being to the accomplishment of a purpose, till every faculty moves harmoniously with every other faculty? Why is man fitted by his work to do something higher than his work, and to lie down in the dust at last, capable of a greater deed than he has ever performed? Why is it, that, great as the record of man upon the earth is, it must be forever unworthy of man, and convey but a hint of his power?

I am not a preacher, nor is this an occasion for preaching; but this is a Christian congregation, which claims from me the noblest view of this subject—the key to its whole meaning. You and I believe that man is immortal, and your knowledge of yourselves will readily bring you to the admission that an immortality of rest must be, beyond all conception, horrible —more repulsive, in fact, than an immortality of work. The mind that ceases to act without an object, must forever feed upon itself. If I am taught anything by the intimate association and the mutual relations of work and play in this sphere of being, it is, that a period will arrive when they will be blended in one; when out of rectified conditions, and purified dispositions, and rationally apprehended schemes and objects of good, impulses will rise to spur the will and all the faculties trained under it into an eternal play that will be essential work, and an eternal work that will be essential play.

Thus introduced to the object and the meaning of this development and discipline, what wondrous music do the din and discord of business become! How magnificent the thought that, running parallel, or intertwining, with our own limited purposes, and even our careless play, there is a limitless divine purpose threading each object and achievement, and passing infinitely on into the unseen! Hammer away! thou sturdy smith, at that bar of iron, for thou art bravely forging thy own destiny! Weave on in glad content, industrious worker of the mill, for thou art weaving cloth of gold, though thou mark not its lustre! Plough and plant, and rear and reap, ye tillers of the soil, for those brown acres of yours are pregnant with nobler fruitage than that which hung in Eden. Let Commerce fearlessly send out her ships, for there is a haven where they will arrive at last, with freighted wealth below, and flying streamers above, and jubilant crews between! Working well for the minor good and the chief good of life, and wisely making play tributary to your ends, you shall all win your way to the great consummation I have indicated, and find in your hands the golden key that will open for you the riddle of your history.

WORKING AND SHIRKING.

THE disposition to shirk seems to be constitutional with the human race. The first recorded act of the primal pair, after they had eaten the fatal fruit, was an attempt to shirk a moral responsibility. The man tried to shift the burden of his guilt upon the woman, and the woman charged the serpent with being her beguiler. From that day to this their descendants have shown that sinning and shirking are inseparable companions.

There is a prevalent disposition in this country to shirk the hardships of useful and productive labor, and to shirk personal, social, and political responsibility. Very few men make a straight path for themselves, dodging no duty, avoiding no burden that legitimately belongs to them, and cheerfully and manfully assuming every responsibility that Providence places in their path. I think that we shall find it both interesting and profitable to discuss this fault and failing of mankind, especially as illustrated by American character and history, and to say a few words of the remedy which Providence prescribes.

Let me begin with the proposition that all mankind are naturally lazy. There are probably some men in the world who love to work, for work's sake, as there are some men in the world who love tobacco and pickled olives, having acquired a taste for them; but, generally, men work because they are obliged to, for the procurement of the necessaries of life, or because they are impelled to by the wish for wealth or some other desirable good. I do not suppose that any considerable amount of stone-fence was ever laid "for the fun of it," or that the boy lives who prefers raking after a cart to flying a kite. Labor is embraced by the majority of men as a lesser evil than that from which it purchases exemption.

Now what is labor? It is the price we pay for everything that is not free and common to men. For air, we pay no price. It is with us and about us everywhere. For the water that bathes our faces and slakes our thirst, we have only to go where it is—and it is everywhere—to find it bursting from the ground in perennial springs, or leaping down cataracts, or murmuring to itself in brooks, or spreading itself out into rivers, lakes, and oceans. Nay, it will come to us from the sky, and we can catch it in our hands, if we will.

It is possible that some special disposition of air and water may cost labor, but both are intended to be without price; and they are made free because they are so immediately essential to the preservation of life. It will be found also that those articles of food which are absolutely essential are cheap. A few nuts, to be had for the gathering; a few roots, to be obtained for the digging; a few sheep and goats that will take care of themselves, and yield milk and meat and peltry—these cost but little labor; but the moment we pass beyond the simplest essentials for the preservation of animal life, we must pay the full price in labor for every article we obtain.

I say *we* must pay: *somebody* must pay. A bushel of wheat represents a certain amount of labor—the preparation of soil for the seed, the sowing, the covering, the reaping, gathering, threshing, winnowing, and transportation. A barrel of flour represents a still greater amount of labor, both in its quantity and condition. Every bushel of wheat and every barrel of flour represents certain processes of labor without which it could never have been produced. So, every ton of iron cost somebody a certain price in labor, and an ounce of gold, if it will pay for the ton of iron, cost somebody just as much labor as the ton of iron cost.

All values are based on labor—the labor they originally cost, or the labor it would cost to duplicate or reproduce them. A necklace of diamonds will sell for ten thousand dollars because it would, roughly and generally speaking, cost ten thousand dollars to duplicate the gems and their setting, drawing them from the original stock of nature. There are exceptions to this rule in the lucky stumbles that are made upon extraordinary deposits of the precious stones and metals; but, speaking in the large way, everything costs its value in labor. California makes no more money in digging gold than Illinois makes in growing wheat; Georgia gets no richer in producing cotton than Massachusetts does in spinning it. Nature is so nicely adjusted to this basis of values, that intelligent labor thrives as well on a mountain as in a valley; thrives as well on the water as on the land; gets just as much for its pains in a quarry of granite as in a vein of gold-bearing quartz; and finds equal profit in working a coal-mine and washing for diamonds.

I look over my audience, and I see silks from China, ribbons from France, cloths from England and Germany, brooches from California, gloves from the feet of the Alps—the work of thousands of weavers and spinners and dyers and cunning artisans and artists—and all these represent labor. All these cost the labor of somebody, and the money that bought them cost the labor of somebody. The money which you gave for these things may not have cost you anything, but it cost somebody its value in labor. There are some of you, possibly, who have never been obliged to labor, and who have earned nothing that you possess; but somebody has earned it. That wealth of yours was dug out of the ground, or drawn from the sea, by somebody; perhaps it required ten thousand somebodies to do it. You or your ancestors may have won this wealth at comparatively little cost; but it all came originally from the marrow and through the muscles of labor.

The fact that some persons are rich proves that the labor of the world is more than sufficient for the wants of the world. That everybody lives, and that some have wealth who produce nothing, shows that there are various ways of securing the results of productive labor without engaging in that labor. There is a large number of men and women in the world who live upon the labor of others—a large number besides those who are naturally or necessarily dependent. Many secure a share of this surplus of production by entirely legitimate means. They take a just contribution from it as it passes through their hands in various commercial exchanges. They fill some office or perform some service for the producers, and secure a proper payment for their work; but the great strife of the world is to see how much of this labor of production can be shirked, and how great an amount of its results can be secured without paying their legitimate price. Every employment that gives heavy pay for light work, every scheme of gain that promises large rewards for little labor, every profession, trade, or calling, that secures the results of productive toil without paying their full price, is filled to overflowing, in every community.

The great centres of commercial exchange are points of attraction for the shirks of the world. They stand wherever the producers and consumers meet, ready to grasp some portion of the profits of trade—men who live by their wits—men who minister to the vices of wealth for a consideration—men who are content to be the well-dressed slaves of capital—men who speculate in the necessaries of life, though thousands starve—men who gamble in stocks and invent fancy schemes of plunder—knaves who eat the flesh and drink the blood of needle-women—Peter Funks, beggars, thieves—men who prefer to simper and smirk behind a counter to doing a man's work behind a plough—women who sell their bodies and their souls for luxury and ease—suckers and swindlers and supernumeraries and sinners generally.

Nor are these all the shirks of the city. If we could know the real motive that brings the reputable people of a city together, we should, very generally, find it to be the desire to win wealth without producing it, and without paying in labor the full price for it. The able-bodied farmer's boy leaves the hoe for the yard-stick to save his back from labor; and there are hundreds of thousands of men in our larger cities who have relinquished manly employment, manly aims and ambitions, and manly independence, for the sole purpose of securing the results of the labor of others at a cheap rate. I do not say that they accomplish their object, for there is great competition in shirking, and pretty hard work is made of it sometimes. I am talking simply of their motive and their aim.

You will not understand me to have any reference to the legitimate commerce and the useful professions and callings which engage large and honorable numbers in every city, when I say that the shirks of the city are very great curses of the country. They have contrived to make labor disreputable, or, at least, unfashionable. They have erected a false standard of respectability. They have helped to establish the opinion that the laborer—the producer and the artificer of the wealth of the nation—cannot possibly be a gentleman, and that the only gentle pursuits are those of trade and commerce, and the professions and callings which more immediately serve them. It is in these false ideas—offspring of pretentious laziness—that American productive labor is educated; and it is sad to think how much of it grows up to despise itself, and to look upon its lot as equally severe and degrading. The city is the beautiful and haughty

Estella that tells poor Pip that his hands are coarse, and poor Pip gets ashamed of his hands, and feels very sadly about himself.

But it is not in ideas alone that the shirking classes of the city curse the country. Let us look for a moment at that paradise of shirks, the stock-exchange—a place where not the first particle of wealth ever was produced or ever will be produced; where great games of chance are played in a strictly legal and a superlatively immoral way; where men combine to break down the credit of worthy corporations, conspire to give a fictitious value to that which is valueless, and make a business of cheating each other and swindling the world. I can perceive no difference between a professional gambler in stocks and any other professional gambler. Both are men who produce nothing; who play at games of skill and hazard for money; who never win a dollar that does not leave some other man poorer; and who strive to over-reach each other, and burn the fingers of unsuspicious outsiders. Professional speculating in stocks is organized and instituted shirking. Sin, we are told, "when it is finished bringeth forth death." Shirking, in its ultimate development, bringeth forth the stock-exchange.

Think of the influence of this institution upon the country. To leave out of account the temptations it holds out to those who are greedy for sudden wealth, or to those who are in desperate circumstances, think of the false standard of values it sets before the country. Think how the trade, the commercial confidence, and the business enterprise of the nation rise and fall with the varying influence of the bulls and the bears in the stock-market, while the real value of the fluctuating stocks may not materially change from one year to another. A panic in the stock-market, produced by professional speculators, is felt from one end of the country to the other; and all this disturbance is caused that a set of professional shirks may *make* an opportunity to steal a dollar out of a railway-bond, or filch a dirty dime from an honest man's share of bank-stock. Would it not be, indeed, a blessing to the country if this legal gambling-shop were shut up? Would it not be better, on the whole, that the men who get their living there should take to similar pursuits in private, where they use a thicker variety of paper—pasteboard, in fact—and where they have only four knaves in a pack? I think so.

Perhaps the most humiliating exhibition which the shirks make of themselves is on the occasion of a change in the national administration. A hundred dollars in money (borrowed), three clean shirts, a long petition, an anxious face, and a carpet-bag, form the outfit of something less than a hundred thousand able-bodied men who make a pilgrimage to Washington every four years. And what do these men want? They want a clerkship, a collectorship, a postmastership—any sort of a ship that will save them the trouble of rowing, and that will furnish them with pay and rations. The majority of these men are shirks, who wish to be released from the necessity of productive and useful industry. They swarm around the centres of patronage like bees around a sugar-cask, every one after something sweet which others have collected. Alas! let me confess that the shirks are not all in the city. Rip Van Winkle lived in a country-village under the Catskills, and we are told by Mr. Irving that "the great error in Rip's composition was an insuperable aversion to all kinds of profitable labor." There is more than one Rip Van Winkle in every American village; but instead of decently lying down in the field, and sleeping for twenty years, he prefers to take a nap equally long in a government-office, and waking up with better clothes on, instead of worse.

The genuine shirk, wherever he lives, has no honor, no conscience, and no patriotism. In the nation's hour of trial, when everything good in an American's nature was appealed to, he clothed our troops with shoddy, and cheated them in their rations, and took advantage of his country's need to fill his coffers, every dollar of which must be patiently worked out by his fellow-citizens. Certainly a swindling government contractor, in a time of national peril, deserves the most infamous place among the shirks and scoundrels of the world.

Let us look at some of the more obvious and ordinary results of shirking. All kinds of business that promise large results at little cost are overdone. The country drives straight into financial wreck at brief, irregular periods, simply because there are too many men trying to get a living without producing anything. If we look over the list of our acquaintances, we shall be astonished to see how large a number of disappointed men it embraces, and how large a proportion of this number is made up of those who tried to win wealth cheaply. Generally, disappointed and broken-down men are those who have failed in trade, or have run through some fancy scheme of gain, or, to use an expressive Yankee phrase, have "flatted out" in a calling or profession which was intended to draw money in some way from the producing and commercial interests.

I repeat, that all kinds of business that promise large results at little cost are overdone. The haste to get rich—the desire to acquire sudden wealth without being obliged to pay in labor the legitimate price for it—is the principal cause of the financial calamities that at brief intervals have befallen our country during the last fifty years. It is not that we have not been a nation of workers. To get rich rapidly, we have been willing to work intensely and immensely; but we have been shirks all the while—striving to get out of our work ten, fifty, or a hundred times more than it has been worth. America can never become a truly happy, stable, and reliable nation, until its views of life become more sober, and a much larger proportion of its people become willing, by patient, manly labor in the useful or productive arts of life, to earn every dollar they receive.

I ought to add to all this, that much of the failure in commercial and professional life is due to a lack of preparation for it; and this neglect of preparation for success is a part of the universal system of shirking. Lawyers are made in a day. Physicians there are in abundance who are as innocent of any knowledge of science as they were when they were born. Men enter the various avenues of trade without a decent familiarity with the forms of business, and without any business habits at all. Trades are adopted, not acquired—adopted at the suggestion of a natural knack. Indeed, I believe that the habit of shirking the work of thorough preparation for the business of life is well-nigh universal in the country. Long periods of training for the professions, and patiently pursued apprenticeships to the arts and trades, are almost unknown. In short, we choose a pursuit which will enable us to shirk labor as far as possible, and then shirk the necessary preparation to win success in it. When a boy changes his roundabout for a coat, he is ready to "stick out his shingle," as he calls it, and the shingle usually "sticks out" a good deal longer than he does.

It is among men who try to get a living by some shift or trick of laziness that we hear the familiar words: "the world owes me a living." A loafer who never did a useful thing in his life; who dresses at the expense of the tailor, and drinks at the cost of his friends, always insists that "the world owes him a living," and declares his intention to secure the debt. I should like to know how it is that a man who owes the world for every mouthful he ever ate and every garment he ever put on, should be so heavy a creditor in account with the world. The loafer lies about it. The world owes him nothing but a very rough coffin, and a retired and otherwise useless place to put it in.

The world owes a living to those who are not able to earn one—to children, to the sick, to the disabled and the aged—to all who in the course of nature or by force of circumstances are dependent; and it was mainly for the supply of the wants of these that men were endowed with the power to produce more than enough for themselves. To a genuine shirk the world owes nothing; and when he tells me with a whine that the world owes him a living, I am assured that he has the disposition of a highway-robber, and lacks only his courage and his enterprise.

I pass now to the consideration of the disposition to shirk special duties of life; and first, the duty of personal self-assertion. We live in a country where, more than in any other, public opinion domineers over the minds of men. Americans generally dread singularity in sentiments and opinions as much as they do in dress; so that if they cannot quite reflect the changing phases of the public mind, they modify their moral clothing sufficiently to avoid attracting the attention of the boys. We dread to appear in the street with a hat or a coat five years old; and we dread just as much to appear in an opinion which has gone out of fashion.

Sacred convictions, deliberately formed opinions, long-cherished sentiments, are clipped and rounded and shortened in, or pieced out in accordance with the popular style, so that we may be enabled to pass for men who are up with the times. The men are comparatively few who are willing to take the responsibility of the full assertion of their personality; who will stand or fall by their convictions, sentiments, and opinions; who will insist on being themselves, even when that is equivalent to being singular. This despotic public opinion, which, without doubt, has a legitimate limited field of influence, shapes our whole national life and character, through its influence upon the individual.

None escape this modifying power, though some feel it and are moulded by it less than others.

I think you will all be able to call to mind some man of your acquaintance who will sufficiently serve to illustrate by his life and character this prevalent disposition to shirk self-assertion. Perhaps in early life he had a few opinions, and conducted his life after a certain policy; but some damaging collision—a little infirmity of will—a little too large a love of approbation, and a good deal of moral cowardice, have led him to throw overboard everything he can call his own; and he has become the victim and sport of the sea of personalities around him. He has a great horror of a collision, and will hear his most sacred sentiments attacked without replying. He shirks all conflict of opinions as he would shun a personal street-fight. Whenever he ventures to push out any manifestation of his personality which hits anything, or meets a repulse, he takes it back as quickly as he would a burnt finger. He is careful to agree with every man who carries a positive character; and it is astonishing to see the variety of people he can agree with. He is like arrow-root, or certain widely-advertised patent medicines that are warranted to "agree with all temperaments and the most delicate constitutions." One always knows where to find such a man as this; and so does one's neighbor. In a time of quiet, he will be with you, and with anybody who happens to be near him; but in a time of disturbance, when opinions are clashing and a great moral conflict is in progress, the fence is his invariable resort. He takes to a fence as naturally at every sign of tumult and struggle as a squirrel takes to a tree when the dogs are out. We have in every community a considerable number of men who have spent all their years of discretion upon the fence. Such men always affect candor and dignity and freedom from prejudice and passion, but they are invariably shirks and cowards.

Such men as these occupy an extreme, it is true; but how large is the multitude who are only less despicable than they! How many are there who go dodging through life,—shunning a collision here for the sake of peace, sacrificing a sentiment there rather than be guilty of singularity, shirking the assertion of their sentiments, convictions, and opinions, when manhood demands their assertion, allowing themselves to be hampered and paralyzed in every putting-forth of their personality, and clipped and rubbed and rounded and polished, until they become as thin and smooth and scentless as an old cake of soap in a public bathing-room.

Going uniformly with one's sect in religion, with one's party in politics, or with one's clique in social life, is only less mean than occupying the fence. A man who buries his personality in a sect or party because he is afraid or ashamed to stand alone, is quite as much a coward as he who endeavors to preserve neutrality. A bully with backers is quite likely to be the poltroon of his company, and quite likely to be a bully because he is conscious of his cowardice, and wishes to prevent other people from finding him out.

We are every day sacrificing something for peace. Well, peace is good, or may be good. Peace is certainly desirable. If daily peace with all mankind can be purchased by the sacrifice of unimportant things, by the surrender of a few personal notions, by a little inconvenience that affects only ourselves, very well. But peace purchased by running away; peace purchased by avoiding conflicts upon questions of vital importance; peace purchased by yielding a point of honor, or sacrificing a principle; peace purchased by silent acquiescence in wrong, is not very well. Such peace is the most insidious and deadly poison that assails American manhood. It is for this peace that a certain class has parted with its political opinions. It is for this peace that men have practically denied their religion. It is for this peace that numbers have failed to set themselves against great evils that threaten their neighbors, themselves, and their children. It was for this peace that American nationality was sold out by cowardly politicians and cowardly people. Shirking self-assertion and personal responsibility for the sake of personal peace—what else was it that led patriotism to retire from year to year before the on-coming flood of treason, until even in the capital of the nation there was not an ark-load of loyalty left? Ah! cursed peace—ah! fatal peace, that is purchased by the surrender of personal manhood!

We are every day sacrificing something for popularity. Well, popularity may be very good, but it is not the best good, and it can be purchased at far too high a price. Popularity that is secured by meanly withdrawing our own opinions to give place to the opinions of others, or by refusing to give voice to solemn convictions, or by ignoring a popular vice or giving countenance to a popular wrong, is *not* good. It is the basest possession which human meanness can win. A man who only asserts so much of that which is in him as will find favor with those among whom he has his daily life, and who withholds all that will wound their vanity and condemn their selfishness and clash with their principles and prejudices, has no more manhood in him than there is in a spaniel, and is certainly one of the most contemptible shirks the world contains.

Of course, I would not be understood to advocate the idea that every man's personality should so stand out that every other man's personality shall run against it. I do not advocate the gratuitous obtrusion of one's opinions, sentiments, and convictions upon the world, or seeking a collision or a conflict wherever one may be possible. I simply maintain that for no mean consideration, like a cowardly desire for peace or a childish greed for praise or popularity, shall a man refrain, on every just occasion, from asserting himself and all there is in him.

I shall speak next of the disposition to shirk the duties of social life. I will lead you to my lesson in this department of my subject through an illustration. In our New England congregationalism, the parish or society is independent in certain very important respects of the church, and has its own peculiar machinery. The parish raises the money, makes the appropriations, and does all the business. Now, if you will get inside of this organization, and look about you, you will find that its responsibility and its work are upon the shoulders of a very small number of persons, and that by far the larger number have no more interest in the affairs of the parish than they would have in the management of a theatre which they might occasionally visit. The majority of those who attend church look upon the minister and the deacons and the parish committee as a sort of corporation whose business they have no interest in and no responsibility for. I have sometimes thought that they suspected there was an annual dividend of the profits of running the machine which those who handled the crank monopolized. They hire a pew; and, if they pay for it, they imagine that their duty ends there. They are patrons of the institution; and if they do not like it they hire a pew somewhere else. Some of them apparently suppose that they place a parish under obligation to them by purchasing the gospel at its particular counter.

The idea that every man who attends a church should have just as much interest in it and just as much responsibility for it—means, brains, and piety being equal—as any other man, they do not apprehend at all. The fact that the support and the responsibility of a church rest upon all alike, and that the man who is willing to enjoy the privileges of a church without bearing his proportion of its burdens is a shirk, has never come within the range of their conception. I suppose this audience is made up of those who do their duty in the parishes to which they belong,—and those who do not; and if it should be like audiences that I am best acquainted with, the latter outnumber the former ten to one.

In general society we find matters much in the same way. Society differs from the parish, however, in that it has no formal organization, no instituted machinery, no sittings with definite appraisements, and no written articles of constitution. Society is, in the looser signification of the word, conventional. Men can enjoy at least a portion of its privileges—and many do enjoy them—without paying anything for them, or without paying the full price for them.

Society, like the parish, has its burdens; and these burdens are usually borne by a few. We say of one man that he is public spirited, and of another that he is not public spirited. We mean that one is willing to assume his portion of the duties and burdens of society, or of the general public, and that the other is not. If some public enterprise is proposed which naturally appeals to the generosity of men as citizens—lovers of the general good—members of society—then we see who is ready to bear his proportion of the burdens of society, and who is disposed to shirk them. We shall find, I am sorry to believe, that the majority of men shirk the pecuniary burdens of society, and yet are quite willing to share in the results of the sacrifices of others. If a park is to be laid out, or a thousand shade-trees are to be planted, or a public library is to be established, or anything is to be done for the general good, which must be done voluntarily, by men acting as citizens—as members of society—we shall find that a few will contribute generously, and that the many will contribute niggardly, and always among these many, the miserly rich. The shirking multitude are quite willing to believe that what ought to be done will be done by somebody, and quite ready to be pensioners upon the bounty of their betters, with the privilege of abusing them. Most men do what they are obliged by law to do, and no more; and we can ascertain how willingly they do even this by inquiring of the assessors and collectors of taxes.

In a restricted sense, "society" is that indefinite number of individuals and families with which each person is brought into intimate relation. The men and women among whom I find myself in social assemblages, who frequent my house, who form the circle next to that which embraces my family-life, are my "society." This circle will be larger or smaller, better or poorer, according to my social value; and my social value will depend upon what I can give and what I do give for what I receive. If I give a great deal more than I receive, that will make me a social leader, or, in time, lift me into community with a higher grade than that in which I move. If I give less than I receive—though I give all I can—that will make me socially subordinate, or translate me to a grade in which the social requirements are less.

We find a very large number of men and women who are not willing to remain in the social circle in which the circumstances and the natural affinities and proprieties of their life have placed them. They have an idea that their social value is not determined by what they have to give to society, but rather by what society gives to them. They believe that if they can set their feet within some circle that is nominally above them—into that charming sphere which Our Best

Society calls "our best society"—their brass will immediately be transmuted into gold. Let us see what our best society, as Our Best Society calls it, is. There are three elements that constitute it, and that we may remember them the more readily, they shall all begin with a *B*, viz.: Breeding, Brains, and Bullion. These three elements are rarely or never in equipoise, but they mingle in different proportions in different places, according to circumstances. In a town where there is a considerable number of honorable old families, Breeding usually takes the lead, and gives the law. In a town where there is no pretension to hereditary respectability, and there is comparatively little wealth, Brains will be in the ascendant, and men and women of culture and gentle manners will be the leaders. When Breeding and Brains are lacking, Bullion will give the law to society; and those who have the reputation of wealth and the habit of ostentatious display will hold the weight of social influence. These three elements combine, as I have said, in various proportions, to make what Our Best Society is pleased to denominate our best society—that circle to which the socially ambitious always aspire.

Now if there are those before me who stand on the outside of this charming and charmed circle, looking longingly into the inclosure, let me put this single question to them: "What will you give to go in?"

What Our Best Society is pleased to call our best society, is not so unreasonable or so difficult as you may suppose. It simply demands that you take notice of its dominant ideas, and pay for its privileges in the current coin. How much old and honorable blood can you bring to add to its stock of respectability? If you have good blood, it is not so much matter about Brains, provided that your pedigree is so unquestionable that Bullion will lend you money. If you have plenty of Bullion, and will use it in the entertainment of our best society, you can get along quite well without either Brains or Breeding; but Breeding, Brains, or Bullion you must have, or you cannot go in. Tell me: have you a great family-name, or wit or learning, and the power to make exhibition of them in conversation? or excellent manners? or a great house and splendid equipage and a hospitable table, with which to pay for the privilege of entering this society? Can you, and will you, pay the price of admission in the current coin, or do you wish to become one of the pensioners and bores of this society? Are you willing and ready to pay the price and assume the duties of a high social position, or do you wish to enjoy its pleasures and advantages and shirk all its responsibilities? —to be patronized and tolerated as people who give nothing for what they receive?

I suppose there are multitudes of people, whose

great desire and anxiety relate to getting into certain society for the fancied or real privileges of which they have nothing to offer; who do not dream of being anything but beneficiaries; and who look upon good society as a sort of charitable soup-concern for social mendicants, supported by people who have nothing to do, and unlimited means to do it with.

There is a great deal of fault-finding with that very nebulous entity which we call society; but if we examine carefully, we shall find that it is uniformly the shirks who make most complaint. I never heard a man who faithfully and cordially performed all his social duties complain of society; and so society, like the parish, is carried on by the few, while the masses of men do not regard themselves as having any social responsibilities whatever. They are shirks, who are willing to receive all that society has to bestow—shirks, who fold their hands and whine because society neglects them—shirks, who never perform a social duty, or feel that a particle of social responsibility is upon them.

I shall notice in particular but one more variety of shirking of which Americans are peculiarly guilty, and this is political shirking—perhaps the most prevalent and mischievous of all, because it strikes at the very root of the state, and of all individual and social well-being. Social shirking does not damage good society or injure its quality; it only makes it smaller. The better elements of society combine by natural and conditional affinities, and the shirks only fall back into comparatively harmless disorganization. Political shirking, on the other hand, instead of leaving political affairs in good hands, invariably leaves them in bad hands; for it is the more virtuous constituents of political communities, and not the vicious, that shirk their political responsibilities. I should rather say, perhaps, that bad men seize the opportunity which the negligence of good men affords them, to manage political affairs for their own selfish advantage.

Under the American system of self-government—at whose ballot-box all social and individual distinctions are wiped away—it is astonishing to see how many there are who do not feel that they have the slightest political responsibility. They come out to the elections, perhaps, because their party-leaders desire them to come out, or because their party-feelings urge them to come out, or because they delight in the excitement of an election, or, possibly, in some rare and remarkable instances, because they are paid for coming out. I give it as a carefully formed judgment, that not one American voter in five really feels that he has any personal responsibility in the government of the country. All feel, of course, that they have a personal interest in it, but this interest is not associated with a sense of high personal duty. In times of political excitement they may be excited, but their interest is mainly in behalf of a party. They may work very enthusiastically, indeed, for "our side," without giving a single thought to our country. To a certain extent, this is the result of ignorance, or of a lack of power to grasp their real relations to the state, or of a degree of moral poverty which shuts them off from all high, patriotic motives.

I have yet to learn that the American nation is not the equal of any of the nations of the world in the possession of pure morals and Christian virtues; but it is painfully evident that there is not a nation on the face of the earth in which bad men have such facilities for acquiring and retaining power as in ours. They win elections to seats in the national legislature by frauds and briberies; they go to roost like foul birds in the offices of great cities; they batten on public spoil; they disgrace Christian civilization and free institutions; they debase the moral sense of the nation. To them, a country or a city is but a great goose to be plucked and plucked and plucked again, until, sibilant and shrieking, it tears itself from their grasp, to be caught immediately by another set of spoilsmen and plucked to the very quills and pin-feathers.

Now, who is responsible for this? Not the bad man, certainly, or not the bad men mainly. It can hardly be accounted a crime for a vessel to run a blockade if she can, and her interests demand the risk; but it is a crime for a blockading fleet to allow her to do it. If the devil is permitted to manage the politics of a nation we expect him to do it, for politics are in his particular line; and the good men, whose business it is to hinder him from doing it, must be held responsible for the damage that may result from his management. Thus I affirm that the good men of America are mainly responsible for everything evil in American politics. They have the best social influences in their hands; they have the Christian Church; they have the literary institutions; they have the pure sympathies of women; they have reason, conscience, truth, and God all on their side—nay, they have the majority; and the only reason why bad men reign and they are powerless, is that they are shirks.

Yet these political shirks are very respectable men. Let us not allude to them too harshly or too lightly. If they are "fossiliferous" and fussy, they are prudent and pious. Far be it from me to speak disrespectfully of their linen, or to question the whiteness of their fragrant hands. They are exceedingly clean and pure men, their particular fault (if they have one) being an excessive cleanliness and purity that unfits them for having anything to do with politics. They are of that unlucky moral hue that shows dirt on the slightest provocation, and requires them to be carefully dusted and set away. They refuse, year after year, to visit the polls, because politics have become so corrupt that they have ceased to have any interest in them, or because good men are not nominated for office; yet they never dream of attending a primary meeting to make sure that good men are nominated, or of making any attempt to render politics less corrupt. Of all the shirks and sneaks which the prolific soil of America produces, there certainly can be none more despicable than these. America is not suffering from a political evil to-day for which the good men of the country should not be held mainly responsible. Bad men have run the nation upon ruin, because they have been permitted to do it; and good men, instead of leading in the political battles, have fought humbly in the ranks, or run away. Indeed, many of them have come to the conclusion that there is something necessarily demoralizing in politics, and that religion and politics are entirely incompatible with each other.

There is another class of good, or goodish men, who hold political privilege at a cheap price, and who are ready to sell it for personal ease and convenience. They are willing to look after politics a little, or to do anything for their country, if it does not cost too much trouble, or too much money. They are very much absorbed by their own affairs, and have no time to give to their town, or their state, or their country.

They leave these matters to those who have leisure; and those who have leisure happen to be those who are bent on public mischief or private advantage. Bad men always have leisure for taking and employing all the power which the excessive occupation of good men leaves in their hands. While, therefore, one set of men are so good as to be disgusted with politics, and another is so busy as not to have time for attending to them, the very worst elements of society find an easy path to power.

The time was not long ago when there were few—alas! how few!—who were willing to sacrifice anything for their country. The best men have declined office and shunned public duty because they could not afford to hold office. They could afford to see office held by second and third rate men, and to be themselves ruled by vicious men, and to have the institutions of their country cheapened and disgraced by the weak or wicked administration of the laws, but they could not afford to part company with a few dollars to serve the country and the institutions which their children were to inherit! What, in Heaven's name, shall become of a nation whose good men—whose best men—not only refuse to participate in elections, but refuse to be elected to office, when chance, or an aroused moral sentiment, designates them for responsible positions? Let the unhappy condition of the country, and the history of the last twenty years, give answer!

I have thus spoken of several varieties of shirking, and several classes of shirks. I might mention others, but it would be alike tedious and unnecessary.

And now I am ready to ask what the cure for this grand national fault in all its various forms of manifestation may be. What is the medicine for this meanness? What will drive the shirking multitudes that throng all the easier trades and professions back to hard and honest gains in the useful or productive arts of life? What will harden the bones and strengthen the muscles and stiffen the courage of manhood, so that it will assert itself as manhood should—at all times, in all places—yielding nothing of personal conviction or personal power to a weak desire for peace or popularity? What will make us public-spirited, and generous in social life? What will enlarge our sympathies and quicken our activities as members of a national brotherhood? What thing, more than any other, will bring us up to a comprehension of our political duties, and a willingness to perform them? What will teach us that we cannot shirk these duties—that there is not an interest of life on which they do not have a practical bearing? What will make us nobler and more unselfish men—more willing to do or die for that which is god-like in our souls and God-given in our institutions? What will transform all this multitude of personal, social, and political shirks into heroes, and evoke from this mass of sneaking laziness and selfish indifference those virtues which are a nation's noblest wealth? I answer—*A great war for a great cause.*

If the history of America for the last fifty years proves anything with striking clearness, it proves that a long peace, maintained without sacrifice, and held without a sense of its value, is the very breeding-bed of cowardice, cupidity, and corruption. The most heroic blood becomes thin, and the stoutest hearts grow weak and cowardly, in the luxurious atmosphere of a cheap peace. National pride, love of country, patriotic self-devotion —these are not the sentiments and the virtues that thrive among a people that recedes from all sense of national care into the selfish pursuits of gain, or the weak indulgences of ease. Peace is very beautiful; peace may be very safe, indeed, for angels; but for men, with the imperfections, temptations, and tendencies of men, a peace that is not the price of ceaseless vigilance, and the cost of a daily sense of sacrifice, may be a curse so much worse than war, that war may be gladly greeted as a blessing in its stead. It was London, cheaply built and cheaply held, and bent on selfish advantage, that was smitten again and again by the plague. At length, in one brief visitation, it breathed upon and blasted a hundred thousand lives. And then came the furious and all-devouring fire, driving the sickly multitudes from their homes, and licking up and wiping out cheap London forever. Straightway, on the ruins of both plague and fire, rose a new city; and long generations have blessed the fire that banished the plague forever. The question in America has been for many years between plague and fire. With a full comprehension of the horrors and sacrifices of war—with a heart bleeding with sympathy for every soul to which war brings bereavement and sorrow—I thank God for the fire, and the dearer and better peace it will bring us.

Fire is a great renovator and gunpowder a remarkable disinfectant. Already is the influence of war visible for good upon the American people. Men have not only discovered that there is something better than money, but more than this—and greater discovery than this—that there is really something which they love better than money. The universal revival of patriotism in the American heart, and the devotion of a million hands and lives to patriotic duty—is not this a blessing? Could anything but war have won it? That one thrill of patriotic indignation that passed through the American heart when the national flag was insulted at Fort Sumter, by those whom it had protected for nearly a century, was worth more than the whole sum of emotion that had rolled up in lazy accumulation during the previous period of peace. It transformed every man into a hero; it made a heroine of every woman. It was like the sudden flowering of the aloe, after sleeping through a century of suns. It burst upon the world like the comet that followed it—unheralded, unexpected. Men saw the flaming glory, streaming up the midnight sky, and wondered from what depth of heaven it had sprung.

And now there have gone forth a million of men, drawn from every walk of society, with their lives in their hands, to defend American nationality and American institutions. The lawyer has left his briefs, the preacher has left his flock or taken it with him, the physician has forsaken his daily round of duty, the merchant his counting-room, the politician his intrigues, and the rich man his home of ease; the governor and the governed, the high and the humble, have gone together, and all have pressed forward, inspired by a common impulse, to do or die for home and native land. Men who have long been sleeping in their political sepulchres have come forth by a miracle of resurrection, to the surprise of the doubtful and the joy of friends. That great number whose perch has been the fence through years of questionable manhood, have made haste to descend, and to declare themselves for their country against all foes. Women, used only to luxury, have laid aside their frivolous pursuits, and with busy fingers and the noblest charities have prepared mustering thousands of fathers and brothers and husbands and lovers for war. Nay, more: forsaking home and kindred and comfort and peace, they have gone forth voluntarily, at their own charges, and without hope of reward, to breathe the foul air of hospitals, and move among the cots of the sick and wounded soldiery, with the sweet ministries of sympathy and mercy. Capital, timid and careful and compromising through years of political decay, and gathering signs of national disruption, has become bold and defiant. Noblest of all, it has thrown its giant arms around the tottering form of American nationality, and sworn to sustain it forever. It has brought its golden treasures, and laid them all at the feet of its country, and said: "Take them, for without thee they are worthless." If there could be one thing nobler than the eager readiness of a million of men to sacrifice their lives for their country, it would be the bold and unhesitating devotion of capital to the common cause. From its nature, it is the sign and seal of political salvation, and the harbinger of returning political virtue.

There is no lack now of personal self-assertion. All men now have an opinion, and there are but few who have not been stiffened up to a determination to assert and maintain it against all forms of opposition. Political shirking is among the sins of the past. Men feel now, in their consciences and in their personal interests, the burdens of the government, and understand and feel, as they have never understood and felt before, their personal responsibility in public affairs. When men fight for their country, and sacrifice their present prosperity and their accumulated treasure for their country, and voluntarily tax themselves through the remainder of their lives for their country, they will apprehend and faithfully discharge their personal responsibilities in its government.

He would be an unwise and a most unsafe physician who should prescribe war as a specific remedy for each of the national evils I have discussed, considered without relation to their cause; but it must be remembered that they are the offspring of a common parent. It is because we have held our choicest blessings cheaply—it is because we have enjoyed them, like air and water, without price, and with no adequate sense of their value, that we have failed to appreciate the minor good, and, whenever possible, shirked its price. The right to life, liberty, and the pursuit of happiness—a right for the acquisition and maintenance of which many a nation has struggled through centuries of blood and sacrifice—the right which the revolutionary fathers fought through weary years of suffering and privation to achieve—we have enjoyed without sacrifice, without price, and with only the feeblest sense of its value. The right to worship God according to the dictates of our own consciences, under forms of our own choice,—

the right which the pilgrim fathers found in the wilderness after their weary search across the sea—has been ours without question and without cost. The right to govern ourselves—asking no privilege of outside powers, and suffering no interference from them—has been as cheaply held as the right to breathe. It is thus that we have lost the standard by which to measure values, and learned to shirk the price demanded for our humbler wealth.

The war remedy is a radical one. It strikes at the very root of the difficulty; and I have no more doubt of its curative power than I have that Providence prescribes it. Whatever may be the issue of this war, it will leave us a better, a braver, and every way a nobler, people. It will leave us industrious, sober, willing to earn the good we enjoy. It will make us self-respectful, and self-asserting, at whatever cost of peace or popularity. Best of all, it will teach every man the value of the political blessings he enjoys, and place the government once more in the hands of the people, who will restore to power the statesman so long discarded, and displace the politician forever.

HIGH LIFE AND LOW LIFE.

LIFE is high or low according to its pursuits, pleasures, and motives. There may be, and, as a matter of fact, there often is, high life below stairs and low life in the drawing-room. There are palaces into which the conception of what constitutes high life has never entered. There are hovels so radiant and redolent with a high and beautiful life, that we count them courts of the immortals. There was conventional high life, I presume, in Sodom; but the only variety which the angels recognized was found in Lot's tent, at the gate of the city; and, for the rest, the flames disposed of it. There was a good deal of nominal high life, without doubt, among the antediluvians; but there was only one family that was high enough to keep its head above water.

Real high life and conventional high life have rarely been identical; and, although the theme is not new, I have thought that a fresh presentation of it might not be without interest and profit. The preacher, the social reformer, the philanthropist, the philosopher, the statesman, and the moralist, all drive at it from different directions, pushing their ideas toward a common centre, as the Indian hunters sweep the game of the prairies into a single inclosure. It certainly ought not to be irksome to stand where the lines converge, and survey the group as it assembles.

It will be useless for us to enter upon a discussion like this without a measure of honest faith in human nature, and in the perfectibility of human character. I believe there are such things in and among men as honor, virtue, truthfulness, dignity, unselfishness. I neither propose nor oppose any theological dogma when I say that I believe in human nature. It is my nature, and, if God made me, it is the nature He gave me. There may be in it hereditary tendencies to evil—it would be strange if there were not; but the nature itself is the finest and most glorious of all God's work, in this world, itself fitted up expressly for its habitation. Without this faith in human nature, high life is anything we may choose to call such, and low life is simply that which does not please us. I make this statement, in this way, because there are so many who, for various reasons, mostly found in their own hearts and lives, do not believe in the possibility of a human life organized, active, and permanent, above the plane of selfishness and sensuality, forever free from the dominion of sordid motives, and tending only to divine issues.

We shall arrive at a competent comprehension of human nature, and at what constitutes high and low life, by an illustration. Let us regard every rational man in the world as two men. Every individual shall be dividual into a master and a slave. Every man is constituted a man by the conjunction of an angel with an animal. Each has a distinct and characteristic will, distinct and characteristic affections, passions, powers, and destiny. One is limited in life, and dies as the animals die. The other lives as the angels live, and is immortal. There is probably not a man or woman before me who is not conscious of the constant struggle going on between these two natures; and I presume there is not one who is not conscious that all the real dignity of life comes through the thorough subordination of the animal to the angel within him. Let us listen to what our man in white and our man in black have to say to each other.

The man in black, being irrational, and having no law but desire, says: "I wish to gorge myself with meat and drink;" but the man in white is rational, and replies: "No; that would harm you, and, as you are united with me, it would injure me." The man in black howls or whines, and begs for indulgence, but the man in white repeats the prohibition, and shuts his ears. The man in black pleads for the object of his base desires, but the man in white shrinks from the suggestion with indignation and shame, and regards with tender honor her whom the man in black would pollute and ruin. The man in black is vain, and would dress himself in gaudy colors, like the animal or the savage. The man in white objects that he would not be his fit associate thus decorated. The man in black gets angry like a dog, but the man in white holds him by the collar until he is calm. The man in black is constantly calling the attention of the man in white to the objects of sense, and pleading for greater license, and offering sweet rewards for indulgence; and strong and true as the man in white may be, he feels the influence as a persistently degrading power.

But the result of this conference is not always such as I have represented to you. The man in white is sometimes a very feeble man, and the man in black a very strong one. In such cases, the struggle may be as long as life, or it may be no struggle at all, and the man in black may have everything his own way. You have only to look into the haunts of vice—into the drinking-hells, the houses of shame, the prisons, the halls of revelry, the gambling-saloons,—nay, you have only to look into those decent dwellings where the gratifications of sense are sought for, or delighted in, alone, to find the man in white a miserable menial—the slave of the man in black, sharing in his debaucheries, and pandering to his desires. If ever in these places the man in white asserts his will, the man in black tramples upon it. If the man in white says: "This is wrong," or "that is indecent—I will not obey you," the man in black leads him by the nose, and proves to him his hopeless subjection. The man in black blasphemes, or commits murder, or drowns himself in drink, and the man in white serves him in all his crimes and debaucheries, and weeps between his helpless protests, or becomes so tainted by his society that he takes a hollow joy in his degrading service, and grows black with his companion.

I believe in the slavery of this particular black man, and the natural superiority of this particular white man. I do not believe that the black man should be abused and killed, but that he should be properly fed, clothed, and taken care of; that while he is under perfect control he should be indulged in his natural, healthful, and legitimate desires. But he is never to be master, never to take the lead, and never to hold an equal partnership in life with the white man. The latter is to be sovereign, and to give the law of his own life to the life beneath it.

And now I drop my illustration, to make the proposition that high life is born of the dominance of the soul over the body—born of the subordination of that portion of our natures which we share with the animals to the purposes and the welfare of that portion which we share with the angels. There can be no perfection of human character without this. There can be no such thing as good society without this; and this can be, or human life is no more than a sorry jest, practised upon a race of beings called into existence for that purpose. I have no knack at splitting theological hairs, or dodging the knives of those who do; but of this one thing I am as certain as I am that there is a God in heaven, and that He has given me the faculty of reason, viz.: that human ability and human responsibility never part company. It seems the extreme of scholastic idiocy to preach human inability out of one corner of the mouth and human responsibility out of the other,—to erect in the eyes of the world, as the representative of humanity, an effigy of helpless and hopeless pollution, and, shaking the scroll of a perfect law in its face, say: "You must, but you can't; you ought to, but it is impossible." I believe in human responsibility, and with it the essential condition of human ability, or I do not believe in anything. Without these, progress can have no path, and perfection no fulfilment.

I have said that the inferior man is to be properly fed, clothed, and taken care of. This must be, because the superior man lives in him, and, in the present state of existence, by means of him. The necessities of the case put the inferior man to labor under the superior man's direction and constraint. The animal in man is always lazy, and needs to be driven to its work like the animal in the stall: and here we strike the question of labor as it relates to our subject.

We find the whole world engaged in getting a living—getting food to eat, clothes to wear, houses to dwell in, carriages to ride in—comforts, helps, luxuries, for the sole use of the body. This care for the body by the soul has, with great universality, degenerated into a slavery of the soul to the body. The great masses of men and women do nothing else all their lives but labor to supply themselves and their dependents with the means of comfortable subsistence. There seems at present to be no help for this. There is something to hope for in the wider diffusion of wealth and the invention of labor-saving machinery—the multiplication of man-power without an increase of consumption; but even these consummations will amount to little in the relief of labor, in a country where the rewards of material enterprise are limitless, and wealth is regarded as the chief good. The comprehension of the essential distinction between getting a living, and living, is a matter of education.

I do not deny that there is a certain amount of education—of soul-culture—nay, I do not deny that there is a certain amount of spiritual satisfaction, in intelligent labor. The man in black works under the impulsion and direction of the man in white, and, in the exercise, the man in white finds food for his faculties, gains a knowledge of mental and material forces, discovers the qualities of things, and secures a healthful expenditure of his constantly generated energies. It is happily ordained that this shall be so, because it secures a certain amount of development to every man, whatever his circumstances may be. But work of the body is not life, in any high sense; and those who prate of labor and worship as in any way identical are the shallowest of dreamers. Work is the means of living, but it is not living. The aeronaut fills his balloon, and then rises and floats. Floating is what the balloon was made for. It takes in its breath below, and it can be held by a leash to the earth it spurns; but its true life begins when the cords are loosed, and it becomes a companion of the clouds.

I once found myself, on a cold winter morning, in a manufacturing village. At four o'clock—still more than three hours to sunrise, and three hours before dawn—the bells of the factories were rung to waken the operatives to their day of toil. Half an hour afterwards they went to their work, at which they remained until six, when they breakfasted. Half an hour was given to the meal, when work was resumed, and continued until twelve, when they dined. Half an hour was also given to this meal, and then they entered the mills and worked until seven, after which came supper. More than fifteen hours between bell and bell, with only one hour out of the number in which, silently, two meals were bolted, with no more of the dignities and amenities of life at the table than may be found at the manger during cattle-feeding! Strong men, tender women, almost children, kept to this work, not one day only, but six days of every week, and fifty-two weeks of every year, unless the water should fail, when the wages go down with the gate! How much of a chance, think you, does the man in white have in such a life as this?

It is complained that manufacturing towns are low places; that religious institutions do not thrive there; that literary societies are not supported there; that people will not turn out to lectures there; that the Sabbath is sadly broken there, or sadly idled away; that there is no reading and no mental improvement there. Nice people, who own manufacturing stocks and live upon the dividends, lament this. It is further complained that operatives drink, and go on sprees, and throng the circuses, and crowd the halls of the negro minstrels, and support the low places of amusement, to the neglect of all that is elevating and refining. Do you wonder at it? Would you not wonder if they did anything else? A man who works until there is no life left in him, and who feels that to-morrow is to be like to-day, must be amused. I do not wonder that he should prefer to hear a negro minstrel or a clown to hearing me. Nay, nor do I blame him for his preference. If I were in his place, I am sure that I should do as he does; and it is my well-adjusted conviction that the clown would benefit me more than the lecturer; that the hour's relief he would give me from the consciousness of my slavery, would do more to make my lot tolerable than any exercise which would still further tax my weakness, or which would give me glimpses of a life that my lot places beyond my realization.

You will admit that to such a community as this high life is not attainable. There is no time for society but such as may be stolen from the hours of sleep. A man who has been on his feet fifteen hours is unfitted for society, unfitted for intellectual efforts and entertainments, unfitted for religious exercises, unfitted for anything and everything that pertains to a higher life. He is the slave of labor; and although there are a few who have sufficient vitality to stand up against the depressing influence of this slavery, and a few who move upon a higher plane by impetus of early habits, acquired under more favorable circumstances, the masses are bound to low life by a bond which they will never sunder, and which it is well-nigh impossible for them to sunder.

Now that there is a great wrong involved in a system of labor which absolutely compels a class, and that a large one in some parts of the country, and growing larger every year, to a life of low aims, attainments, and enjoyments, there can be no doubt. Perhaps you will say that the case I have cited is an exceptional one. I think it is, but the average hours of labor in our factories do not yield a much better result. The worst of the matter is, that no way seems apparent for remedying the evil. The manufacturing of Great Britain, and indeed of all Europe, is set to this key, and the manufacturing of America comes into competition with it, and, to be successful, must harmonize with it. Reform would, in many instances, be the ruin of the manufacturer, and the loss of all labor to those in his employ. The whole machinery of trade has been adjusted to these hours and the values which are established by them, and change could not come without a revolution in prices. As reform, to be practicable and permanent, must be general, and as so many selfish interests are involved, I confess that the case looks hopeless enough to me. I can only fall back on my faith in the gradual melioration of the condition of society, and the operation of those principles of justice and humanity which are embodied in Christian civilization.

But the factories are not alone in their denial of high life to laboring men and women. The retail stores, the milliners', dress-makers', and tailors' shops—all shops where the work is simple, and devoted to the production of articles of common necessity, compel long hours, and render it practically impossible for their inmates to make much progress in intellectual, social, and religious excellence. It is not possible for them to do more than work and eat and sleep, and get such brief out-of-door relief and amusement as will keep their lives from becoming utterly tasteless.

Now I confess to a deep and tender sympathy with these people. They are found fault with for being exactly what their work, through a natural influence, makes them. They could not be otherwise without a constant struggle against this influence. They are blamed because they do not love reading, because they do not seek elevating society, because they love carousals and gay assemblies and buffoonery, because they break the Sabbath and will not attend church. Why, the great, crying, everlasting need of these men is rest and amusement. The call for these is the voice of God in them. Books do not satisfy it; intellectual society does not satisfy it; preaching does not satisfy it; and when I see one of these pale fellows or pale girls, after having worked through every working hour of the week, walking out among the trees and flowers and grass on Sunday, enjoying the beauty of God's world, breathing the pure air and enjoying the rare luxury of the blessed sunlight, I say in my heart that it is right. It is enough for our cupidity to enslave them in the name of Mammon for six days of the week. It is too much for our bigotry to enslave them in the name of God on the seventh.

And now, if we turn to the consideration of voluntary slavery to labor, we shall find that the man in white has but little better entertainment in it than in that which is involuntary. So far as the effect on the quality of life is concerned, the voluntary devotion of a man's entire energies to bodily labor is as disastrous as if it were compulsory. From the small farmer and the wife who is the partner of his toils and fortunes, to the merchant whose transactions involve annual millions; from the maker of a button to the builder of a navy; throughout the whole range of trades and occupations, we shall witness a voluntary devotion of time and vital resources to labor—to getting a living and to hoarding for real wants or superfluous wealth—which leaves real living entirely out of contemplation, and places it beyond possibility.

But let us understand a little more definitely what real living is. We all know what getting a living is;

now what is it to live? It is to engage in and enjoy intellectual activity outside of, and above, that which is occupied in the provision for bodily needs; to acquire and enjoy knowledge and the power which is born of it; to give free exercise to social sympathy in a pure intercourse with young and old; to have sweet satisfaction in home, so that it shall be the one bright spot of all the earth, never left without a sense of sacrifice; to take delight in those things which rise above the bare utilities of life into the realm of the tasteful and beautiful, and to cultivate the arts which make that realm attractive; to be happy in the activity of the moral and religious nature—in worship and in ministry: this it is to live.

It will be seen that living and getting a living are very different things, and that it requires time to live just as really as it requires time to get a living. A man who labors by compulsion, or by choice, fifteen hours of every twenty-four, has no time to live. If the life of man has any rewards above that of the animal, they must be found in this upper life: yet how few are they who look to this upper life for their rewards! The fact explains the unsatisfactory nature of wealth, and the countless failures in the search for happiness which every man has seen. Let us glance at the career of a representative mercantile man. From the age of fourteen to twenty-one he is a clerk with a mean salary, and with such confinement to long hours that he finds no time for mental improvement, and no time for the development of social and æsthetic tastes. He enters business early, with a limited capital, or with no capital at all, and for twenty-five or thirty years he is certain, unless he dies, to be the slave of his business. For twenty-five or thirty years he feels obliged to hold the man in white within him to unrelieved bondage. He does not enjoy home. He does not enjoy leisure when circumstances bring it. His shop or his counting-room is the centre of his thoughts. Visitors at his house are never welcome, if they interfere with business, or take any of his time. His wife and children see nothing of him. He is not felt or seen in society. He is known only as an active, devoted, business man, and thrifty as a consequence.

Let it be remembered that during all these years he has been carrying in his mind the thought that he is getting ready to live. He knows that he is not living —knows that there is something better in life than what he gets out of it, and expects that after the body is provided for, with an ample margin for the future, he will then begin to live, and enjoy the reward of his industry. So, at last, having acquired money enough, he retires from business, and finds—poor man!—that he does not know how to live. Of all the miserable men in the world, I know of none more hopeless and helpless than a man of acquired wealth who retires from business to make his first experiment in living. Such an experiment usually results in one of three ways, viz., he sickens and dies with the effect of a change of habits and with disappointment, or he returns to his business, or he fritters away his life in aimless activities. The real man within him has been a slave to business so long that he cannot rise into independent life. A man who does not learn to live while he is getting a living, is a poorer man after his wealth is won than he was before. There is no way to learn how to live, and there is no way to live, except by keeping a life organized and in operation above and outside of the labors and enterprises involved in getting a living.

When I see at a cottage-door little patches and pots of flowers, and, entering, I find a row of books upon the shelf, and a newspaper on the table, and a few pictures on the walls in domestic frames; and when, on a Sunday morning, I see issuing from this door a neatly-dressed group which takes its way to the village-church, I know that the inmates have got hold of life—got hold of something better than gold—something which lifts them above their lot. Their time, I know, is mainly spent in getting a living, but they find some time to live, and find something in life that gives them dignity.

It is always delightful to see a man getting at the secret of living; and I suppose we have all witnessed some strange transformations of character consequent upon discoveries of this kind. I have seen men introduced to life by the reading of a poem or a story, which so stirred them, so revealed to them their own higher natures, so discovered to them fresh and attractive fields of pleasure, that they became new men from that moment. Straightway they chose new associates, and bought new books, and sought for new pictures, having already found new meaning in the old ones. New visions met them on the sea, and in the sky, and around them on the earth. That which had been their throne became their footstool. That which they had hitherto regarded as a realm of visions and illusions became their home.

I have seen a man, thoroughly absorbed in business, introduced to life by being compelled for a single winter to care for a few pots of flowers. The flowers became to him teachers, preachers, inspirers. They converted him—transformed him. Now, whenever he can steal away from his business, he is in his garden, where everything he touches thrives. You will see his name in all the horticultural reports of the section in which he lives, and if you enter his dwelling, you will find everything brought into harmony with his newly-born taste; and you will find him living and enjoying life, and preparing to enjoy still more the wealth which his busy hands and tireless enterprise are acquiring.

Mr. Wemmick, in "Great Expectations," understood this matter very well. The office of Mr. Jaggers was by no means the place where he lived, or found the rewards of his life. I think that little castle of his at Walworth one of the most delightful and suggestive of all Dickens's creations. The real flag-staff, the draw-bridge made of a single plank, the gun fired every night at nine o'clock Greenwich time, the arrangements for standing an imaginary siege, and the effort to excite the admiration and secure the contentment of the aged parent, are strokes of real genius. Wemmick's philosophy was even better than his attempt at its embodiment. "The office," says Wemmick, "is one thing, and private life is another. When I go into the office, I leave the castle behind me; and when I come into the castle, I leave the office behind me." His attempt to realize something in life which should reward him for the tedious detail of an unpleasant business was peculiar, perhaps, but his theory was correct.

I do not happen to believe in the ennobling influence of constant physical labor. It is noble and ennobling to labor with a high motive—to labor for personal independence, or for any great and good end which involves the soul's prosperity; but to labor for bodily subsistence, throughout one's life, is not ennobling at all. If I wished utterly to degrade a nation, I would keep it to constant labor for the supply of bodily needs. What such labor as this has done for slaves of all colors, and what it has done for the peasantries of the world, we all know. Strict confinement to such labor as this is necessarily low life. It is bondage to the body; and high life is only to be realized when the body becomes the soul's servant in its high pursuits and its pure satisfactions.

Again, the character of life is determined by its pleasures. I have already incidentally touched upon this, but it requires more definite treatment. There is a natural desire in every soul for pleasure. It begins with infancy and lasts as long as life. And here, as we have already seen, the man in white and the man in black are at variance. All life that seeks and secures its best satisfactions in the pleasures of sense is low, and you may judge how much of that which is called high life is really such. I beg you not to misunderstand me here. I believe that the pleasures of sense are just as legitimate as the pleasures of the soul, and that they may be, and should be, a portion of the pleasures of the soul. God never ordained the pleasure-giving power of the senses for the simple purpose of denying its indulgence. I have no faith in the beneficence of any creed which imposes indiscriminate mortification of the senses as sources of pleasure. Such a creed is alike inhuman and ungodly. I believe that there is not a pleasure of sense, from the least to the greatest, which may not, under legitimate conditions and limitations, be made a minister to the soul's life—to what I have called high life—and which was not intended to be such a minister. It is when the pleasures of sense are sought for and indulged in as the chief satisfactions of life—when the soul devotes itself to the procurement and enjoyment of these pleasures—that they are perverted, and that they taint the character of life with vulgarity and animalism. I believe a keen enjoyment of sensual pleasure entirely compatible with a high life which shall be the master of the senses, and which shall hold them subordinate to itself and its own peculiar delights.

All slavery is low life, of whatever sort it may be, and the most abject of all slaves is he who is bound to his senses as the sole or supreme sources of pleasure. The nature of this slavery can be read in its results. The drunkard and the glutton are always low-lived men. There are some instances in which the soul tries to keep up its life in the midst of sensual slavery. It is a sort of mongrel life, and always ends in the reform of one life or the destruction of the other. There are grosser forms of sensual indulgence, having a peculiar power, when relied upon for satisfaction, to bestialize men, and to impose the lowest life upon their devotees. I say that high life is impossible to any person who relies upon the ministry of sense for his choicest pleasures. Even music itself, divine as it may be made, and purifying and elevating as it is when used aright, may become degrading, as all know who have with sadness marked the low life of many who are devoted to it. The pleasures of sense have no power in and of themselves to lift a man above the brutes around him; and he who clings to them as his chief delight, and makes their acquisition his principal pursuit, is more a brute than a man. It matters not how or where such a man lives, or what his social position may be; he is low-lived—unfit for good society—out of place in any sphere of high life.

The pleasures of the mind, the soul, the heart—of all those departments of the human nature which characterize it as human nature—are the pleasures of high life, and they are as various as the forms and phases of that nature. The difficulty is that, in our absorption in the business of getting a living, we do not have time and opportunity for a culture broad enough to make all these sources of high pleasure available. One man gets a taste of knowledge, and spends his life in the pleasure of acquiring it. Another takes his principal delight in the production of works of beauty, or in the study and possession of them. Another is most delighted with poetry. Another has his highest satisfaction in science or philosophy, while his neighbor has his life in pure society: with strong human sympathies, he delights to mingle with his kind, in the active life of the affections. Another has his highest pleasure in religion, in worship, in the practice of works of benevolence.

Now all these men live a high life, but not the highest possible to them. It is not possible that all men shall grasp all the pleasures of high life, because of the variety in the constitution of their natures; but all can take a broader sweep than they do. Almost the entire high life of the working classes—and, practically, the working classes embrace nearly all of us—is connected with religion. The only time the most of us have for living is Sunday. The remaining six days of the week are devoted to getting a living. By religious people and their families, and—in this country, among those American-born—by the people generally, there is no culture but that which is religious deemed legitimate on Sunday, and none but religious pleasures accounted consistent with the sacred character of the day. To this fact is attributable the dry and unattractive character of a great multitude of religious people. They occupy but a single sphere of high life, and their lack of culture in other directions naturally and almost necessarily makes their religion of the hardest and most ungenerous type. There is no mistaking the fact, that many of the Christian people of the world are held in contempt by men of culture in other departments of high life, because they are so utterly barren, so one-sided, so lacking in all matters of intellectual culture. There is no mistaking the fact, that Christianity suffers in its reputation among a large class of intellectual people because so large a number of its professors lack culture in all other directions. The religion which they represent has no breadth of view, no comprehension of great principles, no grand and all-embracing sympathies and charities, and not only no taste for the pure pleasures of the intellect, but a certain degree of contempt for them, or moral aversion to them. It has seemed to be the policy of some churches to repress the intellect, to decry reason, and to reckon the higher accomplishments of the mind as only ministers to human pride. Now my idea of a Christian is, that he should be the most generous, culti vated, and attractive man in the world; and my belief is, that the more widely he can extend the realm of his pleasures in the domain of high life, the more thoroughly will he comprehend and enjoy his religion, and the more will he be able by his life and character to commend that religion to the esteem of all.

But the man who is devoted exclusively to intellectual pleasures is quite as one-sided and quite as dry and unattractive as he whose only hold upon high life is through his religion—possibly more so. The undevout astronomer is not only mad, but mean. An irreligious man whom a love for intellectual pleasure has freed from the dominion of his lower nature, lacks still the grandest element of high life.

It is a matter of surprise to many that culture in high life is so almost universally partial. There are two facts which lie on the surface of things, patent to common observers, viz., that highly intellectual people are not commonly highly religious people, and that highly religious people are not commonly highly intellectual. I do not state these facts as unvarying rules, but they are common enough to be commonly observed, and notorious enough to be beyond contravention. The great masses of church-members you will find to be simple people. Perhaps the great masses are always simple people; but in the church you will find them out of proportion to those of decided intellectual culture. And is it not true that the majority of intellectual people make no pretensions to piety, while many make light of it altogether, as something weak and childish? The proportion of professional men who are actively religious is small, and those are not usually foremost in mental gifts and accomplishments. It is a matter of popular regret that our great men who rise to important places in the nation's councils, and who have a predominant influence in national affairs, are generally either without religious character, or with strong passions unchastened and uncontrolled. This is so notorious that many have come to regard religion as something that will do very well for humble people, and for women, while men of strength and intellect are above it. This idea prevails not only among professional and highly intellectual men, but it largely pervades the mechanical mind of the country. An ingenious, inventive, and skilful mechanic, who has an absorbing interest in his pursuits, is rarely a Christian—rarely religious—and none are more aware of this than mechanics themselves.

Now why is this? Is an intellectual man or an ingenious man more depraved in consequence of his superiority, or is he by his superiority really raised above religion? Neither. It is mainly because he becomes absorbed by the sources of pleasure which have been opened to him in his intellect, and thus has no room for the motive which would extend his culture to the rest of his higher nature. The religious life of the masses is barren and unattractive for a similar reason. They cultivate their hearts to the neglect, certainly, if not at the expense, of their brains; while those who despise them cultivate their brains at the expense of their hearts. Each class is absorbed in its own sphere of pleasure, and the result is as bad as it can be. The intellectual giants of the world give us a Christless literature, and refuse to treat religion as anything more than a useful delusion, or fail to speak of it at all, while people of common gifts and ordinary culture are left to represent a religion which holds within it the wealth of the world, and the highest and purest sources of pleasure which God has discovered to the race. The world has produced but few Miltons and Newtons, but a number sufficient to show us what a noble creature man is when he consents to drink at all those fountains which have been opened for the satisfaction of his higher nature.

The present age has produced one man whom I accept as one of the most beautiful instances of broad culture and high life with which I am acquainted, through observation or history. I have no fitting words with which to express my admiration of this man. With a power, grace, and brilliancy of poetic expression which place him in the front rank of those who write the English language, an industry that is tireless in its search after and study of truth, a love for and a knowledge of art far surpassing all who live and all who have lived before him, a moral courage that tramples upon conventionalities as if they were chaff, and that gallantly attacks the most venerable errors, regardless of the spite of their petty upholders—with all these, he unites the most reverent adoration of the great Jehovah, the sweetest trust in Jesus Christ, and the sublimest faith in the revelations of the Old and New Testaments. To this man, the intellect of the world bows as to a master. The lovers of art accept his dictum as that of an anointed king. The man of culture is content if he can read, understand, and expound him, and the Christian, whether high or humble, recognizes him as a brother in Jesus Christ.

No man can read the works of John Ruskin without learning that his sources of pleasure are well-nigh infinite. There is not a flower, nor a cloud, nor a tree, nor a mountain, nor a star; not a bird that fans the air, nor a creature that walks the earth; not a glimpse of sea or sky or meadow-greenery; not a work of worthy art in the domains of painting, sculpture, poetry, and architecture; not a thought of God as the Great Spirit presiding over and informing all things, that is not to him a source of the sweetest pleasure. The whole world of matter and of spirit, and the long record of human art, are open to him as the never-failing fountains of his delight. In these pure realms he seeks his daily food and has his daily life.

This man, so full of pleasure, is a reformer. In the domain of art he moves the world. A pagan architecture dies before his sturdy strokes, and in the revival of the Gothic he is Christianizing the face of Christendom. Architecture, emancipated by him, has nothing before it now but progress. Painting, which had bowed so long to the authority of the masters, has been released by him from the degrading servitude, and led back free to its mother nature. Above all, he has sanctified the literature of art, and has demonstrated in his own personal life and character that a man, to be truly great, and to have all his intellectual nature enriched and rendered superlatively fruitful, must be a religious man. I hold up this man as a representative of high life, and as an illustration of the normal union of all the highest pleasures of the intellect and the heart, and of the ministry of these pleasures to the symmetrical development and power of the man.

There is still another point in this discussion. I have treated of pursuits and pleasures as determinative of the character of life. It remains to treat of motives.

What is a motive? It is a source of motion. We enter a mill, and find all the spindles awhirr, and all the shuttles flying, and all the complementary machinery in operation for the production of a certain fabric, the accomplishment of a certain end. At last, we descend to the wheel-pit, where, shut away from common observation, the great wheel, turned by the water of a passing stream, swings its ponderous arms—the source of all the motion we have seen above it. This is the motive of the mill. Thus, is the engine the motive of the steamer; the mainspring, of the watch; the heart, of the vascular system of the living body. And wherever we see a great human life in progress, in the production of notable results, we may always know that there is something within it which drives it—a motive-power. It may be a mixed power, as we sometimes find steam and water joined in the driving of a mill. We have already seen that the necessities of the body are powerful and very prevalent motives of life. We have also seen that our love of pleasure in the various spheres of high and low life is a motive of great power, and by these we may learn how everything that gives action and direction to life is a motive of life. One or two of these motives, in consequence of their prominence and prevalence, call for separate and direct treatment.

The first to be noticed is ambition. There is in the human mind a natural desire for distinction—for being, or acquiring, something which shall lift the individual above the mass, and give him consideration with his fellows. Some strive for power, and these seek it mainly in political place and preferment. Some seek only for notoriety, and resort to many means for keeping their names before the public. Others are greedy for fame, a higher and a better prize than notoriety. In oratory, in literature, in war, in ten thousand fields of human action, it impels to the greatest sacrifices of time and strength and safety. It urges the traveller through dangerous fields of discovery; it inspires Blondin on his rope; it nerves the wrestler at his game, and gives power and patience to the noblest of the workers in art. Indeed, it comes in as an aid to much of the worthiest work of the world. A desire so natural and so universal as this—a desire that so readily joins hands with the highest motives of which we are conscious—must have a legitimate sphere of operation, and must, when confined to this sphere, be entirely consistent with the highest life. When it is united with a sincere love of men, and an honest regard for the claims of Christian duty; when it is held subordinate and subsidiary to the universal good; when it lusts for and grasps at nothing which actual excellence of power and character may not legitimately claim, then it is good in itself and good in its results. It is right for a man to desire to excel in anything worthy of a man. It is right for a man to love high position and to seek it in right ways. It is when ambition becomes the single or supreme motive of life that it is wrong. In such cases it is invariably selfish and base, and gives to the mind in which it has its seat, and the life which proceeds from it, a low and vulgar character.

No man, for instance, can follow politics and place-hunting as the business of his life, impelled thereto by his desire for distinction, without being, or becoming, a low-lived man. The man whose ruling motive of life is the desire for political distinction is a mean man, no matter whether he occupies the bench of a country justice, or the chair of the President of the United States. And this explains fully why it is that our politics are so corrupt, and why, almost invariably, our politicians are men without moral principle. They are self-seeking men, almost exclusively, and the result upon the nation is as bad as it is upon themselves. This accursed selfish ambition is at the root of all the political evils we suffer from to-day, and the parent of the whole series of horrors through which we have passed during the last few years. If only those men had been intrusted with power whose love of God and their country surpassed their love of themselves and their love of place, not one drop of blood, and not one cent of money, which the Great Rebellion has cost would have been called for. But for these men, we should have remained a united and a happy nation. They have dechristianized our politics, demoralized our nation, and dethroned God in the national councils; and nothing but the unselfish virtues of the people have saved the country from irretrievable wreck.

What is Washington life? Is it high life? Do good people love to go to Washington and remain? Like calls to itself like. It is, and it has always been, a home of gamblers and courtesans and corruptionists. I do not question that there are good men there, but I believe that the majority of those in place are, and for the past fifty years have been, low-lived men. The life that is lived there is a selfish one; and a selfish life is always low. I state a notorious fact, when I say that it is almost as much as a decent man's character is worth to become actively engaged in politics. He is obliged to come into association and competition with so many unfair and unprincipled men ; he is obliged to meet and struggle with such meanness and mendacity; he is obliged to adopt or countenance so much immoral machinery, that his moral sense becomes sophisticated. There are offices in this country whose responsibilities are great, and whose honors once corresponded with their responsibilities, that good men decline to accept because of the low life which has lied and cheated and bought its way into them. These men cannot afford the loss of moral and social caste which connection with these offices would inflict upon them.

We live under that which is theoretically a popular government—what we comfort ourselves by calling a popular government. A popular government? What have the people had to do with it? Have they selected their office-holders and their rulers? Have they, with a Christian conscience, sought among the wise and good of the land, and, selecting the wisest and the best, placed them in office and in power? Not at all. Politicians get themselves nominated. They nominate one another. Choice of men is determined in newspaper offices, in little cliques and cabals, composed of men who have axes to grind; in primary meetings, packed and managed by interested demagogues; and when election-day comes, the people, lacking wisdom or organization to do otherwise, vote for the least objectionable political candidate presented to them, and vote blindly at that. The people are simply used for the purpose of effecting the aims of the demagogues. I do not suppose that one man in twenty who votes, ever in his life had anything to do directly or indirectly in selecting the candidates for office whom he has annually assisted in electing, or in trying to elect.

Ours a government of the people? Why, it has been a government of the politicians for half a century—of a set of men who, in the main, are actuated by no higher motives than a love of plunder and of place; and these are the men—low-lived and selfish and mean—who make the laws and preside over the destinies of a Christian nation! With all this selfishness and low life and low motive in politics, is it to be wondered at that we have political convulsions? The grand motive-power in our government has for years been personal and political ambition. Religion, as an element of political power and life, has been persistently counted out; and when its aid has been invoked to secure an election, it has been done selfishly in the main. The people are religious: the politicians are not.

We shall find at the political centres that which claims to be high life, in the highest meaning of the phrase. Fashion and fools fall down before this life, and worship it. This is one of the foulest ills which it breeds in society—that, by the forwardness of its arrogance, it overtops all other life, and holds itself before the public with its intellectual culture, and its low aims and motives, as really and distinctively the high life of the nation. We hear of movements in high life, and scandal in high life. We hear of high life attending church, as if Jehovah had been honored in an unusual way. High life dances, and Jenkins informs the public what it wore on the occasion. High life occupies a box at the theatre, and gets the fact reported. High life gets married, and some toadying press announces that the Hon. Mr. So-and-so, member of Congress from a certain district in Massachusetts, or New York, or Ohio, has led to the hymeneal altar the beautiful and highly accomplished daughter of the Hon. Mr. What's-his-name, of the Cabinet or the Senate. And this announcement goes the round of the newsmongers, as an instance of a "marriage in high life." Does the honorable member, who got his seat by the most dishonorable demagogism, protest? Does the beautiful and highly accomplished daughter of the Hon. Mr. What's-his-name, who is a played-out belle and a mercenary husband-hunter, blush at her vulgar notoriety? Does the Hon. Mr. What's-his-name, who is very happy to shift the expenses of his lovely daughter to other shoulders, and grind a political axe at the same time, object? Oh! no; this is high life—dignified life—the life most directly associated with the government—the social life that goes with successful politics. *You* would blush, and so would your modest and Christian daughters; but high life, such as we find at the political centres, never blushes. It has no thought that is not selfishly devoted to personal aggrandizement.

A gambler is a gambler; and I know of no moral difference between the gambler in politics and the gambler in money, to whom he is so fond of playing away his little salary, and the profits of his little jobs. There *is* no moral difference between them; and there is no reason why one should be regarded as belonging to high life more than the other. Life takes the character of its motive; and all selfishness is irredeemably low.

The desire for wealth is a great and almost universal motive of life. There is nothing necessarily wrong, or low, in the desire for wealth. As a means of good to the possessor and to the world, when rightly used, the usefulness and desirableness of wealth are hardly to be over-estimated. Wealth fills the world with beautiful architecture, hangs halls and walls with pictures, fills libraries with books, builds churches and colleges, furnishes the life-blood of great charities, relieves from the slavery and the hard economies of labor, commands time for culture and for living, procures the comforts of independence, furnishes the sinews of war, constructs railroads and navies, and gives wings to commerce. The pursuit of wealth under right motives, or, rather, for right ends, is as legitimate as the pursuit of competence. It is only when wealth is pursued for its own sake, or for the sake of the distinction or the low delights which it secures, that it becomes vulgar. How generally wealth is pursued with these low aims, I leave you to be the judges. How often the claim to respectability is based upon material possessions, we all know. Society holds many men and many families, whose sole claim to a respectable position is based upon the possession of money. Mr. Jones, the grocer, was a common sort of man enough when he was poor, and his family were not recognized in the conventional high life around him. But Mr. Jones, wishing to get into high life, with his family, kept very busily at work, drove sharp bargains, and used his little capital so wisely that he became rich. He moved into a splendid house, bought expensive equipage, put on airs, and, though high life turned up its nose a little superciliously at first, it brought it down, and dipped it in Mr. Jones's wine, and then opened its drawing-rooms to Mr. Jones and his family. Mr. Jones bought his place in society, and a share in conventional high life, as he would buy a box in a theatre, or a share of railway-stock. Even this is better than the pursuit of wealth for the sake of wealth—better than piling up money for the sake of counting it, or to see how large a pile can be made one's own. Wealth, as the servant of high life, is good; but wealth as the end of life, or as the basis of any life, whether nominally high or low, is bad.

But these are commonplaces, and the argument needs to be pursued no further. I have attempted to define natural and necessary distinctions between that which is true and false in life—between that which is high and low. I have tried to show you that the character of life is determined by its pursuits, pleasures, and motives. It has been a plain task—so plain and so obvious in every statement, and so trite, withal, that it must have seemed to many of you like the recitation of a school-room. Yet you know, as well as I, that the propositions I have made, though accepted by the judgment, are practically rejected by the life, of society.

Who are those, generally, in society, whom society itself regards as enviable,—as, indeed, representatives of the highest life of society? Are they the men of intellect, the men of accomplishments, the men of pure morals and pure motives, the Christian men; or are they the men of wealth, or the occupants of place? Who are those who give to society its shape—who pull down one and set up another? Who arrogate to themselves the distinctions and the prerogatives of high life? I answer, the men of power and the men of money. It matters not what their pursuits are; it matters not what their pleasures are; it matters not what their motives are—whether a love of power, or distinction, or money: they claim, receive, and hold the highest place. Low life rides and high life walks. Low life assumes the leadership, and high life modestly, though with many inward protests, acquiesces. Low life throngs the market-places, throngs the watering-places, throngs political conventions, throngs the halls of legislation, throngs all the fashionable assemblies. It has a low and vulgar desire to be seen of men, while high life is modest, and shrinks from contact with so much that is meretricious and base. The animal is rampant and regnant, and the angel hangs his head and folds his wings.

Can we not build better than this? Shall not Christian manhood and Christian womanhood have and hold their place? Shall social and individual values forever depend upon material conditions? My friend, if you are a man of brains, a man of culture, a man of taste, a man of pure and true life, a man acting and living under the impulsion of high motives, bow no more to false gods. Demand that a man shall be a man before he shall be your associate. Do what you can to establish juster social values, so that a man shall stand for a man, however poor and humble he may be, and a brute shall pass for a brute, however proud and high. Do what you can to make high life possible to all, and to bring the low life of the world to do it homage.

THE NATIONAL HEART.

IT has always been the folly of the wise to undervalue the wisdom of the common people. The lawyer despises the jury that he flatters, and the politician shows, in the tricks by which he endeavors to deceive and mislead the people, the contempt he feels for those whom he affects to honor. All the orators have their little compliment for the people—for what they call "the hardy yeomanry," "the intelligent masses," &c. The matter has really become conventional, and the compliment is tossed out as a gallant tosses a pleasant word to a pretty woman, partly because it is his habit, and partly because she expects it.

It was the very wise and brilliant Carlyle who accused the British nation of being mostly fools; yet it must be admitted that, for a nation of fools, it has got on remarkably well. Somehow, British commerce, British manufactures, British agriculture, British power, British wealth, British charities, and British literature, suggest magnificent national acquisitions, resources, and characteristics.

An old-fashioned New England town will give us, perhaps, as good an illustration of the wisdom of the common people as we can find. I presume that there cannot be found elsewhere, upon the earth, communities so well regulated, so pure, so equal and just in all departments of municipal administration, as among some of the older and humbler towns of New England. Once a year they assemble in town-meeting. They are usually fortunate enough to possess one man who understands parliamentary usage, and who presides, year after year, as moderator. They vote their appropriations, elect their town-clerk, selectmen, and school-committee—their road-surveyors, fence-viewers, pound-keepers, and hog-reeves—and go home. Among the thousand persons, more or less, who live in the town, there is not one pauper, not one man or woman, or child over six years of age, who cannot read; not one drunkard, not one place where a drunkard can be made, and not a man except the minister and the physician who has had anything more than a common-school education. Are these men fools, or wise? How much would their condition be improved, think you, by the importation of brilliant men who would despise their simplicity?

But we can find illustrations of popular wisdom in

more important assemblies than New England town-meetings. My impression is that State legislatures have not been remarkable, either in New England or elsewhere, for the native gifts or the learning of their members. Indeed, it has been more than intimated to me that the majority of those who find places there are not so dazzlingly brilliant that they cannot be regarded safely by the naked eye. The boy who emigrated to the West, and wrote back to his father, inviting him to follow, persuading him thereto by the assurance that "mighty small men get office out there," evidently did not understand the composition of Eastern legislatures as well as his father did. Yet, without learning and without experience, these men come together, and legislate for the States composing this Union; and it must be confessed—nay, it may be proudly claimed—that, in the main, they do it well; that, when left to their own good sense and conscience, they do it always well. Under the laws enacted by these men, we have liberty, protection, and prosperity; and we shall find the reason for this as we advance further in our discussion.

It must be apparent to all, that, in the national life, there are certain men, institutions, agencies, and movements, which monopolize the popular attention, and which alone find record upon the page of history. Great men, political institutions, administrations, parties, wars, intrigues of politicians, theories and policies of government—these occupy the surface of the national life; these are what men see and talk about; these produce material for the newspapers; these furnish the staple from which the historian weaves his varied record. In the issue of a war, in the result of a political campaign, in the success of a man, in the triumph of a policy, in the progress of an institution, it is our habit to recognize the results of independent agencies which produce the sum of national life and the stuff of history, and to lose sight of that grand vital power, abiding in the heart of the people, which hides itself by throwing to its surface these shows which cheat our attention.

The child that stands upon the river-bank and sees a great steamer go by, sees only the long and graceful sweep of her decks, the revolution of her wheels, the rise and fall of her working-beam, the smoke pouring from her tall chimneys, her crowd of passengers, and the beautiful flag that floats over all. He does not dream of that heart of fire which throbs in her bosom, without whose mighty pulsations the boat would be only a mass of useless lumber. So, when we enter a garden, we only interest ourselves with that portion of it which occupies the sunlight and the air. Stems and foliage and flowers and fruits—these absorb our attention; while the under-world of soils and roots and vital chemistries, in which all the secrets of the upper beauty hide, are unthought of.

The heart of the people—the national heart—out of this are the issues of the national life. We talk of institutions, and policies, and state-craft, and international reactions, and imagine that we are touching grand realities and vitalities; and while we talk the national heart beats on and the national life flows on, and bears us all upon its tide. There is probably no man so unobserving as not to have noticed a certain drift of events, altogether independent of apparent forces,—a certain drift that the wisdom of the wisest cannot account for—a drift that neither statesmen nor politicians can divert or arrest—for which, indeed, they are in no way responsible. Events march, or seem to march, in solid column, pricking each other forward with crowding spears; and the men and the parties which pretend to marshal them, and which have a certain show of marshaling them, only run with them, or run before them to avoid being crushed beneath their feet. Throughout the sad and terrible war which still engages the energies of this nation, there has been nothing more remarkable than this independent drift of events, baffling all attempts at prevision, breaking up all the schemes of the politicians, making folly to-day of the wisdom of yesterday, and showing how little the apparent actors in the great drama have had to do with its inspiration, and the order of its combinations. I recognize here, reverently and gladly, the presidency of Providence over all our national affairs, and the power of Providence in them; but I see, particularly in this majestic drift of events, which so ruthlessly overthrows policies and prophecies, and theories and men, the tide of the national life as it flows forth from the national heart. It has its birth among the aspirations, the convictions, the affections, and the faith of the American people. It is the product of no man's will. It is not even distinctively the product of the nation's will. It is the product of forces starting as independently of volition as the beating of the human heart itself; and these forces, like springs in the mountain-side, send out their contributions to create that resistless stream which bears the freight of history upon its bosom.

I do not go to the heads of those who compose a New England town-meeting to find the secret of their wisdom, but to their hearts. They are right-hearted, and see clearly; they are right-hearted, and act conscientiously. They aim to do right, and have a common interest in doing right; and the life of the town is that which comes forth from the heart of the town, producing the natural results of peace, order, and prosperity. I do not look for the wisdom of our State legislatures among the brains of the legislators. In the laws and statutes of a State, the learned minds and practised hands of a few have only put into form that which the heart of the majority has pronounced good. Mr. Bancroft, speaking of colonial Connecticut, says that "the magistrates were sometimes persons of no ordinary endowments, but, though gifts of learning and genius were valued, the State was content with virtue and single-mindedness; and the public welfare never suffered at the hands of plain men." And what he says of Connecticut is true generally of all the States. Plain men, in responsible positions, act as they are moved to act by their hearts, and live in a close and fruitful communion with conscience. Sometimes, designing men may lead them away from the right, but they always come back to it with renewed loyalty.

The present period of our national history is marked by such great events, by such antagonisms of opinion in high places, and by such prominence of individual men, that we are more than ever liable to forget the real source of the national life and power, and to judge shallowly and mistakenly of its developments and phenomena. We say, that if this or that policy shall be pursued, if this or that man succeed, if this or that party prevail, if some institution be saved or overthrown, or a battle be lost or won, then shall we have unity, peace, and prosperity, or the opposite of these; whereas, these are not dependent upon any man, or institution, or policy, or party. They must come, and come to stay, as the product of permanent forces, starting in the national heart; as the product of an inspiring, moving, governing, and conservative power, whose fountain-head is among those affections which are highest and nearest heaven. Ambitious men, and interested and selfish parties, and brute force, may for a time pervert the legitimate issues of this power; but it is certain, if it save itself from perversion, to overcome all these, and carry its quality into every act and event which goes to make up national history.

I propose to speak a few words concerning the national heart, as the residence of those forces which move and conserve the national life.

Every heart that is of value to itself and others is identified with a home. There is, somewhere, a group of hearts to which each heart belongs, or it has no strong hold upon the world—a group that is usually bound to a certain spot by all its interests and affections. A boy grows up to manhood in a home, and, choosing to himself a companion, builds a new home for himself and for her. Children are born to him, and at length a home-circle is formed, made up of kindred hearts, and held together by natural affection. Looking into this home, we shall find that all its ambitions, aspirations, and industries, are inspired by this affection. The husband strives to give a worthy home to the woman of his love, and the wife returns his devotion with all love's sympathies and ministries, while both labor for the comfort, the education, and the prosperity of their children, who, themselves, are helpful toward the general welfare. Love is the vital air on which this home lives—on which home as an institution lives. It is both motive and satisfaction—inspiration and reward.

Now let each man before me measure, if he can, the influence of his home-affections upon his individual life. How much of any sort of effort do you put forth that is not inspired, or suggested, or aided, by your love for the persons and the things that make up your home? Where do you look for your sweetest satisfactions? Where does your life centre? Around what spot does your life revolve? Ah! when you lose home and that which home holds, do you not lose that which hallowed the name of country? that which endowed the world with value? Nay, do you not lose that which made you valuable to yourself?

Well, a neighborhood is made up of homes, and, in the main, one home is like another in its characteristic influence upon the individual life. A town or a county is made up of neighborhoods, and a State is composed of counties and towns, and a group of States constitutes the federal Union. So we come, by a very short path, as you see, to the conclusion that the nation is only a grand aggregation of homes, and that the mainspring of the national life is the love that inspires the home-life. A nation is a thing that lives and acts like a man, and men are the particles of which it is composed. If these particles obey the law of their home-life—each one pervaded and controlled by the power of home-affection—then it is easy to see that home-life enters very essentially into the constitution of the national life. We can understand, at least, that we are not to look for the staple of national life in cabinets or congresses, in armies or institutions. We can understand, at least, that in the homes of the nation—under the control of home-affections—the nation lives.

We often wonder how it is that a nation whose government has made it responsible for great crimes can survive those crimes—how a nation debauched in public morals, and corrupted by the prevalence of personal vice in high places, can live—why it does not fall into anarchy by the weight of its guilt pressing upon its rottenness. It is because the great national heart is not guilty, and because the national life is not in the government at all. No nation can be destroyed while it possesses a good home-life. My lawn cannot be spoiled so long as the grass is green, no matter how many trees may be prostrated—no matter how many flowers may be trampled under feet by unclean beasts. The essential life and beauty of the lawn are in the grass, and not in the trees, and not in the flowers, and not in any creature that passes over it; and the life of a nation is not in political institutions, and not in political parties, and not in political or great men, but in the love-inspired home-life of the people.

Where this home-life thrives best, there patriotism —another offspring of the national heart—grows thriftiest. The love of country is one of the purest and most powerful passions of the heart, and is the constant companion of the love of home. Indeed, country is home in the largest sense, and the nation is the great family of which all of us are members. Country is the home of home itself—the setting of the jewel which we wear next our hearts. We claim as kindred all who were born under our own sky, all who are loyal to the same government, all who share the same national lot, and all who cheer the same flag; and we love the land which gives them and us a common home. I say that this love of country and this national affection are only love of home and love of family enlarged, and that these loves always live and thrive together. The man who loves home best, and loves it most unselfishly, loves his country best.

Patriotism is simple and trustful, like family affection; and its subordinate place in the ordinary life of the nation is seen in the fact that it rarely shows itself except in the national emergencies. When the country is endangered, or insulted, or outraged, then we learn something of the strength and the universality of patriotism, and then we learn something of its inspiring and motive power in national action. In recent years, we have seen it rouse our slumbering nation to arms, and lift our startled and distracted people into harmony and unity in the national defence. Truth, presented to the intellect, and enforced with eloquence the divinest, would only have bred difference and disturbance, when the voice of that first hostile cannon, turned against the flag that floated over Fort Sumter, reached the national heart; and the nation, casting off every fetter, stood up as one man, and called for vengeance. This was at a time when there were fear and trembling in high places; when treason had tainted all the governmental departments; when there was neither army nor navy; when statesmen, insomuch as they could see further than other men, were in despair. It was at a time when popular apathy left no ground hard enough to build a policy upon. Ah! how this wound of the national affections—this insult to the object of the nation's worship—this blow at its unsuspecting loyalty—inspired its life, and shattered the bands by which it had been bound so long! I know of nothing more sublime than this sudden waking of a nation through an outrage upon the object of its love; and it will not be possible for the muse of History to measure its inspiring power in the great events which have followed. That can only be found recorded in blood on a thousand battle-fields, and in tears in a million of sacrificial homes.

Love of country does not burn with so steady and so reliable a flame as love of home. It is not so constant a motive in the national life. In the absorption of home-pursuits, and the selfish struggle for gold and power and fame, the national heart forgets, or is prone to forget, its patriotic fervor, and to consent to the subordination of patriotic motives; but when danger comes, there is nothing it will not dare and do to defend the object of its affections. Patriotism—inferior to Christianity as it is—has had a longer life than Christianity and a broader hold upon mankind, and numbers a hundred martyrs where Christianity can claim but one. And patriotism, let me insist, is not confined to the noble few. It is the commonwealth. I believe in the patriotism of the American people—the loyalty of the national heart. It may be tampered with and deceived and misled, but it lives as an irresistible motive-power in the national life.

It is the habit of some over-charitable people to say that, in the present struggle between the loyal people of this country and those in rebellion, the latter are actuated by just as good motives as the former. This may be true to a very limited extent; but it is notorious that the grand motive-power of the rebellion is hate; and hate is not so good a motive as love, and, thank God! it is not so powerful a motive as love. I see arrayed on one side of this struggle those who hate democracy, who hate labor, who hate the idea of human equality, who hate their country and its constitution, who hate the political mother that bore them—the mother under whose fostering care they had lived in wealth, independence, and peace—and who, more than they hate democracy, and more than they hate free institutions, and more than they hate their country, hate the North and the universal Yankee. If you can find any love that operates as a motive of rebellion besides the love of power and the love of slavery, you will be more successful than I have been.

It is patent that the motive-power of the rebellion is hate—hate, fostered and fed in every possible way. It breathes its foul breath through the rebel newspapers; it finds utterance in every speech; it comes forth with bitterest venom from the lips of women; it pollutes and burns the hearts and tongues of even the little children. Extinguish the hatred that glows in the heart of the rebellion to-day, and you extinguish the rebellion itself.

Now, can any sane man think of comparing this motive with that which has poured out for the national redemption its untold millions of treasure, and its hundred thousand lives? Have the men whom we have sent to Southern camps and Southern battle-fields and Southern graves been moved to enlist by feelings of enmity toward those against whom they went to fight? Has there been a bitter hatred of the Southron in the Northern heart? Has it not been notorious, not only here but abroad, that the loyal people of the country—especially those of the North—have carried no bitterness of feeling into this contest? I tell you that it was only because love of country was stronger than brotherly sympathy, that the nation was not ruined years ago. Our troops will not, cannot, be bitter; and I have no question that, if the armies of the rebellion should give up their cause to-day, our loyal forces could not be restrained from the expression of their fraternal feelings for them. We have fought for the country; we have fought for the flag; and love has been the motive-power with us in all the contest; and just as certain as God is stronger than all the powers of evil, and truth is stronger than falsehood, and virtue is stronger than vice, is love stronger than hate in any contest. One is supremely, everlastingly positive, allied to God and heaven; the other is infernally negative, born of hell and bound for it.

There is still another motive-force in national life which claims our consideration, and this is religion. I am inclined to think that we undervalue the power of religion upon the heart of this nation. In saying this,

I contemplate no narrow definition of religion, though I embrace in it, of course, all the forms of Christianity. Religion existed before Christianity, and of course can exist outside of Christianity. It may exist without any written revelation of God, flowing naturally and necessarily from the constitution of the human soul, and its rationally apprehended relations to the Father-Soul. We know there are multitudes of men and women who never enter a Christian church—who have no adequate Christian knowledge—who do not pretend to be Christians; yet who, through the indirect teachings of Christianity and the outworking of their religious natures, entertain the thought of a Supreme God within whose providential reign they come; a God to whom they pray in times of peril, and to whom they owe a certain sort or degree of obedience. This religion may be shallow, and it doubtless is so. There may be very little of love in it—very little of worship in it—very little of comfort and joy in it; but, shallow and loveless and joyless as it may be, there is something in it which gives significance to the word *duty*. It recognizes and acknowledges certain duties, growing out of the relations sustained by man to man and men to God; and this religion, shallow but broad, embraces a nation. It may be that the highest form it ever reaches is a simple sense of duty; but this sense of duty is strong and universal. As I understand the word duty, it always has direct or indirect reference to God and everlasting good. We do that which is due from us to God—due from us to others—due from us to our country—because God's constitution of things makes it due, and God's constitution of us makes us feel it to be so, and urges us to a practical acknowledgment of the fact.

Now permit me to illustrate the peculiar power of this sense of duty, as a motive, from our recent national history. I am aware that, like patriotism, it often sleeps in times of peace, but, when danger comes, it ·prings to its office with an energy that is really sublime. At the opening of the present war, when all the country was a camping-ground, and volunteers were rushing to rendezvous by tens and hundreds of thousands, there was one question which nearly every man was called upon to answer; and that question received but one reply—"What induced you to enlist?" This question, put to rude and rough men by sympathetic friends and visitors—put to men who were often profane and intemperate—put to men who had never been moved to do a heroic deed before—put to the simple-hearted boy from the farm, and the delicate-handed clerk from the counting-room—elicited but this response: "*Somebody must go.*" It was not the love of home entirely that made this "must go," for many of them had no home that they loved, or that loved them. It was not patriotism alone, for many of these men had little that bound them to their country, and feeble interest in its prosperity and safety. This "must go" sprang from a sense of duty, and this sense of duty was born of that which was essentially religion. It was so imperative that it gave them no peace until the uniform was on and the march begun. Now this religion may not have been pure and powerful enough —may not have been intelligent enough—to produce in these men a good personal character, but, appealed to by this great emergency, it made this great and beautiful response. If there are any who doubt the essentially religious character of this response, they will, at least, admit that the nation's life was indebted to the nation's heart for it, and not to its intellect.

"Somebody *must* go." Here was a full recognition of duty, and this recognition has placed two millions of men in fields of action which now hold five hundred thousand of them in the sleep that knows no waking. "*Somebody* must go." American, German, Irishman —Catholic and Protestant—all gave the same suggestive reply; and in that sense of duty which dictated it lay the national safety.

But it can be hardly necessary to illustrate the power of religion in national life in a country whose origin and history are, themselves, the most striking illustrations of it. It was religion that directed the Puritans to Plymouth Rock. It was religion that inspired and sustained them throughout their colonial struggle. Religion constituted so much of their life, that it really ordered the affairs of the State. It had been, in other countries, the habit of the State to take religion under its patronage, that it might be regulated and used for State purposes; but here, religion was the dominant power, and the State was used for religious purposes, as an instrument of the church. Religion found its way into every statute, and every municipal regulation, and every political institution. Before home-life was well established, and while yet the country waited to be loved and to be made worthy of patriotic affection, religion was the ever-present, ever-prevalent motive. Ministers stood side by side in public honor with magistrates, and the people were governed by them in harmonious companionship.

When, in critical moods, we look back upon those men and those times, we find much uncharitableness to condemn, much ignorance to lament, and much superstition to pity; but we know, after all, that the reigning motive of all that early life was the religion of Jesus Christ. It was this religion that crystallized into our political, educational, and charitable institutions. There is not a State constitution in this Union—there is not a college or a public school—that does not testify, directly or indirectly, to the power of religion as the motive of the early life of the nation.

And here permit me a single word on the subject of Puritanism, about whose malign influence in national affairs we hear so much in these latter days, from the lips of mountebanks and demagogues and traitors. Of what crimes does Puritanism stand convicted before the bar of History? It persecuted Quakers and hung witches, and did both in the fear of God and for His glory—which, perhaps, was the most lamentable part of the matter. What else did Puritanism do? It planted one of the most remarkable nations of the world in the wilderness. It gave that nation a love of freedom and justice, a regard for the moral government of God, an open Bible and a free pen and tongue. It impregnated a continent with the democratic idea, and the continent has borne to it a great family of republics. It built the school-house by the side of the church, and the college among the school-houses, and educated, and taught the world how to educate, the common people. It governed social life by the rules of Christian propriety, and carried its religion into every sphere where religion has an office to perform. When the oppressor came to extort tribute, and crush the free spirit of the nation, it rose the first in rebellion; and throughout the long years of the Revolution it poured out its blood like water for the national salvation. It sent from a single little State—the State that holds the everlasting rock on which it first planted its foot—eighty thousand men to the Revolutionary war; and I stand here as the son of a Puritan, and of Puritan New England, to declare with grateful pride that the triumph then achieved over the mother-country was not only a victory of the Puritans, but a victory of Puritan ideas. A belief in the right to life, liberty, and the pursuit of happiness—this is Puritanism. A belief that God rules in the affairs of men; that man has a right to himself that cannot be bought and sold without sin; that the golden rule is the best rule; and that loyalty to freedom and a free government is laudable, and that traitors ought to be hanged—this is Puritanism.

And New England is to be left out in the cold for its Puritanism! New England cold! Why, the only way New England has kept comfortably cool for the last half century has been through her contact with other States, of great conducting power. Leave New England out, and she would come up to a white heat in twelve months. But you cannot leave New England out; you cannot leave Puritanism out. New England is in; Puritanism is in—mixed in; and so long as they represent freedom, and pure morals, and patriotism, they will stay in.

But it is not necessary to refer to the general religious sentiment of the nation, or to historical Puritanism, to learn that religion is a powerful motive in the national life. Its Christian spire rises wherever a hamlet gathers. The cities are crowded with its costly architecture, and into these churches gathers the best and most highly vitalized society of the nation. The Christian pulpit is the greatest moral lever of the age. It holds the highest culture of the country and the best intellect; and its power cannot be measured.

The love of home is strong, and the love of country is strong; but the love of God is supreme, and fertilizes and vitalizes all other loves. Ah! how little do the unthinking realize the power of the religion taught by a free Bible and a free pulpit in such a nation as this! Think what it is to have twenty thousand men in twenty thousand pulpits, proclaiming every week to twenty thousand congregations, made up of the most influential society of the nation, the truths of the everlasting gospel; preaching justice and purity and truthfulness, and love and freedom and faith; enforcing the claims of duty in all the departments of life; giving constant recognition to the reality of a future existence, and drawing motives from it; and exhorting to daily communion with Him who is the source of life and the spring of inspiration! Can such a power as this be measured?—a power with the highest spiritual forces in it—with God and eternity in it, and love as deep and broad as both? Think what it is to have a thousand presses busy with the production of Bibles and religious newspapers and Christian books and tracts! Think of twenty thousand Sunday-schools and a hundred thousand other schools in which prayer is offered daily and more or less religious instruction given, and of a hundred colleges, every one of which is in Christian hands in the pursuit of Christian ends, and then you can only begin to get an idea of the power of religion in our national life.

I have thus tried to exhibit to you the fact that the heart is the motive-power in the national life, and that this life is essentially love and love's natural offspring—that in the love of home, and the love of country, and the love of God, the nation holds all the motive-forces of its being. The national heart is the birthplace of all generous national enthusiasms, all worthy aspirations, all noble heroisms, and through it everything divine in the national life is breathed. A government may exist without love in it, and it may rule a nation without love in it; but no nation can live, in itself, with the power of self-government, self-development, and self-preservation, save as its life starts in, and is fed by, its heart.

We are naturally desirous of the spread of republican institutions over the world; but we may rest certain that they will spread no faster than the hearts of the nations are prepared for them. The only reason why a republic cannot live in Rome and France is, that the hearts of those nations are not capable of creating and sustaining a republic—that they are not under those motive-forces of love which produce a republic, or any form of self-organized national life. The heart of France, for instance, unless I greatly mistake it, does not possess that home-love, that patriotism, and that love of God, whose natural outgrowth and expression is republicanism. When the heart of France wins those possessions, the imperial crown will tumble, and France will become a republic without essay of arms, or effort of will. France is full, even to-day, of republican theory. Nothing can be more radical than the doctrines of popular rights and self-government taught by some of the brightest and most influential minds of France. Indeed, the head of France has been republican for years; but it takes something more than heads and hands to make and sustain a republic. Look at the old republic of Mexico, and see how it has died out at the heart. Its home-life had become poor, its patriotism had been narrowed down to partisanship, and its religion was in dead forms and dead churches, and not in the hearts of the people. When Mexico died as a republic, she died simply because her heart was dead, and because she could not exist longer as a republic. Venice died at the heart, and though events over which she had no control were busy with her destiny, they hardly hastened her fall. In the striking language of Mr. Ruskin: "By the inner burning of her own passions, as fatal as the fiery rain of Gomorrah, she was consumed from her place among the nations; and her ashes are choking the channels of the dead, salt sea."

And here I am led naturally to speak of the national heart as the conservative power of the national life. You will see that my subject is a difficult one to divide —that is, it is difficult, with my view of the subject, to separate for consideration the motive and conservative forces of national life. The winds and tides that give ceaseless motion to the sea are also the conservative forces of the sea. Its constant sweetness is the product mainly of its constant motion. That vital force in the human body which gives it the power to act upon matter is the same force which preserves that body from decay. It is thus in national life. The heart is the motive-power, and it is also the conservative power, through identical channels of operation; but the politics of the day give us our words, and we must see how much meaning there is in them. There is an idea that the conservative forces of our nation are entirely distinct from the motive forces, and we consequently hear of conservatism, and conservative influences, and conservative men. There has been a feeling afloat that this nation is in great need of being saved by somebody, or something; and there is a class of people who have written and talked and engaged in associated action with reference to an outside scheme of salvation, under the name of conservatives. There are others that do not call themselves by this name, who look for the national preservation to powers that do not inhere in the national life.

I think, for instance, that many of us have been looking throughout all this war for a great man—a great leader—bearing his patent of nobility and sign of authority on his forehead, and taking the national salvation into his own hands. I have not seen him: have you? Why have we not seen him? Because we did not need him. We have seen good men, honest men, honorable men, who did their duty, and who were a fair expression of the national heart; but the great, the commanding man, has not come, and would not be heeded if he had. Great men save feeble nations by harmonizing their will and concentrating their power; but ours is not a feeble nation, its will is sufficiently harmonized, and its power is sufficiently concentrated. The nation is able to take care of itself, and has its conservative power in the sources of its life. Still the call for a great man is kept up, and the newspapers have said "lo here," and "lo there;" and politicians have bruited several distinct discoveries of the genuine article; but, to use the street-slang of the day, the people "don't see it." They have no special anxiety to see it. They are on the right track, and know what they want. They need only honest and efficient men to execute their will. Are we willing, at this date of our national life, to trust ourselves in the hands of a great man—to be led by him—to be moulded by him—to be saved by him, in his way? Are we become so weak, so ignorant, so degraded, as to be looking for a great man to save us? God forbid! and God forbid (I speak it reverently and earnestly) that any great man rise to take the nation's work out of the nation's hands!

There are some, I suppose, who are honest in the belief that the nation is to be saved by party politics. We judge thus by the resolutions passed at their conventions, and by the tenor of their speeches and their newspapers. We hear not unfrequently of assemblies of leading politicians in Washington or New York, which seem to be devoted to the business of saving the nation—in their way. One would imagine, from the airs they put on, that the life of the nation was in their hands, or that it had no life independent of party politics. We have a great crisis, as you know, on the occasion of every national election, in which the national salvation is understood to depend on the triumph of—all parties. First and last all parties have succeeded, and first and last all parties have been defeated, and still the nation lives; and it has manifested more genuine vitality, with a third of its subjects in rebellion, than it ever did while all were united.

The idea of putting a living, intelligent, powerful

nation into the keeping—into the conservative embrace—of a few lean party men, the majority of whom are working for power or for pay, is just as ridiculous as the thought of a great army—whose salvation is in itself, if it is anywhere—consenting to be led by a band of camp-followers and sutlers who had volunteered to save it from destruction.

No nation ever conserved its life by or through a policy. A policy may modify the issues of national life somewhat, and have a reactionary effect upon the life itself; but a mere policy has no life in it, to bestow upon anything. Most nations live—indeed, most nations always have lived—in spite of the policy imposed upon them. A national policy is only a way of national living. The life of a stream does not depend upon the way of its flowing. It may be turned by artificial means out of its old channel, and then turned back again, and then diverted into other channels; but these changes do not diminish the volume of the stream, nor hinder it a day from finding the ocean to which it tends. So a party policy may change the direction of a nation's life, and modify for a time its minor issues; but it has no power to save that life—no conservative power. The nation carries its salvation in its own strong heart, and not in the pocket of any party.

I do not pretend that one policy is as good as another, or offer the opinion that it makes no difference what party manages the government: on the contrary, I think that the mode of national life is of very great importance. I simply hold that it is not of vital importance. So far is the nation from having its life in a party, or a policy, that all parties and policies have their life in the nation.

All parties pretend to conservatism, in one way or another—conservatism as they understand it; and we find in them all, and sometimes outside of them all, a class of men who profess to be distinctively conservative. Exactly what they mean by conservatism does not appear, but—they—are—well, they are conservative. They are general dissenters, protestants, fault-finders, critics. Many of them are bankrupt politicians; some have very stiff backs and very sore heads; some have very supple backs and very soft heads; most of them, for some private reason, don't believe in party politics at all, but would like to belong to a party which is not a party, with politics which are not politics. They usually dine satisfactorily, wear good clothes, and have a little something invested in stocks. They are in favor of things as they are, with one or two trifling exceptions. They would like to have all radicals and reformers hanged. They cherish an abiding affection for every good, old-fashioned, comfortable, respectable wrong, and can have no patience with those who are bent on disturbing it. I may have been peculiarly unfortunate in my field of observation, but I have never known an out-and-out, genuine conservative to be on the humane side of anything; and, to-day, he is notoriously bent on saving that which alone brings the nation into danger—saving that which, for its hideous crimes against humanity, against liberty, against the peace and dignity of this nation, against the loyal and patriotic blood of the American people, ought to be destroyed. His peculiar affection for the Constitution of his country seems to be inspired mainly by the clause which protects those who have spit upon that Constitution, and trampled it under their feet.

This sort of conservatism would save the patient by saving the ulcer that gnaws his flesh; would save the ship by saving the barnacles that hinder her way through the water and drag her downward; would save the tree by saving the caterpillars that consume its foliage. It believes that ulcers are angels, and barnacles blessings, and that caterpillars have a constitutional right to be nuisances. It distrusts—nay, it does not recognize at all—the power of a living nation to rid itself of wrongs by the natural outgoings of its life. It stands still amid the sweep and swirl of the national life like an old stump in a western river, with its feet stuck in the mud—a lodging-place for political drift-wood—while the steadily on-going national life slips under and around it without paying it the compliment of a ripple or an eddy.

There are many who believe in the conservative power of education. Many have, indeed, come to a settled opinion that the public-school system of the North and the universal newspaper are the real safeguards of the national life. I think this matter is not properly understood. Education may or may not be conservative in its influence. It is conservative or destructive according to circumstances. When the culture of the heart keeps pace with the culture of the head, and both are educated together, education becomes a conservative power; but when the intellect alone is developed, and the heart is permitted to lie dead or to become corrupted, education simply sharpens a knife for the nation's throat. Education certainly adds something to national life, but conservative power resides in quality, not quantity. It is the sugar that preserves the fruit and not the fruit that preserves the sugar. Educate the intellect of the common people—educate everybody; only remember that conservative power resides in quality and not in quantity. The legitimate relation between the development of the heart and the brain must be constantly preserved, or education will breed national corruption by a law of nature which cannot possibly be evaded.

I have thus attempted to present to you the great

fact that national life does not abide in the government, does not abide in political institutions, does not abide in political parties or political men—that its source is the national heart. I have endeavored to show you that in the love of home, the love of country, and the love of God, lies the grand secret of the nation's vitality—lies that which is distinctively a nation's life—this nation's life. If the government were overthrown, the nation would live; if its political institutions were destroyed to-day, it would form new ones to-morrow, and better ones; if its political parties and its party men were annihilated, it would only be the stronger for the loss. These are only accidents and outgrowths of national life; but if the love of home and country and God should be destroyed, the nation would at once cease to be an organized, living thing. These loves which inform the national heart are the fountain-head of all motive that has life in it, and of all conservative power. I have endeavored to exhibit to you this nation as a creature of the heart—as having in itself, by virtue of its origin and constitution, an independent life. The government is only its instrument; institutions are only its drapery, or property, or machinery; parties are only its parasites; and great men only its agents or ornaments. Private and public errors—private and public vices—these are diseases, these are agents of death; but so long as the vital fountain remains strong and full, the nation is safe.

I have entertained two purposes in this discussion. The first is, to show that whenever disease attacks the national life, all remedial agents that have reference to a permanent cure should be addressed to the heart. This nation has been, and still is, sick. Treason is a symptom. Sympathy with treason is a symptom. Insurrection is a symptom. Corruption in high places is a symptom. Loveless, selfish, godless politicians are a symptom. I tell you that this nation cannot get thoroughly well, until the national heart shall have been made pure enough and unselfish enough to control these symptoms, and expel the diseases which give them birth. By feeding the domestic affections, by the stimulation and development of patriotism, and, above all, by the cultivation of Christian grace and a sense of responsibility to God, is the nation to be cured of its disease. Policies, politics, men, administrations—these are nothing: all nostrums addressed to mere symptoms can be nothing better than momentary in their effect. Deepen and purify the national heart, and treason and rebellion and corruption and selfish politics will be sloughed off by the power of a better blood. It is simply a question of power between the motive and conservative forces of the national life, and the paralyzing and destructive forces.

Ah! how well the great physician who has this nation in his care understands its case! His treatment has indeed been heroic, but it has been wholesome. Is not home more precious to us than it was before this war began? Do we not hold every domestic joy at a higher value? Is not our love of country strengthened and purified since this war began? Has not the national flag a new significance, and a new power of inspiration? Is not our patriotism deeper and broader and better? Is not the piety of the national heart purified and strengthened also? I declare my belief that there has not been a time within the last half century when, as a nation, we have been so willing to acknowledge the sovereign sway of the King of kings, so ready to see His hand in all chastisement and in all success, and so earnest to seek His favor and do His will, as now. These loves that are our life have been fed by the nation's blood, the nation's tears, and the nation's treasures, until the nation's vital forces are greater than ever before in its history.

The second purpose of my discussion is to exhibit to you the true and only ground of hope for the future. Ever since this war was commenced there have been croakers in every community declaring more or less boldly that the nation is dead; that all the blood that has been shed, and all the treasure that has been expended, have been wasted, and that anarchy and general wreck lie before us. I tell you that, with the development of the national heart that has taken place since the war commenced, the nation cannot die. That question is settled; and neither rebellion at home nor interference from abroad can unsettle it. It is beyond all the contingencies of war and treason and intrigue. The government itself is safe from wreck at this moment, not through any power of its own, but through the power of the people under an impulse of the national heart. At the opening of the rebellion, the government was as powerless to save itself as if it had been no more than the corporation of the city of Washington; and when the heart of the nation could not push its blood through Baltimore, it pushed it around Baltimore, to save the national brain from syncope. And this is exactly my point. It is the national life that upholds and moulds and controls the government. The government is only the coronet upon the nation's brow. The nation is king, and the crown moves only as the king moves, and shines only when the king lifts it high into the light.

I suppose there may be eyes in Europe, greedy with the lust of dominion, that are looking toward our shores for new fields of conquest; but if any power should ever undertake to swallow this nation, it would find itself in possession of a most indigestible morsel. A living nation, capable of self-government, cannot be digested by a nation so dead that it consents to be governed by a despot. Even demoralized Poland, with her comparatively low grade of vitality, lies very hard upon the stomach of Russia. Hungary is a constant disturber of the spleen of Austria, and refuses to be digested. Little Switzerland—living Switzerland—with her two and a half millions, sits among her mountain-homes smiling, over the immunity she enjoys from the rapacious maws of the great nations around her. If Switzerland could have been digested, none of the considerations to which her safety has been so often attributed would have saved her from being swallowed long ago. But Switzerland is alive at the heart, and cannot be killed at the heart, so as to be digested. The American nation is alive at the heart, and could not be killed by a foreign war a hundred years long.

And now, as a final result of our discussion, we may learn why it is that this nation has had, from the beginning of its history, such faith in itself. The faith in itself, which it manifested during those long, long years of the Revolution, filled all the European politicians with wonder. They could not realize the fact that these feeble colonies were already a nation, alive at the heart, and possessing the power of self-organization and self-government. The end taught them something, but the lesson did not last. How constantly, during the present war, have European politicians failed to understand and measure us! They prophesied early success to the rebellion, but the rebellion has not succeeded. They thought they foresaw an early exhaustion of means, but they have seen us prosecute the most gigantic war of the century without going to them for a dollar. Nay, they have seen their own capitalists eagerly buying the securities of our government out of the hands of our own people. They foretold famine, but we have had plenty, not only for ourselves but for them; universal bankruptcy, but we have all prospered; anarchy, but we have had perfect order, save in one or two instances when base European blood has disturbed it. They have wondered that as a nation we did not despair—almost felt like quarrelling with us because we would not see and admit that we were ruined—have begged us for humanity's sake not to fight against fate. As if a living nation, any more than a living man, would consent to the amputation of a limb, so long as there was vitality enough in its heart to save it!

Ah! this faith of the nation in itself! It is grand —it is glorious. It is not in the power of this nation to despair. Its faith is not in its government, its institutions, its politicians, or even in its armies. Its faith is in itself, and in God, and is a natural product of its life. It is born among the affections. It is a child of love; and while the love of home and country and heaven live, this faith will live, rising above all disaster, superior to all difficulty, and, like a winged angel, leading the nation to the grand consummations of perpetual peace, prosperity, and power.

COST AND COMPENSATION.

THE law of compensation, as it is generally held and expounded, is a law of circumstances. Over against every defect in a man's constitution, over against every flaw in his condition, over against every weakness in his character, there is set some compensating excellence which rounds him into wholeness. Mr. Emerson, in his exposition of this law, declares that no man ever had a defect which was not made useful to him somewhere—a comfortable suggestion to that limited number of fortunate persons who have defects!

In the general view of this law, man would seem to be not unlike those gum-elastic heads which amuse our children. A pressure on the cheeks is accompanied by a compensatory thickening of the lips. Bear down the bump of reverence, and up comes the bump of benevolence. Squeeze hard across the temples, and hold closely in the back of the head, and we have Sir Walter Scott. There is compensation for every squeeze in some new protrusion. The head assumes new forms and expressions, but it is never smaller. So, in this philosophy, a man may have any number of defects, but the measure of his manhood is not reduced by them. Indeed, his defects are the measure of his excellences.

Now I do not propose to quarrel with this philosophy, which, I may say in passing, covers not only man in his constitution, but man in all his belongings; for there *is* some truth, or half-truth, in it. It opens a field of observation and thought that will well repay exploration, though the only practical result that can be reached is contentment with the constitution of things and the allotments of life; and this is not a mean prize.

I propose to leave this aspect of the law, for one which has relation directly to life and its motive-forces. Cost is the father and compensation is the mother of progress; and I propose to treat of them as they relate to the grand ends, enterprises, and activities of life.

Exchange, for mutual benefit, is the basis of all trade—it is itself all legitimate trade. The man who does a day's work for me exchanges that work for my money, and we are mutually benefited. He would rather have my money than save his labor. I would rather have his labor than save my money. The story of the two Yankee boys who were shut up in a room together, and made twenty-five cents a-piece swapping jack-knives before they came out, is entirely rational and probable. It is very likely that each found his advantage in his new possession. A merchant in Illinois has wheat which he exchanges with a New York jobber for hardware. The exchange is made at the market value, and is nominally an even one, but, in reality, each finds advantages in it, and each makes money by it. When the business of a nation is in a healthy condition, all men thrive through the means of exchanges of values that are nominally equal.

As a rule of business intercourse, we pay for what we get, dollar for dollar, and pound for pound. Every material good which man produces has its price, and can be procured for its price. Except this price be paid, it can only be procured by begging or stealing—through shame or sin. Everything costs something; and most of the meannesses of the world are perpetrated in various ingenious attempts to get something for nothing, or for an inadequate price.

The history of a dollar has been written, I believe, and it would certainly be interesting to follow any dollar through the endless concatenation of exchanges, and see how it relieves and enriches every hand it touches. I pay a dollar, for instance, for a bushel of potatoes, and the green-grocer pays it to the gardener, who pays it, we will say, to the coal-dealer, who pays it to the mining company, who pay it to the miner, who pays it to the draper for a shirt, who pays it to the manufacturer, who pays it to the cotton-factor, who pays it to the Southern shipper, who pays it to the Southern planter, who pays it to his—no—I believe he doesn't. My illustration is not entirely happy, I see; but, after all, it is the only one that will give me a stopping-place. Everything a man parts with is the cost of something. Everything he receives is the compensation for something.

This, as between man and man, in all business intercourse whatsoever. Now between man and nature there is precisely the same relation. Man, as his own proprietor, understands it, and God understands it as the proprietor of nature. God has commissioned nature to pay for everything that man does for her—imposed upon her this law, indeed, which she never disobeys. To man, He says by many voices: "I have given you all the air you can breathe, all the water you can use, and all the earth you can cultivate; I have given you the ministry of the rain and the dew, and the light of the sun and moon and stars, and spread over you the beauty of the heavens; I have given you brains to design and muscles to labor. These are essentials—these are necessary capital for commencing life's business—these are common and free; but if you want anything else—and you do want everything else—you must work for it—pay for it in labor or its equivalent. You are at liberty to exchange what you have worked for, for that which your neighbor has worked for, but, between you, you must work for what you get."

And here is where we find the basis of all the values by which we regulate our exchanges. Labor—the expenditure of vital effort in some form—is the measure, nay, it is the maker, of values. A pearl will sell for just as much more than a potato as it will cost of human effort to obtain it. Gold is not so useful a metal as iron. Iron can be put to ten uses where gold can only be put to one; but gold is ten thousand times as valuable as iron, and mainly because it costs ten thousand times as much labor to obtain it from the earth.

Expenditure—Compensation: these are the great motions of the world. We are all the time pouring our life into the earth, and the earth is all the time pouring its life back into us. Her great storehouse of treasure is filled for those who will pay for it. Douglas Jerrold said that in Australia it is only necessary to tickle the earth with a hoe to make her laugh with a harvest. That I suppose is when she meets the first settler, and is particularly glad to see him; but she soon gets over her extreme good nature, and insists on rigid business dealing. In New England she is severe, but she is true. There is not a spot of all her sterile soil that will not fairly compensate those who put their life into it. The meanest white-birch swamp only asks for drainage and tillage, and it will pay bountifully in bread. Culture, fertilization, exploration—these are the conditions upon which the earth yields up her treasures to man—and she never fails to pay back all that she receives. The trapper, in his pursuit of furs, travels far and wide, and exercises all his skill and cunning; and he brings back that which pays him for his expenditure. The fisherman throws his net or his hook in all waters, and the sea faithfully rewards his quest. The gold-hunter digs into the side of the mountain, and, when he has probed far enough, he reaches the chamber where Nature sits behind her crystal counter, and deals out the yellow ingots. The sweat of the human brow, wherever it falls, dissolves the bars by which nature holds her treasures from human hands.

Thus we find in fellow-dealing, and in all our search for material good among the resources of nature, this law—that everything costs, and everything pays; that if we make an intelligent expenditure, under essential conditions intelligently apprehended and fulfilled, we receive full compensation in the kind of good which we seek. And this law is not a special one. It is universal, and throws its girdle around everything desirable to the human soul. We give and get, and only get by giving. All the good we win, we win by sacrifice.

There are certain essentials to the soul's life, as there are to the body's life, which God bestows in common upon all the race—necessary spiritual capital on which to set up business. It is as if God had said: "I have given you love for your hearts, senses to yield you pleasure while they do you service, joy in living, aspirations, ambitions, hopes; but if you want anything more than these—and you do want everything that you can appropriate in all my universe—you must pay for it by an expenditure of yourself or your possessions. If you want learning, you must work for it. If you desire to reproduce, or embody, that which is within you in any form of art, you must make great sacrifices for it. If you would make high acquisitions in spiritual and moral excellence, you must pay, measure for measure, for all you obtain. There is not a single good in my realm—not yours in common with all your race—not embraced in your original capital—that can be secured without a sacrifice that corresponds to, and in some degree measures, its value; and there is not a good in my realm that will not reward, and does not wait to reward, your expenditures."

Now what are the treasures that a man holds in his hands, exchangeable for the better wealth?

First, Time. Our life is limited. The average life of men does not exceed forty years; and threescore years and ten measure, except in rare instances, the farthest limit of active life. This matter of time, as one of our articles of exchange, is a very important one. Under ordinary and prevalent circumstances, it is a pleasant thing to live, and, it being a pleasant thing to live, it is a pleasant thing to have leisure—that is, to have nothing which shall so occupy our time as to interfere with the simple enjoyment of living. When, therefore, we are called out of our leisure into labor, we go, if our leisure is comfortable or happy, with a sense of real sacrifice.

Again, time is of great value to us, because so much of it is required for those activities whose aim is the sustenance and protection of the bodily life. The amount of time required for the acquisition of the means of bodily subsistence is very great; and to this must be added all that is necessary for bodily rest and refreshment. A man whose period of active life stretches on to fifty years—say from twenty to seventy—laboring ten hours a day, sleeping and resting and idling ten hours, and spending two hours in eating, dressing, bathing, &c., has just two hours left out of the twenty-four which are at his disposal. These amount to four years and a fraction in fifty, without reckoning the Sabbaths—but, as the average of active life is really not more than twenty-five years, and we are only after a general result, we will let the Sabbaths go; and say that every man has four years of time, as a treasure to be disposed of for whatever the soul may choose to purchase.

Let us remember that we are making a liberal estimate. There are great multitudes of men—aye, and women too—perhaps more women than men—who, even in an active life of fifty years, do not have two years of time at their disposal; who work and eat and sleep throughout the whole period, and then die with absolutely no time with which to purchase that higher good for which they were made. It will be seen, therefore, that time, as one of our disposable treasures, is not measured by the duration of life at all. Divide the number of years we live by ten, and the quotient will give us more than the average of time in our possession, for conversion into the higher grades of good.

The second treasure which a man holds for exchange is Vitality. "No man," says Peter Bayne, "has more than a certain force allotted him by nature. It may be greater or less; but it is measured, and it cannot be expended twice." Every man, I suppose, arrives at adult years with a definite stock of vital power on hand. Before he dies, that stock is all to be expended. It may all be expended in bodily labor, or a portion of it only. It may be expended in a struggle against disease. It may be expended in the illicit gratification of the senses. It may be wasted in the digestion of unnecessary food. Or, it may be expended mainly in the acquisition of intellectual, moral, and spiritual wealth. Like time, much of it must be used in obtaining food and clothing and shelter for the body; but there is a remnant left to be applied by the power of the will to the purchase of that good which is the highest wealth of life and character.

The third treasure is Ease. Beyond the simple pleasure of living, and beyond the passive reception of pleasure through the senses, ease is, and always has been, regarded as a treasure. Men often work through many weary years to obtain it. Labor is not a thing which men love for itself. Men love that which pleasantly engages the activities of body and mind; but that is essentially play. Work is something which both body and mind are driven to. The will is obliged to apply its determining and motive power, before either body or mind will undertake that which is essentially a task. To many men, of fine powers, the ease of those powers is the most grateful and precious of all their treasures, and the one which they are the most unwilling to sacrifice for the higher good which only its surrender can win. The fairest picture of heaven itself, to some souls, is that which represents it as the home of ease. But this treasure must go with the others, as a part of the price of spiritual and all superior good.

There is another treasure, harder than all the rest

to surrender, without which the whole payment is vitiated; and this is the Will, with all its self-love and pride. There is nothing more precious to a man than his will; there is nothing which he relinquishes with so much reluctance. The natural desire of every man is to follow the dictates of his own will, unhindered. Obedience is not easy, until it is adopted as the rule of life. If we had no authority but human experience, it would be safe to say that an obedient and childlike spirit is absolutely essential, not only to the acquisition but to the reception of the highest good. A man must come under the laws of his being, and bow to the laws and conditions of all being—he must place his own will in harmony with the Supreme will—before it will be possible for him even to receive the highest good God has to bestow.

I might enumerate other treasures which every man holds for exchange, but you see the drift of the argument, and can fill out the inventory.

These, then, are our treasures—our stock; and now let us examine some of the ways by which, as individuals, communities, and nations, men win compensation for their expenditures.

And first, let me state the proposition which I hope with some degree of clearness to illustrate in this lecture, viz., that no expenditure of the treasures I have enumerated can ever be made, with earnest truthfulness of purpose, without securing compensation in some form, at some time. Let us understand that there are before every one of us two hoards of treasure—one held by God, the other by man—mutually exchangeable, and that this law of exchange, or this law of compensation for expenditure, is instituted from eternity, and has no suspension and no flaw. Let me present this treasure which God holds for us under the figure of a massive golden vase, filled to the brim with water—a vase that can neither be dipped from nor drawn from, but that overflows to the hand that drops its treasure into it—overflows to that hand always, and overflows to no other hand.

In our consideration of this subject, we shall find that cost and compensation are of two kinds; that they are separable into two departments, each governed by independent laws. In one, compensation is directly sought, for personal advantage. In the other, moved by the power of love, we expend our treasure without hope of personal advantage, and receive it without the seeking. The instinct of infancy is to grasp and appropriate something to build itself up with. It blindly reaches out toward everything its senses apprehend, and fixes its grapple upon evil as greedily as upon good. This impulse, directed with increasing intelligence, follows us throughout the infancy of our being. We work for a direct reward. The hardest trial we have, in the education of children, is to induce them to study when they are unable to see and appreciate the reward which that study will secure. Daily practice of the scales upon a musical instrument, drill in the rudiments of a foreign language—these are tasks which a child tires of, because it does not distinctly apprehend, or does not value, their reward. Set the child to learning a tune, or trying a bit of translation, and the reward for work is so near, and so distinctly apprehended, and so much valued, that it labors with efficiency and enthusiasm.

Grown-up children betray the same characteristic, and it is not to be found fault with. It is the ordination of nature that we shall be something before we can do something—that we shall win something before we can have anything to bestow. We are to be fed, developed, endowed, before we are fitted for ministry; and we must seek directly for those rewards which give us food, development, and endowment.

The second motive of action proceeds from within rather than from without. The personal reward is unsought for, but it never fails. When a man moves under the law of love, he is unselfish, and loses all thought of reward. He has ceased for the time to appropriate, and becomes a dispenser. His life is voluntarily transformed into a channel through which the divine beneficence flows into the world. That which he has won of the higher good becomes generative, and makes manifestation. But here, as elsewhere, he must expend his private treasures; and for this expenditure there is always payment. He must expend time, ease and vitality, and money, perhaps—one of the forms in which all these treasures are preserved. Does the meadow that bears one of God's broad rivers on its bosom get no reward from the river? By bearing the burden of the hills, it is greener than they. Any man who becomes the channel of a divine good, sucks into his own being the juices of that good. Indeed, the reward for unselfish service is better than any other, because the quality of the sacrifice is finer.

And here let me say that there is no such thing in the world—that there never was, and never can be, any such thing in the world—as charity—something given for nothing. There may be abundant charity in the motive—that is, sacrifice may be made from motives of love, or pity, or sympathy, or mercy, without wish or expectation of reward; but this expenditure is subject to the highest grade of compensation. There is no letting up of this law for any motive. Expend, and the compensation comes. One motive is the complement and resolution of the other. They fly wing-and-wing throughout the universe. The operation of the law is like that of those old country-wells which we knew in our childhood. While we empty one of their two buckets, the other is filling: it is impossible that one should be emptied without the other being filled, and equally impossible that one should be filled without the other being emptied.

In the first of these two departments of compensation we need to linger but a moment. Precisely as we dig in the ground for gold, or wash the sand for gems, or sound the sea for pearls—precisely as we cultivate the field to obtain those fruits which feed us, or operate the mill to make those fabrics which clothe us, do we seek for that higher good which supplies and endows our higher life. The recorded wisdom of the world is in our libraries; the truth of God is in our Bibles. We know just where labor will win, moment by moment, full compensation. We know what sacrifices will win wisdom, learning, culture. We know what we must give of time, ease, and vitality, for every excellence in art. We know how much of sensual pleasure and how much of will we must relinquish to acquire spiritual elevation and purity; and we know that, in all these cases, these sacrifices will procure the exact measure of compensation which we seek. We know, furthermore, that there is not a power or possession with which we seek to endow ourselves, which is to be procured in any way but by these specific sacrifices. It is said that there is no royal road to learning.

It may be said with equal truth that there is no royal road to anything desirable. Genius enjoys no immunities. The bird flies faster than the fox runs; but the bird must use its wings or the fox will catch it. God gives us arms and hands, but he does not give us strength and dexterity. These have a price, and we must work with our hands and work with our arms, or we cannot have strength and dexterity. He gives us brains, but he does not give us learning, or wisdom, or power of easy expression, or strength and skill in intellectual labor. All these must be purchased, and all these are a sufficient reward for what we give for them.

We turn to the other department, and find our most direct way to its illustration through an appeal to universal human experience. We find no statistics ready for us. No careful plodder has ever been over the ground, and collected the facts which show that for every unselfish deed of good the doer has received a grand reward; and The Master keeps no accounts that are open to our inspection. Every man, however, who hears me will testify to this: that he never fed a beggar, or ministered to a helpless or suffering fellow-man, or made a sacrifice for the public good, without a return which more than paid him for his expenditure.

It is not necessary that I should point out the modes in which good comes to a man, as a compensation for unselfish sacrifice. It is enough for me to say that no man ever made this sacrifice without feeling abundantly paid for it.

Still, let us illustrate the point. I choose for this purpose true marriage and happy maternity. In the surrender of her name, her destiny, her life, herself, to her husband, a woman realizes the reception of a blessing greater than she believes it in her power to bestow; for true love is always humble in the presence of its object. This surrender is entire, and glad as it is entire; and the moment it is made, she finds that she is worth more to herself, as the possession of another, than she was when she was her own. And this wife becoming a mother, gives her life to her children. The freshness fades from her brow, the roses fall from her cheeks, the violets in her eyes drop their dew, and her frame loses its elasticity; but in these children and their precious love, she has a reward for every sacrifice, so great that sacrifice becomes a pleasant habit, and ministry the passion of her life. She expends, under the motive-power of love, all her treasures of time, ease, vitality, and will, and feels pouring back into her heart, through numberless unsuspected avenues, such largess of blessing as overflows her with a sense of grateful satisfaction. Does that Christian lover of his kind who spends his life in hospitals and prisons, in ministry to human need and human suffering, have smaller pay? Has he who gives himself for his country, even if he fall in the front of battle, meaner compensation? Ask him, and hear his noble answer: "It is sweet and glorious to die for one's country." Does he who gives himself in service to the Great Master, even though he die the martyr's death of fire, have a smaller reward? Love is one. It moves to one tune; it works by one law; it leads to one issue.

And now I come to the consideration of this law of compensation as it relates to social communities. Society has material interests and treasures, and society is high or low, good or bad, progressive in culture and goodness or retrograde, refined or coarse, polite or vulgar, as it sacrifices these interests and treasures for social food and social wealth. When we reach the consideration of associated men, we come to institutions. Those who are Christians associate themselves together, and form a church. They build a house of worship, and engage the ministry of a preacher. They start a Sunday-school, and institute all the machinery necessary for securing the best Christian results. Society establishes and supports schools for the education of the young of all classes, purchases libraries for the people, forms lecture associations, establishes institutions for the relief of the poor, and institutes a multitude of agencies for the general good.

Now, while there is a certain number of persons,

in all society, who must sacrifice time, ease, and vitality, directly, for the purpose of elevating its life, the great majority are called upon to sacrifice little more than money; but money itself, as I have already incidentally stated, is an article in which time, ease, and vitality are embodied and hoarded. Some men inherit in money the hoarded lives of many men, and so have much power. Time, ease, and vitality are converted into money, so that a given amount of money represents a day's labor. If my friend, who has a special gift for doing the work of society, spends a day in that work, he sacrifices no more than I do, who give, to forward his objects, as much money as he would earn in that time. Money is a grand, indispensable requisite for all the operations for social improvement. Churches and schools cannot be built and supported without money, and it is a beneficent ordination of Providence that the results of labor can be accumulated and embodied in a form so available for social purposes.

There are three forms in which reward comes for all expenditures made for the higher interests of society. The first is material, and perfectly appreciable by minds actuated mainly by material motives. The Great Rewarder has provided a payment for social sacrifices which the most selfish man can appreciate and appropriate. If a man makes a sacrifice for society, he can, with a common share of brains, see that he gets his money back, so that he may regard his sacrifice as an investment.

Let us, for illustration, suppose the existence of a little city of ten thousand inhabitants, without a church, or a school-house, or a library, or a lyceum, or any institution of any kind for the moral, intellectual, and social culture of the people. Let us suppose this city to be rich in material good, and in facilities and opportunities for augmenting it. Would property be safe in such a city? Would vice be under control there? Would men be industrious there? Would it possess the best elements of prosperity and security? What things, in all the world, would add most to the value of real and personal property in such a city? Would there be a man among its ten thousand—no matter how vile or mean his personal character might be—who could find a better investment for his money than by paying his share toward building five churches and ten school-houses, and endowing a public library and lyceum? Such an investment as this would double the actual market value of all the property of the city. No man there could afford to place his money at simple interest while such an investment waited to be made. Any man who permits institutions like these to go begging, in a city which contains his property, convicts himself of business incompetency. All these institutions bring with them a positive, money-producing and money-preserving power. They are stimulants of industry, foes to all wasteful vices, bonds of harmony among jarring material interests; nay, they are absolute essentials to a safe, steady, and reliable prosperity. It is not necessary that a man should be benevolent to give money for the establishment and support of these institutions. It is simply necessary that he have the instincts and the foresight of an ordinary man of business.

The second form in which reward comes for social sacrifice is higher and better than this; and there are very few minds that cannot appreciate this, and even appropriate it. There are things in the world which cannot be eaten, or worn, or handled, that have a money-value. When a man pays out half a dollar for a dinner, he buys that which he knows to be necessary to his life. A dinner is one of the things that he must have. When he pays out half a dollar for cigars, he pays for that which is not necessary to him, but which, through habit, has become so desirable, perhaps, that he really wins more satisfaction from his expenditure than he did from that which procured his dinner. Here, you see, is a money-value attached to a satisfaction which stands outside the pale of utility. If he pays half a dollar for the privilege of listening to a concert, he concedes that music, or the satisfaction it gives him, has an actual money-value. If he gives half a dollar to hear a lecture, he declares by his act that the satisfaction, or inspiration, or instruction which the lecture yields him is worth half a dollar in money. If he pays a hundred dollars a year for the purpose of hearing a preacher, he recognizes a money-value in preaching, considered with direct reference to himself and his family. There is, then, an actual and well recognized money-value in the satisfactions and acquisitions which come to society immediately through its institutions. We pay out our money, and we get for it a kind of good which we cannot re-convert into money, but which we recognize as worth the money it costs us in the market. Indeed, the value which we attach to this good is measured by the dollars it costs far more than we are generally aware. We talk about free churches, and free schools, and free libraries; but if these were all free—free as air, or water, everywhere—society would be impoverished by them. People do not prize a blessing which costs them nothing, nor care for an institution whose burdens they do not feel. If all these institutions, which do such service for society, should be placed where they would cost society nothing, they would die of inanition.

I have thus discovered to you two distinct and independently competent rewards for all that is expended in the establishment of social institutions. The first is a return in kind, of dollars and cents: a community is actually and demonstrably worth more money after having sacrificed generously for the ordinary institutions of Christian society, than it was before. The second is a reward, in money-value, of the good which these institutions were established to secure, in their direct and immediate result: it is a reward which society feels that it is profited by accepting in place of its money. Yet there is a third reward, not much considered in the expenditure, greater and better than these.

Society, by intelligent sacrifice, not only wins a reward in material good and passing intellectual and spiritual satisfaction, but it builds up for itself a character and a culture, which increase its value to itself and the world. Society grows rich in social wealth, as its sources of satisfaction are multiplied and deepened, and its power and influence are extended. The more society pays wisely for its higher good, the more capacity it has for the reception, enjoyment, and dissemination of that good. Let us, for illustration, take two men, representatives of classes. One is a man of wealth, who hoards his money, or spends it stingily or selfishly. The other is one who spends freely of his means, for the culture of his brain and his heart. The sole satisfaction of one is in accumulating and keeping money. The other delights in intellectual pursuits, in the gratification of his tastes, in the exercise and culture of his religious nature, in all those things which inspire, feed, satisfy, and build up that which is his manhood. Tell me, which of these two men is of the more value to himself? Plainly he who possesses the best and the largest number of sources of satisfaction. If these two men could possibly exchange places with each other, the miser would make an infinite gain, and the man would make an infinite loss. The man is worth more to himself than the miser, because his sources of satisfaction are better, are more varied and numerous, are perfectly reliable, are inalienable, and are constantly deepening and extending. What is true of an individual is true of society. Society becomes rich in power, rich in sources of satisfaction, rich in character, rich in influence, and of value to itself and the world, according to the amount of its sacrifices for those institutions on whose prosperity the progress of society mainly depends. There can never be good society without good social institutions, and there can be no good social institutions without sacrifice.

I ask you to look at this largess of recompense—this threefold reward, touching and enriching every interest, and then be mean in any expenditure for social good if you can.

Thus far in this discussion, even when treating society as an organic, independent entity, I have spoken of this law mainly as it applies to the individual life of men. There is a broader view of the law, remaining to be presented; and this covers its relation to the national life. The painter who composes a picture that is to cover a broad canvas, paints a small one first, which he calls "a study;" the architect who designs a cathedral, draws it first upon a small scale: and both painter and architect do this that they may keep their masses of detail within limits which the eye can embrace at a glance. We, too, shall find it for our advantage, before undertaking to get a view of a nation as a grand, organic life, to study some smaller kindred life—such, for instance, as we may find in a great city.

A great city is a huge living creature, with life and breath and motives, and power and pride and destiny. Its being is just as distinct as that of a man. If we could be lifted above it, and obtain, not a bird's-eye view, but a God's-eye view of it, we should see its arteries throbbing with the majestic currents of life, pushed out from its centre to its remotest circumference, and returning through a multitude of avenues; fleets of winged messengers and ministers hanging and fluttering upon its wave-washed borders like a fringe; breath of steam and smoke rising from its lungs; food received by cargoes, and offal discharged by countless hidden estuaries into the all-hiding and all-purifying sea; grand forces of animal life and grander forces of art and nature harnessed to ceaseless service; couriers of fire flashing forth on their way to other cities, or returning from them with freights of life and treasure at their heels; and, over all, a robe of august architectural beauty, broidered with the thoughts of the ages, and garnished with the greenery of parks and lawns. And this body, embracing all the varieties of human and animal life, and all the matter and material forces whose form and movements are apparent to the eye, is a living organism, and has a soul. Descending into it, we shall find it the subject of laws which it makes, and laws which it does not make. We shall find it a network of interests, with congeries of interests, acting and reacting upon one another. We shall find it with a moral character and a moral influence. We shall find it with a heart, will, and culture, peculiarities of disposition and genius and taste, just as distinct among the great cities of the world as those of a great man among the great men of the world. What a contrast of individuality and character do the two words London and Paris suggest! Light and darkness convey ideas hardly more diverse. New York, Boston, Philadelphia, Baltimore, Chicago, Cincinnati—how distinct the individuality which each of these words represents to us! Bring before your imagination six great men, and you shall not find them more different in all that goes to make up their characteristic manhood, than these cities are in all that constitutes their individuality. They are, I have no doubt, in the eye of God, organic creations, made up of an aggregate of humanity and human powers, peculiarities, and possessions, which have an interest, as such, independent of the individuals which compose them. They have interests that over-ride personal interests, subordinating the man to the city, and a life and development of their own.

It is said that the particles in the human body are changed every seven years. This can almost be said of a city, regarding men and women as the constituent units. Certainly these units are changed every generation, but still the city lives. A man falls dead upon the sidewalk, or dies quietly in his bed. Does the city feel it? His funeral will make part of the life of to-morrow. A few tears around a bier, a few clods upon a grave, a little family draped in black, and new life rushes to fill the place made vacant by his departure! Day brings its roar and night its rest, and there is no pause; there is not even a shudder at the extinction of a life. Twenty generations will pass away, and the great city which we see to-day will be greater still. The giant will be more gigantic, though not a life remains that even remembers the life of to-day.

Thus, in this picture of a city, we have the study for a picture of a nation. I use the word nation, because a nation in healthful life cannot be considered apart from the country which is its dwelling-place, and because the word brings us closer to humanity than the word country.

Take this study now—so small that we can measure it and comprehend its details with a glance of the eye—and spread it upon the canvas. We have here a Colossus, the constituent units of which are men, certainly, but men in cities, men in villages, men in townships, counties, States. Here is a grand organic being, with a range of life reaching through long millenniums; with a character and a manifestation of life peculiar to itself, and just as different from the other nations of the world as London is different from Paris, or Boston from New York, or Henry Clay from Daniel Webster, or Abraham Lincoln from Jefferson Davis. As we look down upon it, we find navigable rivers and lines of railroad and canal taking the place of streets; continental stretches of coast haunted by sail and steam, instead of wharves and harbor bustle; universal production and transportation in place of limited trade; instead of wreathed smoke, the breath of climates, drawn in in storms, and expired in mists that drape the sky with the glory of the clouds; and, shaming into insignificance the sorry piles of brick and stone which we call architecture, grand mountain-ranges, "rock-ribbed and ancient as the sun;" fertile valleys that hold within their broad bosoms milk for a continent; vast forests that bury their feet in the mould of uncounted centuries; lakes that glow alone like gems, or stretch across a continent their chain of silver; and scattered over all, informing all, making its mark upon all, appropriating all, a vast organized human life. This is the nation—body, and soul, and belongings. This is the grandest organized life that the world knows. The life of hundreds of millions is swallowed up in this life. It draws into itself the blood of a thousand generations, and tinctures that blood with its own quality—gives it its own law. What makes a man an Englishman?—birth in England? What constitutes an American?—generation under a Western sky? Why is a Frenchman a Frenchman?—because he drew his first breath in France? Nay. These men are not born into England, America, and France, so much as these countries are born into these men. This great, all-subordinating national life begets and bears its own; so that, meet whom you may where you may, you shall find his national mark upon him, and all over him, and all through him—coloring his skin, characterizing his frame, tinting his eyes, and, in the large view, determining the character of his mental constitution. Climate, food, institutions, pursuits, religion—all contribute to make him what he is.

Now this great creature which we call a nation—one of the gigantic units in God's universe—which, in its aggregate of influences, colors and characterizes the individual life of which it is composed, is, in turn, colored and characterized by that life. Its action is the expression of the sum of individual motives, and its character the sum of individual character. The sum of all Americans makes America, and America makes Americans what they are.

We shall find that a nation's constitution and law of life are at least fairly illustrated by those of the individual man. A nation has grand material interests; and it may become mean and miserly like a man. It has lusts and passions, and it may commit all crimes to gratify its greed for power and its passion for glory. It may be so fond of ease that it will permit its liberties to be stolen from it. It may have a will so stubborn and unreasonable that it will sacrifice for its gratification peace and prosperity, in quarrels with other nations. It may have the vice of pride, so that it will take offence at every fancied insult, and be haughty and insolent in all its intercourse. It may be under the control of the lowest grade of motives; and, on the other hand, it may bow loyally to the highest. It may hold wealth subordinate and subsidiary to those institutions and policies which tend to popular competence and comfort. It may sacrifice its passion for power to national comity, and the desire for the peace and the good-will of the world. It may subordinate its love of ease to the vigilant guardianship and defence of its rights. It may give up its will and its pride for the security of its peace and prosperity, or from higher motives of Christian principle.

In the case of a nation, as in that of a man, an inferior possession is to be sacrificed as the price of a superior good, and this superior good can be had at this price, and cannot be had without it. Whatever of true glory has been won by any nation of the earth; whatever great advance has been made by any nation in that which constitutes a high Christian civilization, has been always at the cost of sacrifice—has cost the price marked upon it in God's inventory of national good.

Now what are the items in this divine schedule? I will name some of them; and first, freedom—freedom of person and pursuit, freedom of thought and worship, freedom of expression by type and tongue. Where freedom is wanting, the highest national good is wanting, for it is not only a good in itself, but it is the condition of all other national good. Without it, there is nothing in national life that is not base. After the freedom of the citizen, intelligence and virtue; then good, competent, Christian rulers, selected because they are competent and Christian, and because they secure justice and humanity in the administration of law, and purity in office. Then peace and security, without which no national possession, high or low, is valuable. And with security and peace and a Christian administration of law, a studied and consistent policy which shall encourage all that is desirable in morals, education, literature, and art. Then fraternal concord, and harmony of sections and interests. I do not need to mention a humane, honorable, and Christian character, for it is alike the source and sequence of all this desiderated good. Still less do I need to mention patriotism—the warm and devoted love of all the nation's children for their government and their fatherland; for such a nation as this must be made of patriots, who glory in their national name, and who are willing to sacrifice everything to that which is truly national glory.

All the good which has been named, and all that is related to it, or associated with it, has a price; and this price must be paid, or the good cannot be secured. Glance with me, for a moment, at one or two points of our early national history, that we may have convenient illustration. Look at that little band of pilgrims that planted their feet on Plymouth Rock, nearly two centuries and a half ago. Watch them throughout the trials of that first winter, when half of them laid down their lives; and watch them still through all their subsequent struggles with the native tribes. See them winning their bread by the hardest, lodging in rude cabins, and ground almost into the earth by small economies, and, at the same time, planting schoolhouses and building churches. Mark how every act of their lives was a sacrifice—how every foundation-stone of this national temple of ours was laid in sacrifice. Mark, further, how whole generations of associated colonial life built in sacrifice upon these foundations, cementing the whole structure with sweat and tears and blood. Did it pay? I do not ask now whether it paid them. That question has already been disposed of. Regarding the nation as an organic individual, I ask whether these sacrifices secured any commensurate national good? Was it a wise and profitable investment on the part of the nation? There is but one answer to this question.

If there is one fact that shines out with unquestioned radiance from the history of all time, it is, that by the pangs of that mother-period—as necessary, as unavoidable, as the pangs of human birth—was the fairest nation born that Time counts among her children. All down these two long centuries has the nation been reaping in joy what then she sowed in tears. There was not a hardship endured, not a drop of blood shed, not a life laid down, in vain. There was not one sacrifice for principle, not one unselfish effort for the general good, not one treasure of time, or ease, or vitality surrendered, that miscarried of its purpose.

Still later came those sacrifices that won our national independence. Independence was a good that had a price, and a heavy price it proved to be. Those brave, enduring, patient three millions paid it. Seven years of war, for what? What was a little tax on tea? What mattered the stamp on paper? It did not amount to much—not a thousandth part as much as a war would cost. Ah! but a principle was involved. Here was taxation without representation—tribute demanded, and a voice in the government and even respectful petitions denied—and this was oppression. Popular rights were not only unrecognized, but trampled upon. The colonies which had already sacrificed much to establish their life as colonies, determined to be independent of a power that abused them, and bent themselves patiently to the task of paying the price which their independence would cost them. Seven years of war! Seven years of blood, of hardship, of crippled prosperity, ending in total financial wreck; seven years of weeping and watching, of scanty food and scantier clothing; seven years of anxiety and difference in the public councils, and of quarrels with public servants, even the spotless Washington being accused of the grossest political crimes; seven years of vigilance against the intrigues of tories, who worked in the interest of the enemy, and clamored for peace; seven years of what seemed to the observing nations of the world to be the hopeless struggle of a colonial handful with the most gigantic military and naval power of the earth.

The end finally came. The price was all paid to the last drop of blood and the last tear—to the last hardship and heart-ache; and the coveted boon was won. From this long struggle the nation rose a bankrupt in everything but that one prize it had sacrificed every material good to obtain. It was independent, and had its destiny in its own hands. Was the new possession worth its cost? Let the history of the last eighty years answer. We have grown from three to more than thirty millions. Never in the history of the world has a nation had such enormous growth, or such marvellous prosperity. The oppressed of all nations have found an asylum with us. It is no idle boast, but sober fact, that we stand to-day, as a nation, without a rival in the world in general intelligence, morality, and material resources.

The American nation developed in its symmetry from the point of its independence. Colonial life was childhood; independent life was manhood. If we, for a moment, suppose that this price had not been paid, we shall get a suggestion of the measure of good we should miss. It would reduce our thirty millions to ten, and make a contemptible Canada of our magnificent empire. Time would fail me to indicate the variety of good which the nation has received from the sacrifices of the Revolution, and imagination could not compass the amount. It is enough that none can deny that the reward for these sacrifices has been unspeakably munificent.

These illustrations are two, among the thousands furnished by the history of the world. I choose them because they need no treatment. You are familiar with all the facts, and these facts teach us that this law of cost and compensation, beginning, as we have seen, in the life of the individual man, runs up through all the social and civil organizations and institutions of men; that all those treasures which a nation holds dearest—its freedom, unity, independence, peace, security, prosperity, character, and position—have their price in the free sacrifice of inferior good; that those treasures are not only won at a cost but kept at a cost; and that no national sacrifice can possibly be made, in the right spirit, for high ends, that does not, by an immutable law of God, procure a grand reward.

Give and get; sacrifice and win; expend and grow rich; minister and be helped—this is the lesson of our lecture; and it is a lesson necessary to be learned before the first step can be taken in individual, social, and national progress. For our own good, God puts us on a business footing with Himself; and he is the only reliable paymaster. Do not be deceived by appearances. If payment does not come at once, in return for a sacrifice, it is because you have only paid an instalment. Italy paid for her unity in instalments. Rome has made one instalment of the price for her liberty. When the price is all paid, she will have it. Hungary has paid one instalment. Wait until she pays another, and another, and perhaps still another, and we shall learn, at last, the price of her independence.

As I come to my closing page, I cannot choose but think of him whom the nation loved—the pure, the wise, the gentle, the true—stricken from his high place by the hand of the assassin—every man's father, brother, and friend—the sweetest, noblest, costliest sacrifice ever laid upon the altar of freedom. I cannot choose but think of half a million of men who, alive four years ago, sleep in the soldier's grave to-day. They perished, some of them, beneath the fiery crest of battle, some of them after the wave had passed, and only the stars saw and pitied them, some of them in hospitals, some in ambulances, some of them in the sea—all of them for their country and its holy cause, with a patriotic enthusiasm that rose to a sublime faith in their country's future, and a prophecy of its permanent glory and peace. I see, too, a million women draped in black—mothers, daughters, sisters, wives, lovers, of those who have given their lives to the great cause. There is mourning in the land—mourning all over the land. Not a battle has been fought that did not shake the nation's breast with one great sob of sorrow. I see a great sacrifice of treasure—time, industry, money, vitality, ease—more than I can compute; more, indeed, than will ever be computed. I see a long period of taxation for ourselves and our children; but I see beyond all these, piled quietly against a golden sky, mountains of compensation, bright with the hues of a glorious peace, and holding within their purple bosoms treasures for the endowment of all the coming generations of men.

ART AND LIFE.

PRIMITIVE art must have been as humble, and its character as simple, as the life from which it sprang and to which it ministered. It was the creature of rude utility, having relation only to man's material necessities—to the dressing and keeping of a garden, and the stitching of fig-leaves. It was entirely natural and rational that Jabal, Adah's first-born, should be the father of such as dwell in tents and have cattle, and that her later son, Jubal, should be the father of such as handle the harp and organ; though I doubt not that Tubal-Cain wrought brass and iron, and was a favorite in the family for a good many years before Jubal effected much in instrumental music.

It may be presumed that the arts necessary for securing food and raiment and shelter were those which had first development. They lay nearest the outreaching life of a new race. They were born of the natural, animal want to which they ministered.

They were the first things on which the instinct of self-preservation laid its hand. Ideas were an after-growth, and their expression in sound, and form, and color, and language, an after-fact. When Jubal played his first tune, he opened the golden gate to a new realm. Music was a thing of the soul—a rose-lipped shell that murmured of the eternal sea—a strange bird singing the songs of another shore. In this first expression of the soul, high art had its birth. The art which had preceded it had its origin and end in the material; high art began and ended in the spiritual; and this later development is so exalted above the former, that we make the generic title specific, and call it Art.

I propose to address you upon art and life—art as the expression of life, and life as the end of art. My first proposition is, that God and his creation, or God and nature, are the first facts in all life and all art. Nature is the expression of God's self and of God's life; legitimate art is the expression of that which is godlike in man and in man's life. I only need to assume, what you will all admit, that man is God's child, bearing His image, and partaking of His essence, to show that the expression of himself and of his life, when both are in their normal estate, must necessarily be after the order of nature and in the style of nature. If that which is greatest and best in man be like

God, then that which is greatest and best in art must be like nature. It is from this fact, and from no other fact, that nature becomes in some respects a standard by which to test the forms and qualities of art; that is, of the highest art, which is essential creation.

To develop my idea of art in its higher manifestations, I begin at its lower. God expresses an idea in a beautiful landscape; man, admiring it, expresses himself by painting its picture. God makes a man of bone and brawn and blood; man imitates the form as closely as he may in marble. God builds a forest, and man repeats the sweep of its arches and the lines of its tracery in cathedrals. In the rolling thunder and the hoarse cataract, God speaks to man with audible voice, and writes his thoughts in woods and mountain-ranges, and stars and grass and flowers. So man speaks his thoughts to men by audible sounds and visible signs. God makes instruments of music, and His great life plays through them. The sounding shore, the gurgling brook, the roaring storm, the plashing waterfall—beasts, birds, and insects—weave their separate melodies into august harmonies. Man, too, makes instruments of music, and breathes through them the melodies and the harmonies of his life.

So far, man expresses the life in him through his faculty of imitation. He simply takes in from nature, and gives out what he receives. Nature is his nurse and his teacher. She speaks, and he faintly and imperfectly repeats her words. At this point, what we call talent in man stops; beyond this point talent never goes. It may flutter and mount with many a graceful gyration, but it cannot surpass it. Genius may imitate, and even in imitation show its divinity; but it goes alone into the higher realms of art. Genius only can create and compose. Nature may educate and correct genius; but its expression is the expression of a life unborrowed from nature—a life instituted, informed, and inspired by God Himself. If genius lays nature under tribute, it is for materials—not inspiration. It chooses from nature, and moulds to its will; it assimilates nature to itself, and then utters it as its own expression. Nature is the master of talent; genius is the master of nature. Genius acts from the centre to the circumference, as a power of creation and order; talent gathers from the circumference, and utters only what it gathers. Genius originates ideas and invents forms; talent adopts ideas and imitates forms. Talent is instructed; genius is inspired.

My second proposition is, that nature, which is an expression of God's life, is not an end in itself, but is addressed to life, and has its end in life. The whole structure of the universe—the blue expanse above our heads, the sun, the moon, the constellations, the atmosphere which invests us, the great ocean, trackless, fathomless, boundless; all of inanimate nature that we see —is utterly without significance and without value, save as it relates to life—the life to which it ministers and from which it proceeds. Not only inorganic but organic nature, in all its subordinate forms, relates to a life above and beyond itself. The earth feeds the grass, and the grass feeds the ox, and the ox feeds the animal life of man, and the animal life of man serves the higher life of the human soul. We find life rejoicing in every element of nature—swimming in the sea, flying through the air, and rejoicing on the land. Even the old rocks of far-retired ages are records of the great fact that they were that life might be; and they even now bow their Titan shoulders, with patience and purpose, to sustain the burden of that which lives in the sunlight above them.

There is not an atom of matter, not a form of beauty and grace, not a star in heaven nor a flower on the earth, not a rill that cleaves the sod nor a sea that chafes the shore, that does not appeal to life for the justification of its existence.

Thus God becomes transitive through nature, into life. There is no such thing in nature as beauty for beauty's sake; all beauty is for man's sake. The procession of the seasons, the phenomena of revolution and change, all the magnificent machinery operative in the natural world, are the ministry of the life of God to the life of men. We drink that life from these cups. When I take a flower into my hand, and mark its wonderful beauty of form and color, and inhale its fragrance, I know that it is a thought of God expressed to me, and that one end of its value is upheld by God's thought and the other end by mine—that, save as the expression of one life, and the apprehension and appropriation of another life, conjoined, it is as valueless as utter nothing.

Upon this basis I rest my third proposition, and from this I propose to develop the lesson of the hour. This proposition is, that art is not an end in itself, and that it cannot be justified, save as it ministers to a life beyond itself. In other terms, art intransitive, without an object, is a monster, illegitimate in its origin and unjustifiable in its existence. A work of art, in any department of creation and composition, that has no ministry, is either a thing utterly without value, or a thing of discord and mischief. It is not enough that art be true to nature, for nature is not an end—it is a means. It is not enough that the artist be true to himself, for he is not the end of art. It is not enough that he be true to art, which simply means being true to certain conventional ideas and arbitrary rules, for art is not the end of itself. Art has a mission to life, and can only be true art when true to life through a well-administered purpose. The question which every true artist will ask himself before he undertake expression will be, "What have I, in me, as the development of my life, which is susceptible of embodiment, and which I can embody, in a form of art that shall minister to the growth or the wealth of other life?"

Thus I take the standard of art out of the hand of the artist, out of the hand of art, and out of the hand of nature, and place it in the hand of life, and bid the artist be true to that. He is not to bow to art, for art is his servant. He is not to bow to nature, for nature is God's servant. He is not to bow to himself, for he is life's servant. He is to bow to life—that to which he owes service—that which is necessary to give to art the slightest significance and value.

The question of ultimate purpose becomes, then, the very first question in all sound and rational criticism. Primarily to be settled is the question of intent upon one side of a work of art, and of legitimate or actual effect upon the other. If the intent and the effect both be good, then the existence of the work is justified, and the work itself may be approached critically from both sides;—from both sides, I say, for the life of the author and the life of the age or the people that he addresses, furnish the only standpoints from which a work of art may legitimately be criticised. The justification of a work of art existing only in its intent and effect, criticism may only decide whether the intent have its best possible embodiment in the work—whether the work embrace perfectly the artist's idea, and whether the end secured be the highest to be secured by the idea. Thus, if these principles are genuine, are laid aside the arbitrary rules of the schools, the notions and conventionalisms of a pestiferous dilettanti, the tests and standards born of the usages of the masters; and the very soul and substance of criticism is brought within the compass of a nutshell, and the comprehension of all.

To illustrate: we find spread over our heads a canopy of blue. If, for the nonce, we assume the interpretation of the purposes of the Creator, this color was selected through the reach of His contrivance to present to the eye a soft and pleasant tint to meet its outlook into space. This sky is a work of nature, marvelously beautiful. The intent is good; the end is good; and its existence is justified. Now let us approach this work as critics. We are now ready to ask whether blue, of all the colors of the spectrum, is the best to paint a sky with—whether blue, of all those colors, is the most agreeable to the eye when looking into space, or whether some other color, or combination of colors, would be better. If we can prove that some other color would be better for this purpose, then we can prove that the work, as a work of nature, is imperfect. But no: we say that it is the embodiment of

God's best thought, in God's best way, for the best achievement of a great and good purpose, relating to the life of His children. This conclusion would, of course, follow the critical examination of every other work of nature with which we are acquainted. And this is my key not only to all art but to all criticism.

I have exhibited these principles, as the ground of my justification in declaring the prevalent ideas of art to be mainly a mass of crude conceits and inconsistent notions. I have exhibited them, that the people may assume for themselves a rational judgment of art, and enter upon a domain from which they have hitherto been excluded—upon which they have not even presumed to enter. Hitherto, this domain has been the domain of mystery. Art itself looms upon the popular apprehension as a phantom—a great, shadowy, sublime something, into whose presence only a favored few may come; into whose counsels and secrets only the world's *élite* may be admitted. It cannot be approached through any of the ordinary channels of knowledge. Science, laden with the spoils of nature's arcana, stops embarrassed before this phantom, and bows and retires. Philosophy confronts it with boldness and determination, only to see it vanish into the impalpable and the incomprehensible. Wisdom, that has gathered into its storehouse the wealth of all lands and all languages, may not even give it good-morrow without betraying the accent of the unsophisticated. Only those whose eyes have been anointed may see; only those whose ears have been touched may hear; only the mind that has been miraculously quickened may conceive the marvels of a world the brightest glories of which found their birth in the inspirations of paganism, and were addressed to an age of sensuality and shame.

Homage to the old, the useless, and the arbitrary, is the price of that which is called the artistic sense. At the shrine of this absurd trinity, Christian manhood, truth, and purity must kneel with votive offerings. On its altar must they sacrifice their first-born sense of the tasteful and truthful, in order to procure a vision of that which is inscrutable to natural eyes, and a love of that which appeals to no natural appetite or aptitude. . So true is this that the conviction is almost universal that artistic sense, or artistic taste, is a thing never inborn, but always acquired—that it is itself a thing of art, or something which proceeds from art. The multitude acknowledge that they know nothing of art. They see an old painting that they would hesitate to give a dollar for at an auction-shop, sold for a hundred guineas—"a phantom of delight" to critics and connoisseurs—and they shake their heads in profound self-distrust. They see a select few go into raptures over the long-drawn, dreary iterations and reiterations of a symphony, and confess that they know nothing of music. They read a literary performance which stirs and inspires them—which elevates and enlarges them—which fills them with delight and satisfaction; and are shocked and chagrined to learn, at the end of the month, by the shrewd critic of the review, that they have been so vulgar as to be pleased with something that tramples upon every rule of art.

So the people sit down, and heave the sigh of humble despair. Art is something beyond them—something above them. It is high; they cannot attain unto it. It is profound; they may not fathom it. Now this idea of art, as it is held alike by the initiated and the uninitiated, has its birth in distrust of the great truth that art is alike without meaning and without value save as it ministers to life by direct purpose; the great truth that all true art is but a life-bearer from him who utters to him who receives. Art, as I have said before, is not an end in itself; and the only reason why art has done no more for the civilization and exaltation of mankind is that artists, and the self-constituted arbiters of art, have hedged it in from the life of mankind. They actually put a work of art under ban which bears a mission to life, for the reason that it bears a mission. In their view, a work of art is actually prostituted by the burden of a mission. If a lesson of life is to be conveyed, they would let the schoolmaster and parson bear it. It must not profane the backs of the dapper gentlemen who do the sublime and beautiful for them. The art-critic of to-day contemns and derides a work which has any intent in it beyond the satisfaction of the critical judgment of himself and his precious fraternity.

You will readily apprehend, from this train of reasoning and remark, the ground of my claim that the people—the great world of hungry life—are the only competent judges of art. They recognize, know, and love the hand that feeds them—the hand that ministers to their want; and they are the grand court of final judgment on all art and its authors. No artist ever won an immortality that was worth the winning, that he did not win from the people, by a ministry through direct purpose to the life of the people. This is no new doctrine, even if it be not commonly accepted. "The light of the public square will test its value," said Michel Angelo to the young sculptor whose work he was examining; confessing, master of masters as he was, his own incompetence to decide whether it should be immortal.

You will remember that fifteen or twenty years ago two musical artists—players upon the same instrument—visited this country respectively to make a professional tour. One was the pet of the musical critics; and he was undoubtedly more thoroughly versed in the technicalities and intricacies of his art, and possessed more of manual facility, than his rival. We were told that he was true to his art—truer by far than his competitor—and that the latter was a charlatan and a trickster. Well, this charlatan breathed out upon the people the life that was in him—the very pathos and passion of his soul; and the people drank it, and were blest. One of these artists was a man of talent and education; the other, a man of genius and inspiration. Vieux Temps returned across the Atlantic, chagrined and disgusted; Ole Bull remained to win the admiration and the plaudits of a continent.

Every year or two the musical critics are exercised with ecstacy by the miraculous performances—the runs and roulades, the trills and tricks—of some imported contralto or soprano, and bemoan the low state of art that hinders them from winning attention to that which they miscall art; but when a pure and generous life, a noble womanhood, a soul of strength and sweetness—gushing with life in every expression, and sympathetic with life in every fibre—breathes through the lips of Jenny Lind, the people drink the nectar with greedy lips, till it overflows in tears. The immortality of Grecian art sprang from its truth to the highest life of its time, and of its ministry to that life. The Christian art of later centuries addressed also the highest life that lived, and the highest department of that life.

The entire artist-life of Raphael was devoted to feeding the highest religious life of his country and his age. Hardly a picture of this master remains that was not born of religious inspiration, and intended to reproduce in the beholder the exaltation out of which it proceeded. Raphael is immortal. The people did not ask then, and they do not ask now, what were the characteristics of his school—whether this or that master modified the development of his genius—whether he learned this thing of one and that thing of another. They know that he gave his most exalted life to them embodied in forms of art; that those forms enter into their life, elevating their conceptions and exalting their sensibilities, and that they have received a blessing.

For the illustration of my position, I have dwelt thus far among the confines, the suburbs, of art. I have spoken only of that which resides in sound and form and color. Music may be divine, but its living is its dying. It gushes, and is drunk up by the thirsty silences. It bursts in blooming harmony, and the whole flower is at once exhaled. The great song that entranced the ears of the simple shepherds of Bethlehem went back into heaven with the vocal host. The literal sentence was saved, but the pearls that glorified the sacred string were returned to their casket. All that is material perishes. Pigments fade, canvas decays, and marble crumbles. The long path of art is strewn with ruins. Thus the great aggregate of life that in the ages gone has sought embodiment in form and color will waste away, age after age, until only hollow names remain, to be read as we read the names on gravestones set over life and beauty turned to dust. It is only words that live, immortal representatives of everything evolved by the processes of thought, the experiences of life, and the operations of the imagination. The temple of art is built of words. Painting and sculpture and music are but the blazon of its windows, borrowing all their significance from the light, and suggestive only of the temple's uses.

To me, words are a mystery and a marvel. There is no point where man so nearly touches God as in creation by words. There is no point where art so nearly touches nature as when it appears in the form of words. What are these words? They are the very nothing out of which God spoke creation into being. "Let there be light," said the Creator; and there was light. It came of those words; and it comes of ours as well. He spoke to perception; we speak to imagination. We pronounce the word light, and the imagination sees the atmosphere flooded with sunshine. We pronounce the word night, and straight the sky is studded with stars. Words paint the flower beyond the faculty and facility of the pencil. Words weave and wind the very harmonies of heaven. There is nothing that man knows, there is nothing that the heart has felt, there is nothing the imagination can conceive, that may not, and does not, find in words its highest revelation. Ah! this is impalpable, invisible, plastic nihility—this formless mother of forms—this vitalized nothingness—this matrix of all being—words! When the artist works with these, he works with that by which God made the universe; and there is no genuine embodiment of the highest life of man which passes so directly into the life of other men as that which takes the form of words. The pencil and the chisel are but clumsy things by the side of the pen—the choicest and noblest of all instruments ever placed in human fingers.

In sculpture and picture, man speaks to man by signs, to which the receiver of the utterance is unaccustomed. Into those channels of expression the popular life does not flow; but words are familiar—the dies in which all daily life and thought are fashioned. Through words, life flows freely and exactly into life. Picture and sculpture are fixed and formal, and strive to make us understand them by attitude and expressive dumb-show. Words are vocal and vital, active and flexible, and enter the door of our perception whether we will or no. Words, in short, are not only the highest representatives of thought and life, but they are the representatives, the sources, the expounders, and the preservers of all that is highest in picture and sculpture.

I approach this field of art with profound interest, for the first book upon which I lay my hand is the Bible. In this book God condescends to speak to men in words. Even He must come to this. The burning stars, the everlasting hills, the infinite sea, forests and streams and flowers—all his sublime sculpture, and infinitely varied picture, even when informed with vitality and instinct with action—are not sufficient for His purpose, not sufficient for His self-expression, and not sufficient for our satisfaction. He comes to convey to us something more of His life than He can convey through nature. He comes to us with a mission. Now, I ask, will He be simply didactic, or will He convey His life to us through forms of art? If we examine the volume critically, we shall find that He embodies all His highest truth in these forms. The life He would convey is moulded into the form of human life, endowed with the spirit and the motives of humanity, and then passed over to us. He does not say in two words, "be patient," but He builds the trial and triumph of Job into an exquisite form of art; and Ruth inculcates the lesson of filial love and duty in the sweetest pastoral that lives in language. He does not read to us dry lessons of morality, but he gives those lessons vitality in parables, in which "a certain man" is made to live what He would have us learn. The sweet singer of Israel pours out his life to us in Psalms —divine life breathed into him, and breathed through him—and we drink in that life to feed the springs of our devotion. On the wings of exaltation and adoration furnished by the art of the Psalms, the praise and the thanksgiving of Christendom rise to heaven.

I ask myself, why this huge volume of poems and allegories, and songs and narratives, and parables and pastorals? Why this waste of type and paper? Why all this wonderfully varied machinery for the conveyance of a definite number of simple and sublime truths? Why this exhibition of the same truths in wonderfully varied forms? I find the answer, and I find it only, in my theory of the mission of art; and I claim the Bible as a divine recognition of the fact that art is the ordained vehicle for the conveyance of that which is divine in the life of man to the life of men.

True art is that which is true in life, organized in the idea, in its relations to human motives—abstract truth, assimilated to life, and thus made food for life. Abstract truth is no better fitted to feed the soul's life than the abstract elements which enter into the composition of the body are fitted to feed the bodily life. Chemistry will tell me all the elements contained in the food I eat; but if I take my food at the hand of chemistry, I shall die. Vitality must organize these elements, and then my vitality will feed upon them. So, if my soul try to live on abstract truth, it will starve. I cannot take my spiritual food from the hand of spiritual chemistry. It must be organized for me by a vital process—it must be lived in fact or in idea—before it can come into healthful relation to my spiritual vitality. I cannot take even God Himself until He is manifested to me in human life.

Thus, this book of books is a depository of the highest truth, all assimilated to life by the processes of art. Out of this exhaustless magazine of all that is divine in human life do the nations of Christendom draw their food. Forth from this has sprung our civilization. Out of this germinal mass have grown and will grow all good institutions; and by it is human life to be wholly regenerated. We find in this book that when God works in the field of art, He works precisely as He does in that of nature—with direct reference to life. He never makes art an end of itself. As in nature, so in revelation, there is no such thing as beauty for beauty's sake; all beauty is for man's sake. Every form of art contained in the Bible is but a vehicle for the conveyance of divine humanity to a life that needs it.

But we leave the Bible, and take up a humbler volume—a volume which I suppose the majority of literary men would conspire to place upon the lowest shelf of art, and open the pages of The Pilgrim's Progress. From my point of vision, you will see that as a work of art this book must be regarded as one of the most remarkable ever written by mortal pen. More truly than any uninspired book with which I am acquainted does it spring out of life, and answer the end of art—passing into other life. An illiterate tinker sits in Bedford jail, and embodies in an allegory his own religious life. In this allegory he gives his highest self-expression—organizes the truth that he has lived, for the nourishment of other life. It will be seen that the origin of the work is strictly legitimate, and that the intent is, beyond question, beneficent. What has been its effect? It has been the grateful food of millions. It has been translated into a multitude of languages, and will live immortally in the heart and life of Christendom. Yet Bunyan did not know what artistic sense meant. He was innocent of all knowledge of classical models; but he had something in him, knew what he wanted to do with it, invented the best possible way of doing it, and did it. Many of the greatest minds, though entangled by false theories of art, have not failed to recognize the angel in his pilgrim form, and have rendered him just tribute. When Southey and Cowper, Radcliffe and Franklin, Coleridge and Johnson, Jamieson and Macaulay, bring their offerings to such a shrine, the author may well spare the worship of smaller minds. I grant that, as a work of art, this great vehicle of Bunyan's life is roughly finished, but that may well be rough which comes from the hand of a giant.

We now come to the consideration of an acknowledged master—crowned by the critics and the people alike as the world's master. What is Shakspere's secret? What was the material with which he wrought? Life—always life. In some, perhaps many, respects, he is indeed the world's master. More than any other man has he drunk in, assimilated and organized in forms of art the life of the world. The king and the courtier, the prince and the peasant, the fop and the fool; manhood and womanhood pure and simple and beautiful—manhood and womanhood black with impurity, passion, and craft; every form of life that came within the range of his far-sweeping vision—he appropriated to his uses. These he associated and informed with life and motive; and then he embodied in language the dramas which their life played in his wonderful brain. This is the life he has transmitted to us; and in it, and in it alone, resides his power over us. Bunyan and Shakspere are very different; yet both are masters. Shakspere was a highly vitalized medium through which the life of humanity passed into artistic organization for the use of other life; Bunyan was a medium hardly less vitalized, through which the divine life passed into form for the nourishment of the same life.

Though the field is tempting, the lack of time forbids the further illustration of this point. I cannot leave it, however, without recalling for a moment my proposition that the people are the true judges of art, and that all immortality worth the winning must be won from the people. All the critics in the world cannot kill the Bible. All that philosophy and science and learning can do to effect this object has been done; but it is stronger to-day than ever before, because the people find a life in it which they need, and which they can find nowhere else. I speak of the book now simply as a collection of works of art, without reference to its origin. Bunyan was immortal long before the critics of art found it out. Shakspere would have been forgotten centuries ago if he had not had a ministry for the people. When the people will not come to the support of the critics—when they fail to find anything in a work of art which ministers to their growth and wealth—that work, in my judgment, is competently condemned. It answers no purpose in the earth. It has no apology for existence. A fictitious halo of glory may be thrown around it, and its author's name may descend to posterity in books, and a feeble and foolish dilettanti may make it the theme of encomium; but it is a dead thing, which must ultimately descend to a burial too profound for resurrection.

Although I have recognized with sufficient directness the popular want with relation to the ministry of art, I have failed to consider that want distinctly in the light of a demand which has a place in the basis of my theory. I have stated, as a general fact, that no man wins immortality in art save by ministering to the life of the people; but I have not stated that the demand for life at the hand of the artist helps to fix—nay, independently of everything else, fixes—the province, and defines the mission, of art. In the whole range of nature, every want has placed over against it an appropriate source of satisfaction. If there be a well of water in the desert, and a crowd of thirsty Arabs around it, the office of that well is defined by that thirst. So if a town need bread, and there be only one man who can bake it, that man's province and mission are as well defined by that want, as by the power and skill he has within him. If such a man should say, "I have nothing to do with this want—I did not make it; I am to be true to the highest faculties I possess, and the glory of my trade; I will make patty-cakes and pastry; if the people will not buy these, the worse for them; as for ministering to this clamor of popular want, I will do no such thing"—I say that if such a man

U of M

should say this, we should call him a fool or a madman—possibly worse names than these.

Now, in the consideration of this subject, I see before me two classes of men. One is comparatively small, but it is full of vitality, and rich with life. The other is large, and poor in these elements. The artists are opulent; the people are in poverty, and in need of the overflowing life which the artists possess. I know that there is no way for the administration of this life save through forms of art. "Give us of your wealth," say the people; "give it to us in a vehicle by means of which we may be enabled to appropriate the whole of it, for we are poor, and in need of that of which you possess an abundance." When I see and hear this, and learn that this want can only be supplied by the artist, I am left in no doubt touching the character of his mission, and the direction of his duty.

Mark how this appetite for life is pronounced—this need of life declared. Mark how the newspaper has become the universal fire-side companion—how its morning visit is as necessary for the satisfaction of a daily arising want, as the coffee and the rolls of the breakfast-table; and mark, too, how everything—marriages, deaths, and all—is read before the dry and didactic leader. Mark how the personalities of the press—kind or otherwise—are first devoured in the greedy appetite to get at the life of others. We may deplore this devotion to the newspaper, but it can neither be checked, nor diverted, until a better life can be drunk in from other sources. The newspaper is only fascinating and absorbing because it feeds better than the popularly available forms of art this demand for life.

Mark, too, the interest of old and wise men in the books written for children—books, by the way, the truest to the mission of art of any to be found in our literature. I do but give voice to the common experience in the assertion that a first-class juvenile is as interesting and as instructive to the mature mind as to the immature. The truths elucidated may be familiar —even trite; but the life in which they are cast ministers to this ever-open want, and confers a fresh vitality upon the truths themselves.

Rising into a higher range of literary art, we find almost the whole world engaged in novel-reading. Many of the wise and good shake their heads over it. Careful and conscientious parents place fiction under ban in their households. The pulpit fulminates against it, even if the church fail in terms to proscribe it. Signal instances of its sad effects upon the mind and the morals are portrayed in the issues of the Tract Society, but still the reading goes on; and from one to one hundred editions of every work find buyers and readers. If the novel is not read openly, it is read in secret; if not by sun-light, by gas-light; if not in the house, or under genial sanction, then in the barn, or under a green tree. Why all this swallowing of so much that is trash? Why this almost indiscriminate devotion to worth and worthlessness? Is this all from a debased or a morbid appetite? By no means. You will find the high and the low all agreed upon a work of fiction from the pen of genuine genius, true to its mission. Of living, active writers, Mr. Dickens and Mrs. Stowe will have the most convenient shelf of the library of him who reads "The Devil's Darning-Needle —a Tale of Love, Madness, and Suicide," as well as that of the man of high and chastened tastes.

Life! Life! This is the cry of the multitude—life, true and chaste and beautiful—life that shall nourish and enrich us, if we can get it, but life of some kind—life of any kind—rather than none. This great world of common life, bound to the work-bench, the farm, the counting-room, the four walls that inclose the domestic circle, the factory, the ceaseless routine of daily toil and care in every sphere, cries for the wealth of other life. It cannot go out, and gather life; so it eagerly grasps that which comes to it. It cannot mix in multitudes, and travel, and enter into varied society; so it must buy multitudes, and buy travel, and buy society, in books—so art must bring them into communion with life. This cry for life cannot be stifled. It can only be hushed by satisfaction. History, narrative, biography—all these—are laid under tribute in accordance with individual tastes for the supply of this want.

If you will go up and down this land, and, when you find him, place your hand upon the shoulder of the preacher who draws the largest audiences, has power over the greatest number of minds, and moulds and sways public sentiment more than any other, you will find him to be one who exhibits his truth organized in the form, and instinct with the breath, of life. You will not find him the expounder and the champion of a creed—the retailer of second-hand dogmas, and ready-made rules and formulas, but the promulgator of a life —a life which he has in him, fed by every fountain that God and humanity open to him.

So I say that in the want of the world, no less than in the vital wealth of the artist—in the want of the world, no less than in the economy of God in creation and revelation—is the true mission of art defined. Never, until this mission shall be comprehended and practically entered upon, will art rise to be the power in the earth that it ought to be, and is destined to be. We mourn over the decadence of art in its Italian home. We lament the insignificant position that it has achieved in this country. We cross the seas, or go back to a dead literature, to gather from the old masters their secret. We strive to filch from a burnt-out life the light and inspiration which may only be invoked from a living present and a possible future. We look to decayed nationalities and effete civilizations for ideals and ideas upon which those very nationalities and civilizations have starved. We refer to the old models of thought and art with slavish deference to classic authority. We strive to cast the burning life, molten in Christian love, of this latter day of grace, into the old moulds of pagan art and literature—outgrown, outlived, and outlawed. We bow to the life behind us, and not to that within us and before us. We stand upon the mountain-tops of life, and peer down into the valleys for light.

Pray Heaven we may have no art in this country, until we can learn to be as true to the life within us and without us as those whom we have learned to call masters were true to their own life and that of their age! We have the same foundation to build upon that they had. We have a hundredfold richer materials than they had. Our civilization and institutions are purer and higher than theirs. Into all our life and thought have been infused the fertilizing influences of Christianity; and what shall prevent an unprecedented development of art save blind obedience to artificial standards, reared among the ancient schools, standing half way between us and chaos, rather than half way between us and the millennium?

I have repeatedly said that, save as art ministers directly to the life of the people, by definite purpose, it is illegitimate. I have nowhere said, directly, that the beautiful in art has a mission to life and a ministry for it; and this I wish to say here. I do not propose to speculate upon the nature of the beautiful, presuming that your minds are already sufficiently confused on that subject. Driving after practical truth, I go back to my first facts—to God and nature—to find the legitimate mission of beauty. Only in subordinate departments of nature do I find beauty a leading element, or a principal purpose. In a pansy, a daisy, and a rose, as in a wide sisterhood of flowers, I find no object consulted higher than the pleasure of vision, or the excitement into activity of the sense of the beautiful; and when I find millions drinking in this beauty with exquisite pleasure, and see that it has a refining and harmonizing power upon their life, I conclude that beauty in nature, independently of all other elements and properties, has a mission from God to the life of men—that through it something of God's life passes into man's life.

I look upon a wheat-field, spread like a sheet of gold upon the hill-side, and as the shadows of the clouds chase each other over it, and it bends, and swells in soft undulations, to the will of the wandering wind, I say and feel that it is very beautiful. It moves me more than the rose that I hold in my hand; but I see at once that the beauty of the wheat-field is a subordinate element—that it is no more, in fact, than the glory, the efflorescence, of the element of fitness. It is eminently fit that that sheeted aggregation of plants which have sucked up from the soil, and, by vital elaboration, have prepared for my hand that which feeds my life, should be beautiful. The beautiful is a proper dress for that to appear in which is the very staff of my life.

I look out upon the ocean when the sun is bright and the wind is still; when spectral spars and sails flit along the edge of the horizon, and the sea-birds toss the sunshine from their wings in flakes of silver, and the surf gently kneels at the feet of the headland where I stand, and bathes them with its tears, and wipes them with its flowing hair, and I say that it is all very beautiful: but this beauty is not what the ocean was made for. It is only the fitting garb of the infinite storehouse of waters from whence arise the clouds that spread the heavens with glory, and rejoice the earth with showers. It is only the proper physiognomy of the great and wide sea, which defines nationalities and races; upon whose bosom buoyant Commerce weaves the meshes of human interest, that bind clime to clime, and unite universal man in universal brotherhood.

With the lesson which these my first facts teach me, I come back to art; and if this be a legitimate lesson, drawn from the only legitimate source, I am prepared to tell exactly what the mission of beauty in art is. In art, as in nature, beauty has a subordinate mission. If art be simply the medium by which life is transported from those who are rich in gift and grace and goodness to those who are not equally rich, or not rich in identical wealth, the simple question to be settled, is, whether beauty be the highest evolution of life on one side, and the greatest need of life upon the other. I assume that there can be but one answer to this question, and that beauty never is, and never can be, more than the shell of the highest art—the appropriate dress of vital values. I find beauty as the supreme end of art justified in nature, but only in miniature forms and limited instances. Always, as nature rises toward high ends and important issues, beauty ceases to be an element, and takes the subordinate position of a quality or property, with relations to that which is essential.

Now you will bear me witness that the slavery of art to beauty is universal. The aim of nine-tenths, at the least, of all the forms of art that have been uttered in the departments of picture, sculpture, and poetry, has been ministry to the sense of the beautiful. The voice of universal art is—beauty first and at any sacrifice;

beauty exclusively if necessary. Beauty has been compelled to come in. If the palaces of thought would not furnish it, then the highways and hedges have been laid under compulsory tribute, while the highest end of art has been forced into the lowest seat, or thrust out of the house for lack of a becoming garment.

Thus has art been cheated out of its sinews and its soul. Thus has it failed, where it has flourished most luxuriantly, to preserve the life of nations from decay. Thus are we, in this country, drinking the breath and toying with the curls of beauty, and all the while wondering why, in an age far in advance of all its predecessors, in power, activity, civilization, culture, freedom, and positive goodness, art has made no greater progress. I only wonder that it has a name to live—that it has not utterly starved upon the husks which have been its food. Thank God for the few great souls, scattered here and there, along the track of history, that were a law unto themselves, and revealed all the life that was in them, in such forms as that life naturally assumed.

I have been obliged by the limits of an effort like this to deal in broad generalities, and these relating entirely to the highest departments of art. I might profitably spend another hour in exhibiting the bearings of my theory upon the range of art that lies below my theme—upon that which is simply imitative and adaptive; but my pen respects your patience, and I will only add a few practical conclusions.

My first conclusion is, that there is, and can be, no such thing as a general standard of art and criticism, having relation to form and management. There is no such thing in nature. A horse is made for fleetness: so is a swallow; so is an antelope; so is a greyhound. An elephant is made for strength: so is an ox; so is a lion; so is a bull-dog. Suppose a critic of nature should set up his standard at the side of the horse, and insist that a swallow should have four legs, a greyhound hoofs, and an antelope a switch tail. Or suppose he should set it up at the side of the elephant, and insist on tusks for the ox, a trunk for the lion, and a greater show of ivory on the part of the bull-dog. We should all laugh at such a critic as this; yet a critic like this is just as ridiculous in the domain of art as in the domain of nature. In nature, we always find the form of each creature exactly adapted to the life that is in it; and both life and form are adapted to their mission. Every creature of God is sent into the world to live a certain life, and do a certain thing, and is endowed with precisely that form which will best enable it to live that life, and do that thing. Forms, varying almost infinitely, combine the same elements. The greyhound and the swallow are fleet, yet one is borne upon feet and the other upon wings. Therefore I say that the life embodied in a form of art, and the mission to other life on which it is sent, must always determine and define that form, without regard to any arbitrary standard whatsoever—without regard to any other form in the universe of art. Therefore I say that a man who condemns a work of art because it is not like something else, does not know what he is talking about. Every work of art has in its centre a germinal idea, which has, in itself, a law of development, and this development cannot be cramped or interfered with in any way, without damage to the work. I know of no way by which such a work may be judged save the one I have already given to you. Does it embody the artist's idea in the best form for producing the effect at which he aims? That is the question, simply and solely. It has nothing to do with schools, precedents, authorities, and general rules whatever.

This leads me to another practical conclusion which has, in substance, already been affirmed, viz., that you and I, and everybody who has brains and uses them, are competent judges of art, in the measure that we are competent judges of anything. If I display a picture, or unveil a statue, or read a poem or a story, or exhibit any form or creature of art to you, and you experience no thrill of delight, and drink in no thought that feeds in any way the life that is in you, so that you feel enriched by it, I declare that work of art to be competently condemned, notwithstanding a single connoisseur, judging by his arbitrary standard, may pronounce it a gem. So far as you and I are concerned, it is a failure, and so far as we represent the world, it is a failure before the world. There is nothing in it that we want; there is nothing that the world wants. In short, if there be nothing in a work of art save that which is addressed to the critical judgment of a few dawdlers and dilettanti, professional wine-tasters who cluster about the spigots of art—experts, who have no life that was not born of art, and no life out of art—then that work has no apology for existence, save the ignorance or the hallucination of its author.

Another and a most important practical conclusion, is, that the life must be rich which produces art, or it will have no wealth to convey to other life. Many young persons—men and women—with genius in them, and with all the natural yearning of genius for self-expression, write books, and give them to the world only to be disappointed, and to sink back into disgust with a public which is not capable, as they think, of appreciating them. But does not this stupid public appreciate Shakspere and Milton? Ah! the trouble is that the public does appreciate them. They have nothing, and can have nothing, to give the world, and why should the world be grateful? They have only dealt with books and dreams. They have only become imperfectly prepared to live, themselves, and what have they to give to other life? The struggles, the sorrows, the patient toil, the collisions, the ten thousand polishing, chastening, softening, fertilizing, and strengthening influences which give them symmetry, power, knowledge of human motive, and sympathy with the universal human heart, are all unexperienced. I believe that the world, in the main, sooner or later, is just; and that it will weave a crown for every man and woman who by ministering to its life deserves it. I believe that every man who gives the results of a rich life to the public, in higher or humbler forms of art, will be recognized by the public—that the public will turn to him as one of the benign sources of its life; and this, not so much from a sense of justice, as from unthinking obedience to a natural law—the law that turns the infant's lips to its mother's bosom, and the dying saint to his Redeemer's promises.

And now for a practical conclusion of a more grateful character—the conclusion of this address. If I apprehend the signs of the times, in their true aspect, a brighter day is dawning upon the world of art. In all departments of thought and life we are cutting loose from the old, and thinking and doing for ourselves, in obedience to the life within us, and with reference to the living realities of to-day. More and more distinctly pronounced is the call of the world for help, and more and more is that call respected; for the world of life is beginning to take judgment into its own hands. More and more is the patronage of art, in all its forms, passing from the hands of the church—from the hands of royalty and wealth and power—into the hands of the people. Less and less is art the servant of the great, and the pensioned glorifier of doughty names and doubtful institutions. Art has now to deal with the people more than ever before in the world's history. The critical middle-men bless and curse with less effect than formerly; and artists of every class will be compelled to give the world what it needs.

I believe both in the law and the fact of progress; and as life is more opulent now than ever before, so a higher art is possible now than has ever existed. I believe, too, that the ages which are to follow this will surpass our richness of life, and our possibilities of art, as they will transcend this and all preceding ages in expression. The art of to-day should embody the highest life of to-day for the use of to-day; for those who have gone before us need it not, and those who will come after us will have something better. The art that now lies in glittering piles upon the shore of achievement was deposited by waves which started near the land, and found but insignificant spoils as they rolled in and burst upon the beach. Closely behind us press other billows, with mightier bosoms and loftier crests, surging in from further climes and richer seas, with contributions that will shame our unproductive age.

I not only believe in progress, but in communion as its vital condition. It is the condition of progress in religious life, and it is the condition of progress in all life. Those who are great, and those who would be great, must serve. Those who would win for their names a wreath of glory, must expend their lives in ministry. The name that is above every name belongs to Him who communicated His whole life to the race. Universal progress is impossible, save as the barren many become partakers of the life of the fertile few.

Painter, sculptor, poet,—worker in words of whatsoever name—minister of the life which is—prophet of that which is to be,—have I not shown to you your mission? Hungry waiters at the door of art—thirsty loiterers at the fountain of life—hold to your right, and demand that that mission be fulfilled!

THE POPULAR LECTURE.

THE popular lecture, in the Northern States of America, has become, in Yankee parlance, "an institution;" and it has attained such prevalence and power that it deserves more attention and more respect from those who assume the control of the motive influences of society than it has hitherto received. It has been the habit of certain literary men (more particularly of such as do not possess a gift for public speech), and of certain literary magazines (managed by persons of delicate habit and weak lungs), to regard and to treat the popular lecture with a measure of contempt. For the last fifteen years the downfall of what has been popularly denominated "The Lecture System" has been confidently predicted by those who, granting them the wisdom which they assume, should have been so well acquainted with its nature and its adaptation to a permanent popular want as to see that it must live and thrive until something more practicable can be contrived to take its place. If anything more interesting, cheaper, simpler, or more portable, can be found than a vigorous man, with a pleasant manner, good voice, and something to say, then the popular lecture will certainly be superseded; but the man who will invent this substitute is at present engaged on a new order of architecture and the problem of perpetual motion, with such prospect of full employment for the present as will give "the lecture system" sufficient time to die gracefully. An institution which can maintain its foothold in the popular regard throughout such a war as has challenged the interest and taxed the energies of this nation during the last three four is one which will not easily die; and the history of the popular lecture proves that, wherever it has been once established, it retains its place through all changes of social material, and all phases of political and religious influence. Circumstances there may be which will bring intermissions in its yearly operations; but no instance can be found of its permanent relinquishment by a community which has once enjoyed its privileges, and acquired a taste for the food and inspiration which it furnishes.

An exposition of the character of the popular lecture, the machinery by which it is supported, and the results which it aims at and accomplishes, cannot be without interest to thoughtful readers.

What is the popular lecture in America? It will not help us in this inquest to refer to a dictionary; for it is not necessary that the performance which Americans call a lecture should be an instructive discourse at all. A lecture before the Young Men's Associations and lecture organizations of the country is any characteristic utterance of any man who speaks in their employment. The word "lecture" covers generally and generically all the orations, declamations, dissertations, exhortations, recitations, humorous extravaganzas, narratives of travel, harangues, sermons, semi-sermons, demi-semi-sermons, and lectures proper, which can be crowded into what is called "a course," but which might be more properly called a bundle, the bundle depending for its size upon the depth of the managerial purse. Ten or twelve lectures are the usual number, although in some of the larger cities, beginning early in "the lecture season," and ending late, the number given may reach twenty.

The machinery for the management and support of these lectures is as simple as possible, the lecturers themselves having nothing to do with it. There are library associations or lyceum associations, composed principally of young men, in all the cities and large villages, which institute and manage courses of lectures every winter, for the double purpose of interesting and instructing the public and replenishing their treasury.

The latter object, it must be confessed, occupies the principal place, although, as it depends for its attainment on the success of the former, the public is as well served as if its entertainment were alone consulted. In the smaller towns there are usually temporary associations, organized for the simple purpose of obtaining lecturers and managing the business incident to a course. Not unfrequently, ten, twenty, or thirty men pledge themselves to make up any deficiency there may be in the funds required for the season's entertainments, and place the management in the hands of a committee. Sometimes two or three persons call themselves a lecture-committee, and employ lecturers, themselves risking the possible loss, and dividing among themselves any profits which their course may produce. The opposition or independent courses in the larger cities are often instituted by such organizations,—sometimes, indeed, by a single person, who has a natural turn for this sort of enterprise. The invitations to lecturers are usually sent out months in advance, though very few courses are definitely provided for and arranged before the first of November. The fees of lecturers range from fifty to a hundred dollars. A few uniformly command the latter sum, and lecture-committees find it for their interest to employ them. It is to be presumed that the universal rise of prices will change these figures somewhat.

The popular lecture is the most purely democratic of all our democratic institutions. The people hear a second time only those who interest them. If a lecturer cannot engage the interest of his audience, his fame or greatness or learning will pass for nothing. A lecture-audience will forgive extravagance, but never dulness. They will give a man one chance to interest them, and if he fails, that is the last of him. The lecture-committees understand this, and gauge the public taste or the public humor as delicately as the most accomplished theatrical manager. The man who receives their invitation may generally be certain that the public wish either to see or hear him. Popularity is the test. Only popularity after trial, or notoriety before, can draw houses. Only popularity and notoriety can pay expenses and swell the balance of profit. Notoriety in the various walks of life and the personal influence of friends and admirers can usually secure a single hearing, but no outside influence can keep a lecturer permanently in the field. If the people "love to hear" him, he can lecture from Maine to California six months in the year; if not, he cannot get so much as a second invitation.

One of the noticeable features of the public humor in this matter is the aversion to professional lecturers,—to those who make lecturing a business, with no higher aim than that of getting a living. No calling or profession can possibly be more legitimate than that of the lecturer; there is nothing immodest or otherwise improper in the advertisement of a man's literary wares; yet it is true, beyond dispute, that the public do not regard with favor those who make lecturing their business, particularly if they present themselves uninvited. So well is this understood by this class of lecturers that a part of their machinery consists of invitations numerously signed, which invitations are written and circulated by themselves, their interested friends, or their authorized agents, and published as their apology for appearing. A man who has no other place in the world than that which he makes for himself on the platform is never a popular favorite, unless he uses the platform for the advocacy of some great philanthropic movement or reform, into which he throws unselfishly the leading efforts of his life. Referring to the history of the last twenty years, it will readily be seen that those who have undertaken to make lecturing a business, without side pursuit or superior aim, are either retired from the field or are very low in the public favor. The public insist, that, in order to be an acceptable lecturer, a man must be something else, that he must begin and remain something else; and it will be found to-day that those only who work worthily in other fields have a permanent hold upon the affections of lecture-going people. It is the public judgment or caprice that the work of the lecturer shall be incidental to some worthy pursuit, from which that work temporarily calls him. There seems to be a kind of coquetry in this. The public do not accept of those who are too openly in the market, or who are too easily won. They prefer to entice a man from his chosen love, and account his favors sweeter because the wedded favorite is deprived of them.

A lecturer's first invitation, in consonance with these facts, is almost always suggested by his excellence or notoriety in some department of life that may or may not be allied to the platform. If a man makes a remarkable speech, he is very naturally invited to lecture; but he is no more certain to be invited than he who wins a battle. A showman gets his first invitation for the same reason that an author does,—because he is notorious. Nearly all new men in the lecture-field are introduced through the popular desire to see notorious or famous people. A man whose name is on the popular tongue is a man whom the popular eye desires to see. Such a man will always draw one audience; and a single occasion is all that he is engaged for. After getting a place upon the platform, it is for him to prove his power to hold it. If he does not lecture as well as he writes, or fights, or walks, or lifts, or leaps, or hunts lions, or manages an exhibition, or plays a French horn, or does anything which has made him a desirable man for curious people to see, then he makes way for the next notoriety. Very few courses of lectures are delivered in the cities and larger villages that do not present at least one new man, who is invited simply because people are curious to see him. The popular desire is strong to come in some way into personal contact with those who do remarkable things. They cannot be chased in the street; they can be seen only to a limited extent in the drawing-room; but it is easy to pay twenty-five cents to hear them lecture, with the privilege of looking at them for an hour and criticizing them for a week.

It is a noteworthy fact, in this connection, that, while there are thousands of cultivated men who would esteem it a privilege to lecture for the lecturer's usual fee, there are hardly more than twenty-five in the country whom the public considers it a privilege worth paying for to hear. It is astonishing, that, in a country so fertile as this in the production of gifted and cultivated men, so few find it possible to establish themselves upon the platform as popular favorites. If the accepted ones were in a number of obvious particulars alike, there could be some intelligent generalizing upon the subject; but men possessing fewer points of resemblance, or presenting stronger contrasts, in style of person and performance, than the established favorites of lecture-going people, cannot be found in the world; and if any generalization be attempted, it must relate to matters below the surface and beyond the common apprehension. It is certain that not always the greatest or the most brilliant or the most accomplished men are to be found among the popular lecturers. A man may make a great, even a brilliant speech on an important public question, and be utterly dreary in the lecture-room. There are multitudes of eloquent clergymen who in their pulpits command the attention of immense congregations, yet who meet with no acknowledgment of power upon the platform.

In a survey of those who are the established favorites, it will be found that there are no slaves among them. The people will not accept those who are creed-bound, or those who bow to any authority but God and themselves. They insist that those who address them shall be absolutely free, and that they shall speak only for themselves. Party and sectarian spokesmen find no permanent place upon the platform. It is only when a lecturer cuts loose from all his conventional belongings, and speaks with thought and tongue unfettered, that he finds his way to the popular heart. This freedom has sometimes been considered dangerous by the more conservative members of society; and they have not unfrequently managed to get the lectures into their own hands, or to organize courses representing more moderate views in matters of society, politics, and religion; but their efforts have uniformly proved failures. The people have always refused to support lectures which brought before them the bondmen of creeds and parties. Year after year men have been invited to address audiences three fourths of whom disagreed utterly with the sentiments and opinions which it was well understood such men would present, simply because they were free men, with minds of their own and tongues that would speak those minds or be dumb. Names could be mentioned of those who for the last fifteen years have been established favorites in communities which listened to them respectfully, nay, applauded them warmly, and then abused them for the remainder of the year.

It is not enough, however, that a lecturer be free. He must have something fresh to say, or a fresh and attractive way of saying that which is not altogether new. Individuality, and a certain personal quality which, for lack of a better name, is called magnetism, are also essential to the popular lecturer. People desire to be moved, to be acted upon, by a strong and positive nature. They like to be furnished with fresh ideas, or with old ideas put into a fresh and practical form, so that they can be readily apprehended and appropriated.

And here comes the grand difficulty which every

lecturer encounters, and over which so many stumble into failure,—that of interesting and refreshing men and women of education and culture, and, at the same time, of pleasing, moving, and instructing those of feebler acquirements or no acquirements at all. Most men of fine powers fail before a popular audience, because they do not fully apprehend the thing to be done. They almost invariably write above the level of one half of their audience, or below the level of the other half. In either event, they fail, and have the mortification of seeing others of inferior gifts succeed through a nicer adaptation of their literary wares to the wants of the market. Much depends upon the choice of a subject. If that be selected from those which touch universal interests and address common motives, half the work is done. A clear, simple, direct style of composition, apt illustration (and the power of this is marvellous), and a distinct and pleasant delivery, will do much to complete the success.

It is about equally painful and amusing to witness the efforts which some men make to write down to the supposed capacity of a popular audience. The puerilities and buffooneries that are sometimes undertaken by these men, for the purpose of conciliating the crowd, certainly amuse the crowd, and so answer their end, though not in a way to bring reputation to the actors. No greater mistake can possibly be made than that of regarding an American lecture-going audience with contempt. There is no literary tribunal in this country that can more readily and justly decide whether a man has anything to say, and can say it well, than a lecture-audience in one of the smaller cities and larger villages of the Northern States. It is quite common to suppose that a Western audience demands a lower grade of literary effort, and a rougher style of speech, than an Eastern audience. Indeed, there are those who suppose that a lecture which would fully meet the demands of an average Eastern audience would be beyond the comprehension of an average Western audience; but the lecturer who shall accept any such assumption as this will find himself very unpleasantly mistaken. At the West, the lecture is both popular and fashionable, and the best people attend it. A lecturer may always be certain, there, that the best he can do will be thoroughly appreciated. The West is not particularly tolerant of dull men; but if a man be alive, he will find a market there for the best thought he produces.

In the larger cities of the East, the opera, the play, the frequent concert, the exhibition, the club-house, the social assembly, and a variety of public gatherings and public excitements, take from the lecture-audiences the class that furnishes the best material in the smaller cities; so that a lecturer rarely or never sees his best audiences in New York, or Boston, or Philadelphia.

Another requisite to popularity upon the platform is earnestness. Those who imagine that a permanent hold upon the people can be obtained by amusing them are widely mistaken. The popular lecture has fallen into disrepute with many worthy persons in consequence of the admission of buffoons and triflers to the lecturer's platform; and it is an evil which ought to be remedied. It is an evil, indeed, which is slowly working its own remedy. It is a disgraceful fact, that, in order to draw together crowds of people, men have been admitted to the platform whose notoriety was won by the grossest of literary charlatanism—men whose only hold upon the public was gained by extravagances of thought and expression which would compromise the dignity and destroy the self-respect of any man of character and common sense. It is not enough that these persons quickly disgust their audiences, and have a brief life upon the list. They ought never to be introduced to the public as lecturers; and any momentary augmentation of receipts that may be secured from the rabble by the patronage of such mountebanks is more than lost by the disgrace they bring and the damage they do to what is called "The Lecture System." It is an insult to any lyceum-audience to suppose that it can have a strong and permanent interest in a trifler; and it is a gross injustice to every respectable lecturer in the field to introduce into his guild men who have no better motive and no higher mission than the stage-clown and the negro-minstrel.

But the career of triflers is always short. Only he who feels that he has something to do in making the world wiser and better, and who, in a bold and manly way, tries persistently to do it, is always welcome; and this fact—an incontrovertible one—is a sufficient vindication of the popular lecture from all the aspersions that have been cast upon it by disappointed aspirants for its honors, and shallow observers of its tendencies and results.

The choice of a subject has already been spoken of as a matter of importance, and a word should be said touching its manner of treatment. This introduces a discussion of the kind of lecture which at the present time is mainly in demand. Many wise and good men have questioned the character of the popular lecture. In their view, it does not add sufficiently to the stock of popular knowledge. The results are not solid and tangible. They would prefer scientific, or historical, or philosophical discourses. This conviction is so strong with these men, and the men themselves are so much respected, that the people are inclined to coincide with them in the matter of theory, while at the same time they refuse to give their theory practical entertainment. One reason why scientific and historical lectures are not popular, is to be found in the difficulty of obtaining lecturers who have sufficient ingenuity and enthusiasm to make such lectures interesting. The number of men in the United States who can make such lectures attractive to popular audiences can be counted on the fingers of a single hand. We have had but one universally popular lecturer on astronomy in twenty years, and he is now numbered among the precious sacrifices of the war. There is only one entirely acceptable popular lecturer on natural sciences in New England; and what is he among so many?

But this class of lectures has not been widely successful, even under the most favorable circumstances, and with the very best lecturers; and it is to be observed, that they grow less successful with the increasing intelligence of the people. In this fact is to be found an entirely rational and competent explanation of their failure. The schools have done so much toward popularizing science, and the circulating-library has rendered so familiar the prominent facts of history, that men and women do not go to the lecture to learn, and, as far as any appreciable practical benefit is concerned, do not need to go. It is only when some eminent enthusiast in these walks of learning consents to address them that they come out, and then it is rather to place themselves under the influence of his personality than to acquire the knowledge which he dispenses. Facts, if they are identified in any special way with the experience and life of the lecturer, are always acceptable; but facts which are recorded in books find a poor market in the popular lecture-room. Thus, while purely historical and scientific lectures are entirely neglected, narratives of personal travel, which combine much of historical and scientific interest, have been quite popular, and, indeed, have been the specialties of more than one of the most popular of American lecturers, whose names will be suggested at once by this statement.

Twenty years ago the first popular lectures on anatomy and physiology were given, and a corps of lecturers came up and swept over the whole country, with much of interest and instruction to the people and no small profit to themselves. These lectures called the attention of educators to these sciences. Text-books for schools and colleges were prepared, and anatomy and physiology became common studies for the young. In various ways, through school-books and magazines and newspapers, there has accumulated a stock of popular knowledge of these sciences, and an apprehension of the limit of their practical usefulness, which have quite destroyed the demand for lectures upon them. Though a new generation has risen since the lecture on anatomy and physiology was the rage, no leaner field could possibly be found than that which the country now presents to the popular lecturer on these sciences. These facts are interesting in themselves, and they serve to illustrate the truth of that which has been stated touching lectures upon general historical and scientific subjects.

For facts alone the modern American public does not go hungry. American life is crowded with facts, to which the newspaper gives daily record and diffusion. Ideas, motives, thoughts, these are always in demand. Men wish for nothing more than to know how to classify their facts, what to do with them, how to govern them, and how far to be governed by them; and the man who takes the facts with which the popular life has come into contact and association, and draws from them their nutritive and motive power, and points out their relations to individual and universal good, and organizes around them the popular thought, and uses them to give direction to the popular life, and does all this with masterly skill, is the man whose houses are never large enough to contain those who throng to hear him. This is the popular lecturer, *par excellence.* The people have an earnest desire to know what a strong, independent, free man has to say about those facts which touch the experience, the direction, and the duty of their daily life; and the lecturer who with a hearty human sympathy addresses himself to this desire, and enters upon the service with genuine enthusiasm, wins the highest reward there is to be won in his field of effort.

The more ill-natured critics of the popular lecturer have reflected with ridicule upon his habit of repetition. A lecturer in full employment will deliver the same discourse perhaps fifty or a hundred times in a single season. There are probably half a dozen favorite lectures which have been delivered from two hundred to five hundred times within the last fifteen years. It does, indeed, at first glance, seem ridiculous for a man to stand, night after night, and deliver the same words, with the original enthusiasm apparently at its full height; and some lecturers, with an extra spice of mirthfulness in their composition, have given public record of their impressions in this respect. There are, however, certain facts to be considered which at least relieve him from the charge of literary sterility. A lecture often becomes famous, and is demanded by each succeeding audience, whatever the lecturer's preferences may be. There are lectures called for every year by audiences and committees which the lecturer would be glad never to see again, and which he never would see again, if he were to consult his own judgment alone. Then the popular lecturer, as has been already intimated, is usually engaged during two thirds of the year in some business or profession whose duties forbid the worthy preparation of more than one discourse for winter use. Then, if he has numerous engagements, he has neither time nor strength to do more than his nightly work; for, among all the pursuits in which literary men engage, none is more exhaustive in its demands upon the nervous energy than that of constant lecturing. The fulfilment of from seventy-five to ninety engagements involves, in round numbers, ten thousand miles of railroad-travel, much of it in the night, and all of it during the most unpleasant season of the year. There is probably nothing short of a military campaign that is attended by so many discomforts and genuine hardships as a season of active lecturing. Unless a man be young and endowed with an extraordinary amount of vital power, he becomes entirely unfitted by his nightly work, and the dissipation consequent upon constant change of scene, for consecutive thought and elaborate composition.

It is fortunate for the lecturer that there is no necessity for variety. The oft-repeated lecture is new to each new audience, and, being thoroughly in hand, and entirely familiar, is delivered with better effect than if the speaker were frequently choosing from a well-furnished repertory. It is popularly supposed that a lecturer loses all interest in a performance which he repeats so many times. This supposition is correct, in certain aspects of the matter, but not in any sense which detracts from his power to make it interesting to others. It is the general experience of lecturers, that, until they have delivered a discourse from ten to twenty times, they are themselves unable to measure its power; so that a performance which is offered at first timidly, and with many doubts, comes at length to be delivered confidently, and with measurable certainty of acceptance and success. The grand interest of a lecturer is in his new audience—in his experiment on an assembly of fresh minds. The lecture itself is regarded only as an instrument by which a desirable and important result is to be achieved; and familiarity with it, and steady use in its elocutionary handling, are conditions of the best success. Having selected the subject which, at the time, and for the times, he considers freshest and most fruitful, and with thorough care written out all he has to say upon it, there is no call for recurrence to minor themes, either as regards the credit of the lecturer or the best interests of those whom he addresses.

What good has the popular lecture accomplished? Its most enthusiastic advocates will not assert that it has added greatly to the stock of popular knowledge, in science, or art, in history, philosophy, or literature; yet the most modest of them may claim that it has bestowed upon American society a permanent good of incalculable value. The relentless foe of all bigotry in politics and religion, the constant opponent of every form of bondage to party and sect, the practical teacher of the broadest toleration of individual opinion, it has had more to do with the steady melioration of the prejudices growing out of denominational interests in Church and State than any other agency whatever. The platform of the lecture-hall has been common ground for the representatives of all our social, political, and religious organizations. It is there that orthodox and heterodox, progressive and conservative, have won respect for themselves and toleration for their opinions by the demonstration of their own manhood, and the recognition of the common human brotherhood; for one has only to prove himself a true man, and to show a universal sympathy with men, to secure popular toleration for any opinion he may hold. Hardly a decade has passed away since, in nearly every Northern State, men suffered social depreciation in consequence of their political and religious opinions. Party and sectarian names have been freely used as reproachful and even as disgraceful epithets. To call a man by the name which he had chosen as the representative of his political or religious opinions was considered equivalent to calling him a knave or a fool; and if it happened that he was in the minority, his name alone was regarded as the stamp of social degradation. Now, thanks to the influence of the popular lecture mainly, men have made, and are rapidly making, room for each other. A man may be in the minority now without consequently being in personal disgrace. Men of liberal and even latitudinarian views are generously received in orthodox communities, and those of orthodox faith are gladly welcomed by men who subscribe to a shorter creed and bear a broader charter of life and liberty. There certainly has never been a time in the history of America when there was such generous and general toleration of all men and all opinions as now; and as the popular lecture has been universal, with a determined aim and a manifest influence toward this end, it is but fair to claim for it a prominent agency in the result.

Another good which may be counted among the fruits of the popular lecture, is the education of the public taste in intellectual amusements. The end which the lecture-goer seeks is not always improvement, in any respect. Multitudes of men and women have attended the lecture to be interested; and to be interested intellectually is to be intellectually amused. Lecturers who have appealed simply to the emotional nature, without attempting to engage the intellect, have ceased to be popular favorites. So far as the popular lecture has taken hold of the affections of a community, and secured its constant support, it has destroyed the desire for all amusements of a lower grade; and it will be found, that, generally, those who attend the lecture rarely or never give their patronage and presence to the buffooneries of the day. They have found something better—something with more of flavor in the eating, with more of nutriment in the digestion. How great a good this is, those only can judge who realize that men will have amusements of some sort, and that, if they cannot obtain such as will elevate them, they will indulge in such as are frivolous and dissipating. The lecture does quite as much for elevated amusement out of the hall as in it. The quickening social influence of an excellent lecture, particularly in a community where life flows sluggishly and all are absorbed in manual labor, is as remarkable as it is beneficent. The lecture and the lecturer are the common topics of discussion for a week, and the conversation which is so apt to cling to health and the weather is raised above the level of commonplace.

Notwithstanding the fact that a moiety, or a majority, of the popular lecturers are clergymen, the lecture has not always received the favor of the cloth. Indeed, there has often been private and sometimes public complaint on the part of preachers, that the finished productions of the lecturer, the results of long and patient elaboration, rendered doubly attractive by a style of delivery to be won only by frequent repetition of the same discourse, have brought the hastily prepared and plainly presented Sunday sermon into an unjust and damaging comparison. The complaint is a strange one, particularly as no one has ever claimed that the highest style of eloquence or the most remarkable models of rhetoric are to be found in the lecture-hall. There has, at least, been no general conviction that a standard of excellence in English and its utterance has been maintained there too high for the comfort and credit of the pulpit. It is possible, therefore, that the pulpit betrays its weak point, and needs the comparison which it deprecates. A man of brains will gratefully receive suggestions from any quarter. That impulses to a more familiar and direct style of sermonizing, a brighter and better elocution, and a bolder utterance of personal convictions, have come to the pulpit from the platform, there is no question. This feeling on the part of preachers is by no means universal, however; for some of them have long regarded the lecture with contempt, and have sometimes resented it as an impertinence. And it may be (for there shall be no quarrel in the matter) that lecturers are quacks, and that lectures, like homœopathic remedies, are very contemptible things; but they have pleasantly modified the doses of the old practice, however slow the doctors are to confess it; and so much, at least, may be counted among the beneficent results of the system under discussion.

Last in the brief enumeration of the benefits of the

popular lecture, it has been the devoted, consistent, never tiring champion of universal liberty. If the popular lecturer has not been a power in this nation for the overthrow of American slavery—for its overthrow in the conscientious convictions and the legal and conventional fastnesses of the nation—then have the friends of oppression grossly lied; for none have received their malicious and angry objurgations more unsparingly than our plain-speaking gentleman who makes his yearly circuit among the lyceums. No champion of slavery, no advocate of privilege, no apologist for systematized and legalized wrong has ever been able to establish himself as a popular lecturer. The people may listen respectfully to such a man once; but, having heard him, they drop him forever. In truth, a man cannot be a popular lecturer who does not plant himself upon the eternal principles of justice. He must be a democrat, a believer in and an advocate of the equal rights of men. A slavery-loving, slavery-upholding lecturer would be just as much of an anomaly as a slavery-loving and slavery-singing poet. The taint so vitiates the whole æsthetic nature, so poisons the moral sense, so palsies the finer powers, so destroys all true sympathy with universal humanity, that the composition of an acceptable lecture becomes impossible to the man who bears it. The popular lecture, as it has been described in this discussion, has never existed at the South, and could not be tolerated there. Until within four years it has never found opportunity for utterance in the capital of the nation; but where liberty goes, it makes its way, and helps to break the way for liberty everywhere.

It is a noteworthy fact, that the popular lecturer, though the devoted advocate of freedom to the slave, has rarely been regarded as either a trustworthy or an important man in the party which has represented his principles in this country. He has always been too free to be a partisan, too radical and intractable for a party seeking power or striving to preserve it. No party of any considerable magnitude has ever regarded him as its expositor. A thousand times have party-speakers and party-organs, professing principles identical with his own, washed their hands of all responsibility for his utterances. Even now, when the sound of falling shackles is in the air, and the smoke of the torment of the oppressor fills the sky, old partisans of freedom cannot quite forget their stupid and hackneyed animosities, but still bemoan the baleful influence of this fiery itinerant. Representative of none but himself, disowned or hated by all parties, acknowledging responsibility to God and his own conscience only, he has done his work, and done it well—done it amid careful questionings and careless curses—done it, and been royally paid for it, when speakers who fairly represented the political and religious prejudices of the people could not have called around them a baker's dozen, with tickets at half-price or at no price at all.

When the cloud which now envelops the country shall gather up its sulphurous folds and roll away, tinted in its retiring by the smile of God beaming from a calm sky upon a nation redeemed to freedom and justice, and the historian, in the light of that smile, shall trace home to their fountains the streams of influence and power which will then join to form the river of the national life, he will find one, starting far inland among the mountains, longer than the rest and mightier than most, and will recognize it as the confluent outpouring of living, Christian speech, from ten thousand lecture-platforms, on which free men stood and vindicated the right of man to freedom.

THE END.

NEW BOOKS

JUST PUBLISHED BY

CHARLES SCRIBNER & COMPANY,

124 GRAND STREET,

NEW YORK.

DANTE,

As Philosopher, Patriot, and Poet. With an Analysis of the Divine Comedia, its Plot and Episodes. By Professor BOTTA. 1 vol. crown 8vo. On tinted paper. $2 50.

It is decidedly the best account of the poet that has appeared in the English language. It is careful, learned, discriminating, and eloquent, written in terse and eloquent English that is remarkable in the pen of an author not native to our soil. The Analysis of the poem is full and philosophical, alive with Italian enthusiasm, yet calm and truly Catholic in its humanity and trust.—*N. Y. Evening Post.*

3d and 4th Vols. FROUDE'S ENGLAND.

Froude, (James Anthony.) History of England, from the Fall of Wolsey to the Death of Elizabeth. From the 4th London edition, in 8 vols. crown 8vo. *Vols. 1 to 4 now ready.* The other four volumes will follow shortly. Per volume, $2 50.

NATURAL HISTORY AND ZOOLOGY.

A Manual of Zoology. By Professor SANBORN TENNEY, A. M., Author of "Geology," &c., with over **500** ENGRAVINGS, in 1 vol. crown 8vo. 540 pages. $3 00. *Also, a fine Edition on Tinted Paper, in an octavo volume. Price* $4 00.

In this book particular attention has been given to a full description of the Quadrupeds, Insects, Reptiles, Fishes, Shells, &c. of North America, and especially of those appertaining to our own country. As a complete Manual of "Zoology," it is believed that this volume surpasses any yet published. The illustrations are on "a scale," and engraved in the very best style.

Dr. J. A. ALEXANDER'S ISAIAH (Unabridged).

The Prophecies of Isaiah, Translated and Explained, by J. Addison Alexander, D. D. The complete work in two vols. 8vo., $6 50. Also, the Abridged Edition, 2 vols. 12mo., uniform with *Psalms, Acts, Matthew, and Mark.*

UNIVERSITY EDITION.

The Fœderalist. A Collection of Essays written in favor of the New Constitution as agreed upon by the *Federal Convention*, September 17th, 1787. Reprinted from the original Text under the Editorial Supervision of Henry B. Dawson. 1 vol, 8vo. $3 00.

Copies sent post-paid on receipt of price.

TIMOTHY TITCOMB'S NEW WORK.

Plain Talk on Familiar Subjects. By Dr. J. G. Holland. Uniform with "*Titcomb's Letters to Young People*," "Bitter Sweet," &c. 1 vol. 12mo., 360 pages. Price, $1 75; full gilt, $2 50; half calf, extra, $3 50; Turkey Morocco, $5 00.

HISTORY OF RATIONALISM.

Embracing a Survey of the Present State of Protestant Theology. By Rev. Jno. F. Hurst, A. M. 1 vol. 8vo., $3 50.

The history of Rationalism is traced through all its stages of development down to the present time. The whole period passed over is about two centuries, and in giving a history of Rationalism during this time, it has been an object of the author to describe indirectly, the state of Protestant Theology at the present time.

A NEW AND REVISED EDITION, (WITH A SUPPLEMENT) OF THE

CYCLOPEDIA OF AMERICAN LITERATURE.

Cyclopedia of American Literature. By. E. A. and G. L. Duyckinck. Embracing Personal and Critical Notices of Authors, and Selections from their Writings, from the Earliest Period to the Present Day. With 225 portraits, 425 autographs, and 75 views of colleges, libraries and residences of authors, and elegant steel engravings of J. Fenimore Cooper and Benjamin Franklin. 2 vols. royal 8vo, cloth, $10 00; half calf, $15 00. The Supplement sold separately when desired. Price $2 50.

This new edition of the Cyclopedia of American Literature, which has been for some time out of print, will include a Supplement, bringing *the work down to the present year.* Many new articles relating to Old and Recent Authors have been added, with numerous Obituaries of Authors already included, and much additional matter respecting living authors and their publications, previously noticed.

By PROF. GEO. P. FISHER.

Essays on the Supernatural Origin of Christianity, with special reference to the Theories of Renan, Strauss and the Tübingen School. By Professor George P. Fisher, of Yale College. 1 vol. 8vo, $3 50.

This work will present a critical examination of the principal theories proposed from the side of Naturalism in opposition to the truth of the Gospel history. The historical speculations of the Tübingen School are fully discussed, and the genuineness and credibility of the New Testament Historical Books are vindicated against the assaults of Dr. Baur, and his followers. The book will also embrace a dissertation upon the Personality of God and the Followers of Pantheism. The work is not a refutation of obsolete errors, but a discussion of living questions and current forms of unbelief. It is adapted not only to meet the wants of ministers and theological students, but also of intelligent laymen.

A NEW WORK BY PROF. AGASSIZ.

The Structure of Animal Life.—Six Lectures. Delivered before the Brooklyn Institute, by Prof. Louis Agassiz. 1 vol. 8vo, 46 Illustrations, $2 50.

REV. DR. H. BUSHNELL'S NEW WORK.

The Vicarious Sacrifice. Grounded on Principles of Universal Obligation. By Horace Bushnell, D. D., Author of "Sermons for the New Life," "Nature and the Supernatural," &c. In 1 vol. octavo, $3.

Copies sent post-paid on receipt of price.

A NEW LIFE OF CICERO.

A New Life of Cicero. By WILLIAM FORSYTH, M. A. Q. C. With Twenty Illustrations. Two vols., crown 8vo. Printed at the Riverside Press, on tinted and laid paper. Price $5. In half calf, $9.

LORD DERBY'S HOMER.

The Iliad of Homer. Rendered into English blank verse. From the Fifth London Edition. Two volumes, crown 8vo, on tinted and laid paper. Price $5. In half calf, $9.

MAX MULLER'S NEW WORK. (Second Series of)

Lectures on the Science of Language. In 1 volume, with a series of 31 Wood Engravings, illustrating the positions of the Organs of Speech, uttering the various articulate sounds of which all language is composed. Crown 8vo, 623 pages. Price. $3 50. (Uniform with first series.)

IK MARVEL.

Wet Days at Edgewood. By the Author of "My Farm of Edgewood." 1 vol. 12mo. Price $1 75.

HENRY S. MAINE.

Ancient Law: its connections with the early history of society, and its relation to modern ideas. 1 vol. 8vo, cloth. Price $3 50.

PRESIDENT T. D. WOOLSEY.

Introduction to the Study of International Law. Designed as an aid in Teaching and in Historical Studies. Second edition, revised and enlarged. 1 vol. 8vo, cloth. Price $3 50.

NEW WORK BY HON. G. P. MARSH.

Man and Nature; or, Physical Geography, as Modified by Human Action. Uniform with "Lectures on the English Language." 1 vol. 8vo, cloth. Price $4.

By HORACE BUSHNELL, D. D.

Christ and his Salvation. 1 vol. 12mo, cloth. Price $2 00.

Prof. JOSIAH P. COOK, Jr.

Religion and Chemistry; or, Proofs of God's Plan in the Atmosphere and its Elements. In Ten Lectures. 1 vol. 8vo, cloth. $3 50.

Copies sent post-paid on receipt of price.

NEW ILLUSTRATED BOOKS FOR 1865-'6.

I.

CHRISTIAN ARMOUR;

OR,

Illustrations of the Christian Warfare as Embodied in the Exhortation of the Apostle Paul,

" Take unto you the whole armour of God."

The object of this unique and novel work is to bring the Fine Arts to the aid of the great spiritual truths of religion, and by presenting them to the eye in a picturesque and attractive shape, to impress them more deeply on the mind. The Illustrations comprise a series of

RICHLY ILLUMINATED PLATES,

Emblazoned in Gold and Colors,

In the style of the Ancient Missal Decorations, improved and chastened by the refinements of Modern Art.

In them the Apostolic emblems are portrayed, and their sacred significance is indicated, each being accompanied by an appropriate Poem, and surrounded by floral and arabesque borders, all appropriately referring to the divine injunctions of the Sacred Text. In one elegant quarto volume, massively bound in Levant morocco, beveled, antique, richly gilt sides and edges. Price $18 00; in cloth, beveled, and extra gilt, $15 00.

II.

THE BOOK OF RUBIES.

A Collection of the most notable Love Poems in the English Language. In 1 vol. crown 8vo, printed by Alvord, in 2 colors, on superfine extra calendered tinted paper, bound in extra illuminated cloth, full gilt, $3 75.

The Same, Turkey morocco, antique, $6 50. The Same, Turkey Morocco, extra, $6 75.

It is believed that this work will be found the most complete and best arranged in its contents, as it is the most elegant in mechanical execution. The author has brought to light the most precious ores he could find in his explorations in the wealthy mines of Amatory Poetry, and the result is a work which sparkles with the love thoughts of all ages.

Copies sent post-paid on receipt of price.

NOW READY.

THE THIRTIETH EDITION OF

BITTER-SWEET.

BY DR. J. G. HOLLAND Author of "Timothy Titcomb's Letters."

1 vol. 12mo, $1 50; in full gilt, $2 50.

J. Russell Lowell, in the *Atlantic Monthly*, says: "It is truly an original poem—as genuine a product of our soil as a golden-rod or an aster. It is as purely American—nay more than that—as purely New-English as the poems of Burns are Scotch. From the title to the last line, it is delightfully characteristic. We mean it as very high praise when we say that Bitter-Sweet is one of the few books that have found the secret of drawing up and assimilating the juices of this new world of ours."

Epes Sargent, Esq., of Boston, in a letter to the publisher, says: "I know of no long poem of American origin that I can place before it. In saying this, I do not forget the productions of Longfellow, so deservedly celebrated. The flow and mastery of poetic language in this work seems to me very remarkable. All the lyrical parts are excellent. The descriptive parts are admirable, original, and thoroughly American."

The *London Literary Gazette*, of December 4, says: "Bitter-Sweet is a dramatic poem *of unquestionable power*, representing the inner life of a Puritan family in New England. It contains many eloquent passages."

The *London Athenæum* says: "It is a suggestive and original poem. Vigor, and force, and imaginative beauty, are to be found in it."

"If we mistake not, our readers will recognize with us *the genius of a true poet*, with a rare wealth of poetic sympathies, profound observation of the workings of human passion, and the creative power to clothe his conception in expressive forms."—*New York Tribune.*

"It is the real *power* of a work which gives it a rank among the *productions of genius, and to this rank Bitter-Sweet assuredly belongs.* Since the days of Gray there has been written no better blank verse, and the songs show a finish and beauty which almost surpass Mrs. Browning."—*New Haven Journal.*

"A dramatic poem which is characteristically American, showing a great command of versification and purity of style. This poem shows that Dr. Holland *is a man of genius.*"—*Boston Post.*

"It is a gem of a book, unique in style and conception, yet touchingly simple and grand. The poem contains passages of surpassing beauty."—*Great Barrington Courier.*

"'Bitter-Sweet' has many exquisite passages, and, as a whole, will have legions of admirers."—*Boston Traveller.*

"It is a *book* of *great originality*—the fruit of a strong, original, and extraordinary mind."—*Boston Transcript.*

"We feel assured that Bitter-Sweet will establish the author's fame *as a poet of genius.*"—*Detroit Daily Advertiser.*

"This panorama, in graceful verse, is a beautiful and original conception, and establishes Dr. Holland among *our first American poets.*"—*Buffalo Commercial Advertiser.*

NOW READY.

THE TWENTY-FIFTH EDITION OF

GOLD-FOIL,

HAMMERED FROM POPULAR PROVERBS.

BY TIMOTHY TITCOMB.

One volume, 12mo.; 360 pages. $1 25; in extra gilt, $2 50.

The homely proverb is but the thread for a string of Pearls. The style is one of simple cast and of chaste beauty. We are free to express our admiration of a volume characterized as this is by sound common sense, manly feeling, a high moral and truly practical tone, and a simple force and beauty of thought and expression which are very rarely combined.—*New York Evangelist.*

A series not only entertaining, but tinged with a beautiful view of moral truths, and expressed in language full of rich thoughts, but powerful against the wrong, mighty in favor of the right.—*Troy Whig.*

This work, admirable for its unity of purpose, and its unusual vigor of thought comes to us laden with rich and rare ideas, clothed in most brilliant language; the exceeding purity of the style is one of its greatest charms.—*Rochester American.*

In the present work, his themes are taken from common life, though the illustrations are suggested by some of the current proverbs, that are familiar to the people. —*New York Tribune.*

Full of good sense and written in good sound English. They are better than the hammered foil—they are the virgin metal, pure, precious, and solid. It is really a satisfaction to find a volume of such intrinsic worth.—*Providence Journal.*

A series that will recommend themselves to the heart of the reader for their truthfulness, simplicity, tenderness, and beauty.—*Hartford Courant.*

It contains good humor, sound philosophy, and solid instruction, in a style which at once makes a captive of the reader.—*Lowell News.*

The diction is smoother, more graceful (than "Titcomb's Letters") and worthy of "Bitter-Sweet." The doctor will gain a more lasting reputation among scholars by "Gold Foil."—*Troy Times.*

A remarkable book, a work of sterling merit, which appeals to every intelligent reader. No doubt it will reach a thousand editions.—*Philadelphia City Item.*

The evident result of culture, reading, reflection, and experience, as practical a series as any of the PRESENT CENTURY.—*Boston Gazette.*

Overrun with beautiful language and happily conceived thoughts.—*Boston Post.*

A book which cannot be opened at any page without throwing to the mental eye a gleam of light from its pleasing surface.—*Hartford Times.*

Sensible and instructive, and deserves to be read and pondered by young and old.—*Boston Advertiser.*

Written in the genial style and the earnest, friendly way which constitutes the secret of Dr. Holland's success in winning attention to his sober teachings.—*Buffalo Express.*

A CHOICE AND POPULAR BOOK.

FORTY-FIFTH THOUSAND—NOW READY.

TIMOTHY TITCOMB'S LETTERS

TO YOUNG PEOPLE, SINGLE AND MARRIED.

1 vol. 12mo., $1 50; or in full gilt, $2 50.

THEIR GOOD SENSE, SOUND ADVICE, AND GENIAL HUMOR COMMEND THEM TO ALL.

"This series is one of the best of the kind we have ever met with. The writer is evidently a shrewd observer, and he gives an infinite deal of wholesome advice in a plain, open, straightforward manner. While he inculcates true religious principles, he indulges in no cant, and his style is such as will at once attract the attention of those for whom the work is written."—*New York Courier and Enquirer.*

"Pleasantly told, and couched in such language that it cannot fail to win its way to the hearts of the young. The subjects treated bear upon all the relations of life; and the moral tone which characterizes every page, the earnestness which is breathed into every line, and the genuine love of the good, the true, and the beautiful, which casts its halo over the whole work, cannot fail to leave their impress on the mind of the reader." —*Buffalo Courier.*

"We have rarely read a volume which contained more plain, good, common sense or practical advice. It is written in a taking style, and will be a treasure in many a household."—*Boston Atlas.*

"Their good sense, sound advice and genial humor, commend them to general perusal." —*Albany Evening Journal.*

The *London Literary Gazette* says:—"We have never read a work which better inculcates the several duties and responsibilities of young men and women, married or single."

"The strong common sense which pervades them, the frank and manly utterance of wholesome truths in pointed and beautiful language, and the genial sympathy which the author has for those whom he addresses, cannot fail to commend the work to general favor.

"FOR PURE ENGLISH DICTION AND BEAUTIFUL IMAGERY IT WILL TAKE ITS PLACE AS A CLASSIC WITH IRVING'S SKETCH BOOK."

"These letters are written with such frankness, honesty and good sense, and exhibit such a wholesome horror of humbug and cant, that we know the author must be a 'good fellow,' and, while pleased to read his book, learn to like him."—*Hartford Press.*

"They contain many truthful and valuable suggestions, presented in the cultivated and attractive style of a practised writer. There is an earnestness and hearty tone to the whole which commends the book to the good opinion of all."—*Hartford Times.*

"Written in a style to both please and instruct. They entitle the author to the lasting gratitude of the young as well as the old."—*Northampton Gazette.*

LESSONS IN LIFE.

BY DR. J. G. HOLLAND, (Timothy Titcomb.)

A companion volume to "Letters to Young People," and "Gold Foil." 1 vol. 12mo. 350 pages. $1 75; in gilt edges, $2 50.

In this volume, the author of "Letters to the Young," and "Gold Foil," has discarded something of the didactic tone of those two popular works, but retained their direct and familiar style, and all those characteristics which have given them so large and so honorable a currency with the public. The "Lessons" are twenty-four in number, and they are not only "lessons *in* life," but *from* life. The topics discussed are those which are of interest to every thoughtful man and woman, and they are treated freshly, clearly, and forcibly, with abundant ingenuity of argument and aptness of illustration. The publisher is convinced that the book will prove to be even more popular than its predecessors, named in this circular, to which it is regarded as a companion volume.

"They remind one of the older and better English Essayists; of Addison perhaps most, and yet they are not at all cast in the same mould. They have the same general spirit, and have wit akin and yet different—not so quiet—and more trenchant; if not so elegant in the liquid flow of words, they are warmer in the glow of humanity, and are more redolent of the highest morality and the purest religion, while wholly free from cant."—*Utica Morning Herald.*

LETTERS TO THE JONESES.

BY DR. J. G. HOLLAND, (Timothy Titcomb.)

Uniform with "Lessons in Life," "Letters to Young People," &c., &c., &c. In 1 vol. 12mo. Cloth, $1 75; in cloth, full gilt, $2 50; in Turkey extra, $5 00.

FROM AUTHOR'S PREFACE.—"If the reader will so far favor the author as to suppose that, when a young man, he taught the district school in Jonesville, 'boarding around,' according to the primitive New England fashion; that he has kept himself acquainted with the lives and fortunes of his old friends and pupils there; that they have known something of him, and, through an officious representative of the family have requested him to write these letters for the public eye, which he had no time to write for their private reading—I say, if the reader will suppose all this, he will supply all the necessary machinery of the book, and the writer will have his ustification for the direct and homely talk in which he indulges toward the family."

MISS GILBERT'S CAREER.

BY DR. J. G. HOLLAND, (Timothy Titcomb.)

An American story. 1 vol. 12mo. 475 pages. $2 00.

THE BAY PATH.

BY DR. J. G. HOLLAND, (Timothy Titcomb.)

A tale of New England Colonial Life. 1 vol. 12mo. 418 pages. $2 00.

Copies sent by mail, post paid, on receipt of price.

NATURE AND THE SUPERNATURAL,

AS TOGETHER CONSTITUTING THE ONE SYSTEM OF GOD.

BY REV. HORACE BUSHNELL, D.D.

1 vol. 8vo., 550 pages. $2 25.

"Whatever misgiving may exist in any mind in taking up this last and greatest work of Dr. Bushnell's, we believe will soon be swept away by its tide of argument and eloquence. It deals with the greatest problems that can engage the mind of man. Dr. Bushnell, with a clear, penetrating sagacity, and with remarkable grasp of thought, seizes at once the most obnoxious and dangerous features of modern scepticism, and submits them to a scrutiny which exposes their inherent native deformity. The author aims at a noble mark, and, in our judgment, reaches it. The work will rank very high among the literary and theological productions of the present century."—*New York Evangelist.*

"The discussion is conducted with great ability, abounding in large views, profound arguments and apt illustrations. It is a quiver full of arrows wherewith to defend the citadel of Truth against the assaults of Science, falsely so called."—*Christian Intelligencer.*

"A noble monument of the earnest and talented author's production to religious science and literature. As a solution of the difficulties which modern schools of philosophy have raised against a supernatural system of grace, we regard this as by far the ablest work which has appeared since Rationalism opened its assaults upon the Christian faith. It should be among the first books purchased by the minister in making up a library, however scanty."—*New York Independent.*

WHAT THE QUARTERLY REVIEWS SAY.

The *North American Review* says:—"The author has rendered a most important service to Christian Faith, both as regards the external facts of our religion, and the more recondite experience of its true disciples. We accept his theory in its essential features, and rejoice in the ability and lucidness with which it is here developed."

The *Princeton Review* says:—"It is quite the most able and valuable of Dr. Bushnell's works on theology. It of course bears the imprint of the author's genius, in its fresh and brilliant diction, its affluent originality and bewitching felicity of illustration, its episodic passages of marvellous beauty and eloquence."

The *New Englander* says:—"To many who care little for the name, but have sighed for the reality of an established faith, it will prove a benison for which their hearts will ever bless the writer. * * * The delineation of the character of Jesus is, in our view, the finest upon its theme in English literature. We do not hesitate to pronounce it a magnificent book, a truly Christian book, and one pre-eminently adapted to the times in which we live."

The *American Theological Review* says:—"We are prepared to say that we have never followed so close and so forcible an argument, that was at the same time so readable. It is one of the freshest books of the season, or of any season."

NOTICES OF NATURE AND SUPERNATURAL CONTINUED.

The *Mercersburg Review* says:—"We welcome this book with all our heart, as a most valuable accession to the theological literature of the age. Dr. Bushnell has contrived to throw into it the full vivacity and freshness of his own nature. It is rich throughout with thoughts that breathe and words that glow and burn. The book is one which deserves to live, and that may be expected to take its place, we think, among the enduring works of the age."

SERMONS FOR THE NEW LIFE.

BY HORACE BUSHNELL, D.D.

1 vol. 12mo. 456 pages. $2 00.

CONTENTS.—I.—Every Man's Life a Plan of God. II.—The Spirit in Man. III.—Dignity of Human Nature shown from its Ruins. IV.—The Hunger of the Soul. V.—The Reason of Faith. VI.—Regeneration. VII.—The Personal Love and Lead of Christ. VIII.—Light on the Cloud. IX.—The Capacity of Religion Extirpated by Disuse. X.—Unconscious Influence. XI.—Obligation a Privilege. XII.—Happiness and Joy. XIII.—The True Problem of Christian Experience. XIV.—The Lost Purity Restored. XV.—Living to God in Small Things. XVI.—The Power of an Endless Life. XVII.—Respectable Sin. XVIII.—The Power of God in Self-Sacrifice. XIX. Duty not Measured by Our Own Ability. XX.—He that Knows God will Confess Him. XXI.—The Efficiency of the Passive Virtues. XXII.—Spiritual Dislodgments. XXIII.—Christ as Separate from the World.

The *Methodist Quarterly* for July says:—"Our American pulpit has lately furnished no volume presenting so deep a reach of thought in the speaker, or presupposing so nigh a moral and intellectual appreciation on the part of the congregation. * * Dr. Bushnell has a deep insight, and a searching power of tracing the relations of great truths to each other. The overmastering trait of his productions is cool, stern, slow, moving *intellect;* yet intellect gently interpenetrated and made malleable by moral feeling—imagination, too, there is, but none for its own sake."

The *Princeton Review* says:—"These discourses, although they apparently differ a good deal in character, bear the clear impress of Dr. Bushnell's genius."

The *North American Review* says:—"In original forms of thought, that highest order of originality, which comes more from nice elaboration than from wayward spontaneity, it is surpassingly rich. Another generation will peruse it as a book that has life in it—the double life of its author and of vital truth."

The *Monthly Religious Magazine* says:—"Nor are these sermons written on the same level with any of the author's preceding productions. They betoken a deeper experience. They speak from a richer knowledge. They are the expression of a faith wrought patiently out by a harder discipline."

CHRISTIAN NURTURE.

By Horace Bushnell, D.D. 1 vol. 12mo. Price $2 00.

Part I.—The Doctrine.—I.—What Christian Nurture is. II.—The Ostrich Nurture. III.—The Organic Unity of the Family. IV.—Infant Baptism, how Developed. V.—Apostolic Authority of Infant Baptism. VI.—Church Membership of Children. VII.—The Out-populating Power of the Christian Stock.

Part II.—The Mode.—I.—When and where the Nurture begins. II.—Parental qualifications. III.—Physical Nurture, to be a means of Grace. IV.—The Treatment that discourages Piety. V.—Family Government. VI.—Plays and Pastimes, Holidays and Sundays. VII.—The Christian Teaching of Children. VIII.—Family Prayers.

"It takes up the difficult problems of Christian education one by one, in a clear, practical manner, with good sense, scriptural knowledge, and devotional feeling."—*Boston Journal.*

"As we have read chapter after chapter of this volume with unmingled delight, we have mentally resolved upon making each the theme of an editorial article embodying the substance of its teachings. But it is impossible to condense Dr. Bushnell's thoughts into fewer words than he himself employs, or to exhaust a subject in briefer compass than he allots to it. And most assuredly it would be impossible to substitute words for his, which would as clearly and nicely express the meaning. We would most earnestly recommend the book to parents, for the profit of themselves and their children."—*N. Y. Independent.*

"We cannot but welcome these earnest and powerful presentations of the influence of the parent over the faith, and character, and whole being of the child, which are fitted to quicken the conscience of every father and mother, and make them more faithful in the discharge of their sacred trust."—*N. Y. Evangelist.*

WORK AND PLAY; OR, LITERARY VARIETIES.

By Horace Bushnell, D.D. 1 vol. 12mo. Price $2 00.

"A variety of themes which are treated with that calm, philosophical and scholastic habit of thought for which the author is distinguished. No one can read him without having his mental pulse quickened, and his mind newly furnished with the results of a deep thinker's study."—*New York Observer.*

The Round Table says:—"There is much in the style of Dr. Bushnell, as well as in the mould and treatment of his conceptions, which reminds us of the stately prose of the older writers, now of Milton, now of Jeremy Taylor, and then again of quaint Sir Thomas More * * * In all his writings, we trace the vigorous workings and the splendid results of a powerful mind, equally moved by a taste for philosophy, for poetry, and for politics."

From the American Theological Review.

"This volume contains the best orations and articles of the author; and this is another way of saying that it contains some of the best literature of the kind which this country has produced. Common things and thoughts are clothed upon with light and beauty. Dr. Bushnell is a poet, in all but form; his mind moves spontaneously amongst the highest subjects of thought, and he adapts these to the general mind so the it is elevated by communion with him."

From the New Englander.

"The reader will here find not less of truth or more of genius, perhaps, than abounds in the author's other writings; but the truth is from a wider and more varied field, and the genius is more free and sportive in its creations. Those who are acquainted with Dr. Bushnell only through his theological writings, will do well to read this volume of literary varieties, and fill out their conception of the theologian and divine, with that of the philosopher, the scholar, and the man of letters."

NATURAL HISTORY:

A

MANUAL OF ZOÖLOGY

FOR

Schools, Colleges and the General Reader.

BY SANBORN TENNEY, A.M.

AUTHOR OF "GEOLOGY," ETC., AND PROFESSOR OF NATURAL HISTORY IN VASSA FEMALE COLLEGE.

WITH OVER FIVE HUNDRED ENGRAVINGS.

1 vol. crown 8vo., cloth, price, $3 00; Library style, large 8vo., on tinted pap. PRICE $4 00.

This work is a complete Manual of Zoölogy, giving a general idea of the whole Anir Kingdom, while it is especially full upon AMERICAN Zoölogy; describing briefly all of o Mammals, Birds, most common Reptiles, Fishes, Insects, Shell-Fish, Sea-Urchins, Sta Fishes, Sea-Anemones and Corals. It is particularly adapted for a class-book in our hi schools, academies and colleges; it gives the general reader the results which he so mu desires, and which, heretofore, he could gain only by wading through the numerous lar and costly volumes of Cuvier and other masters of science. It is almost an indispensab aid to the teacher who would give oral instruction in Natural History.

IT IS JUST THE BOOK:

For the Farmer who wishes to learn about useful and noxious insect
For every Boy who wants to learn the names of all the Nor American Birds and Quadrupeds.
To take to the Mountains and to the Seaside.
For Family Reading; in short, for all who desire to get a clea idea of the leading facts and principles of Zoölogy, and t become acquainted with the rich and varied forms of anima life which abounds on our shores and in our forests, in ou lakes and streams, and in our gardens, groves and fields.

THE PICTORIAL ILLUSTRATIONS,

More than five hundred in number, have nearly all been drawn expressly for this work and surpass everything of the kind before done in this country. Several American Animals are here depicted for the first time. The illustrations alone give a good idea of all the principal groups of Animals, and are worth to any one interested in the subject many times the price of the book. A few specimens are herewith presented.

CHARLES SCRIBNER & CO., Publishers,

124 Grand Street, New York.

Copies sent by mail, post paid, on receipt of price by publishers.

www.ingramcontent.com/pod-product-compliance
Lightning Source LLC
LaVergne TN
LVHW010203110826
845151LV00002B/595

* 9 7 8 1 4 2 5 5 3 5 3 6 0 *